BLAISDON

MEMORIES OF THE
NEW ELIZABETHANS

To Jill & Derek

with best wishes

Stephen White

First Published 2012

Blaisdon Plumlications
The Temple
Longhope
Gloucestershire
GL17 0NZ
Email: blaisdon@hotmail.co.uk

British Library Cataloguing in Publication Data.
A catalogue record for this book is available from the British Library.

ISBN: 978-0-9543775-2-6

Printed by Gomer Press, Llandysul, Ceredigion, SA44 4JL.

BLAISDON

VOL 3

MEMORIES OF THE NEW ELIZABETHANS 1964-2012

STEPHEN WATERS

BLAISDON PLUMLICATIONS

DEDICATED WITH PERMISSION TO

HER MAJESTY

QUEEN ELIZABETH II

ON THE OCCASION OF HER

DIAMOND JUBILEE

BUCKINGHAM PALACE

5th April, 2012.

Dear Ian,

I was pleased to see you at the reception in the Royal Gallery
following the loyal addresses at Westminster Hall recently. I mentioned
then that your letter of 7th March had been safely received and that
Her Majesty would be very touched if a future book about the village of
Blaisdon in the years since 1964 were to be dedicated to her on the
occasion of the Diamond Jubilee. I am writing now formally to confirm
this but also to thank you for your kindness in enclosing a copy of
Memories of a Country Parish, a beautiful book which The Queen was
delighted to receive. I thought that Mr. Waters and all those associated
with the project might wish to know that Her Majesty has asked that the
volume be placed in the Royal Library in Windsor.

Yours ever,

Christopher

Sir Christopher Geidt
Private Secretary to The Queen

The Baroness Royall of Blaisdon, PC.

Jean Waters for putting up with my disappearance from family life for the months involved in producing this book.

Rosemary Wagstaff for her delightful letter and animal artwork throughout the book. Her beautiful work can also be seen on her 'Words of Art' web site (www.words-of-art.com).

Father Sean Murray for allowing access to his vast library of photographs and documents relating to the Salesian School in Blaisdon.

Nigel Hogg and Stuart Baker for their invaluable help.

Last, but not least, a huge 'thank you' to all the contributors who have made this book possible. This book is a lovely record of our time in Blaisdon village, Woodgreen and Nottwood Hill, which can be treasured and passed down to the future generations. To those who I have not been able to contact, please accept my apologies. It was not for want of trying!

Except where indicated, photographs have been provided by the families concerned or from the author's collection. Every effort has been made to locate copyright holders and obtain permission. Any omission or error brought to my attention will be remedied in future editions.

Profits from the sale of this book will be donated to Blaisdon Village Hall.

CONTRIBUTORS

Thanks go to the following people and where relevant, their families, who have contributed to this book and without whom its production would not have been possible.

Peter & Jean Adams
Jack Alcock & Jennifer Griffiths
Steve Allen
Sarah & Jeremy Aston
Stephen & Nicola Atkinson
Angela & Kevin Baker
Christine Barnard
Glenys & Ken Barnard
Lee Barrett
Ian & Tracey Batham
Mike Bayliss
Dorothy Baylis
Blaisdon Old Boys
Peter & Sue Booth
Richard & Zoe Boyles
Shirley Brickel
David & Pauline Brown
Peter Brown
Julie Buckley
Nicky Charlesworth
Peter & Katherine Davis
Ewan Davis
Jules De Bharra
John Dunbar
Clive Edmonds
Terry Elcock
Roger Etherington

Sheila Evans
Mary Evans
Brian Evans
William Faucett
Angela & Keith Foster
N. Funsten
Stuart & Sue Gent
Rev. Ian Gobey
J. Goss
Susan Green
Brenda Hales
Daren Hales
Llivia Hales
Vicki Handley
Heather Harrington
Paul & Penny Harris
Dick & Hilary Hawker
Tony Haynes (Jnr)
Chris Helm
John & Pat Higgins
Elizabeth Higgins
Catherine Higgins
Rev. Sarah Hobbs
Nigel & Lynne Hogg
Andrew Hogg
Sharon Hookings & Rakesh Kaushik
Mark & Ann Hopkins

Mandy Howell

Joyce Inger

Niki Janneh

Roger & Gail Jones

Brian Jones

Megan & Gerald Kear

Joanna Kelly

Roger Keyse

Claire Keyse

Steve & Judith King

Nicola Klaiber

Joan Knowlman

Elaine Lanciano

Christine Leyfield

Joyce & David Lilley

Louise Lisseman

Christopher & Patricia Manners

Amelia Meek

Nathalie Mignotte

Roger & Kate Millis

Don Morgan

Mark Morgan

Fr Sean Murray

Fr Aidan Murray

Sue Oldham

Madge O'Rourke

Elizabeth Perry

Humphrey Phelps

Don & Ann Rich

Ben & Anna Rich

Tom Rich

Max Rich

Abbie Rich

David & Joan Risborough

Dorothy Roberts

Jill & Andrew Rodgett

Lara Rodgett

Clive Rodway

Debbie Rowe

Jan Royall

Harriet Selwyn

Megan Sharp

Venk Shenoi

Helena &Kyriakos Simonidis

Fran Smart

Neil Smith & Jenina Miller

Thursa Smith

Sam & Amanda Spencer

Louise Stoddart

J. Stokes

Liz Tandy

Helen Taylor

Norman Taylor

John & Jill Tutton

Emily Venn

Kyron & Kate Venn

Andrew & Judith Vickers

Rosemary Wagstaff

Waddy Warr

 Erica Warr

Jean & Stephen Waters

Eleanor Waters

Ian Waters

Martin Webb

Westbry-on-Severn Young Farmers

Guy, Louise & Spot Wilkins

Keith & Sarah Wintle

Claire & Chris Woolham

BLAISDON

Most people living in Blaisdon have only known one monarch, Queen Elizabeth II, and the years covered by this volume reflect life in a small country parish during the majority of her reign. The people of Blaisdon are honoured that Her Majesty has given her permission for this book to be dedicated to her on the occasion of her Diamond Jubilee.

Blaisdon is a small community with a wealth of social history. The middle years of the 20th century were explored in Volume 2 through the memories of those who lived in Blaisdon. Now, the story of Blaisdon's 'New Elizabethans' is revealed, looking at those who have made Blaisdon home between 1964 and 2012.

The last volume revealed the great social changes that occurred in rural life as the countryside moved from an era of manual labour to mechanisation. The village was occupied by families who tended to have lived in the area, if not the village, for generations. In 1964, the village lost its railway and village school whilst Blaisdon Hall's Salesian School changed in 1962 from an agricultural school to one caring for children with social problems. Village life was about to change again and this volume reflects a very different way of life.

In the latter half of the 20th century, cars became much more widely owned and people became much more mobile. A place of work no longer dictated where people had to live and those who could, moved to live in what were perceived as more desirable locations, including the countryside. Today Blaisdon has only a few families who can trace their attachment to the village through generations. Most have moved to the village and stay by choice.

The second big change to have occurred is seen in the houses themselves. The years covered by the last volume saw mains water and electricity arriving in Blaisdon. Most houses still had outside toilets and no bathrooms. There is hardly a house in the parish that has not undergone modernisation in the last 50 years to provide the amenities desired by today's residents. Many houses have been extended and in a couple of cases, demolished and replaced by larger residences. However, there have been very few additional houses built in the village itself, as it is a Conservation Area with no infill building allowed. Whether this restriction on the growth of the community is good, future generations will have to decide. For those of us who have been lucky enough to live in Blaisdon during the reign of Queen Elizabeth II, it remains a very special village and reflective of the many changes that have occurred in rural life during her time on the throne.

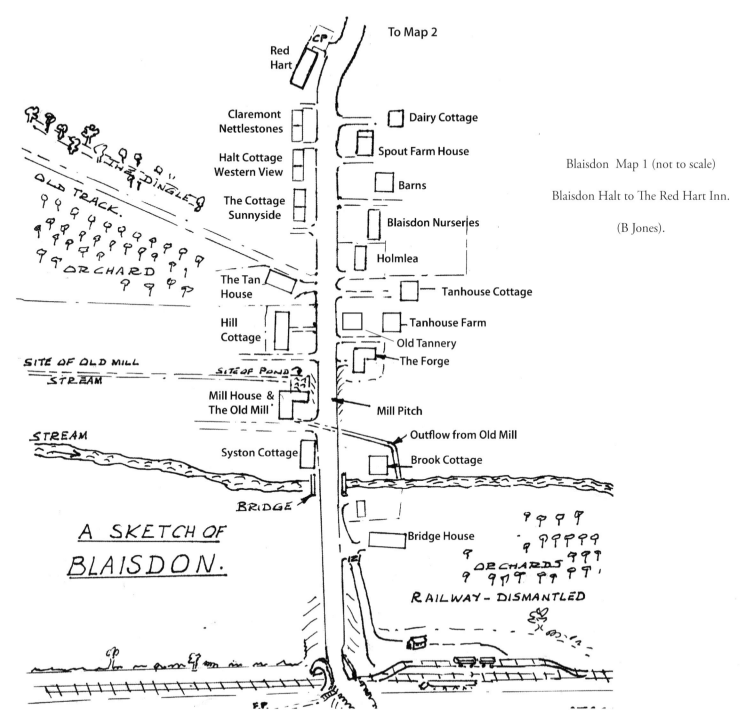

Red Hart

CP

To Map 2

Claremont
Nettlestones

Halt Cottage
Western View

The Cottage
Sunnyside

Dairy Cottage

Spout Farm House

Barns

Blaisdon Nurseries

Holmlea

Blaisdon Map 1 (not to scale)

Blaisdon Halt to The Red Hart Inn.

(B Jones).

"THE DINGLE"

OLD TRACK.

ORCHARD

The Tan House

Hill Cottage

SITE OF OLD MILL

STREAM

SITE OF POND

Mill House &
The Old Mill

Tanhouse Cottage

Tanhouse Farm

Old Tannery

The Forge

Mill Pitch

STREAM

Syston Cottage

BRIDGE

A SKETCH OF
BLAISDON.

Outflow from Old Mill

Brook Cottage

Bridge House

ORCHARDS

RAILWAY - DISMANTLED

F.P.

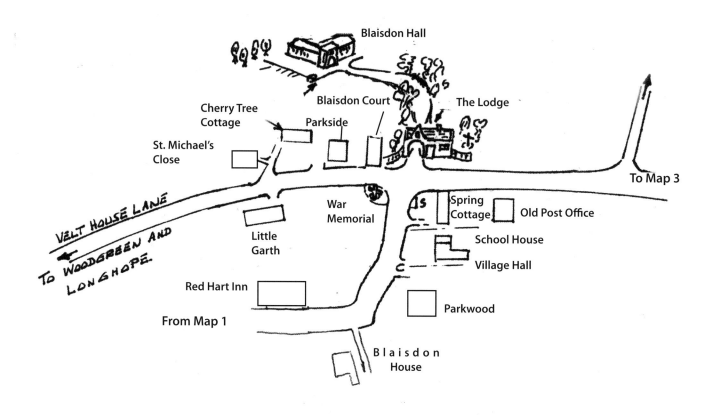

Blaisdon Map 2 (not to scale).

Red Hart Inn to Velthouse Lane & The Old Post Office.

(B Jones).

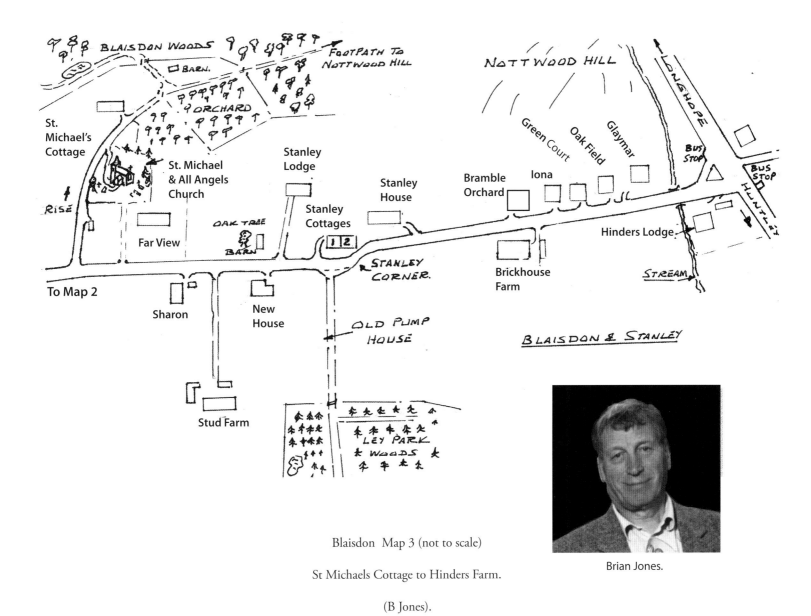

Blaisdon Map 3 (not to scale)

St Michaels Cottage to Hinders Farm.

(B Jones).

Brian Jones.

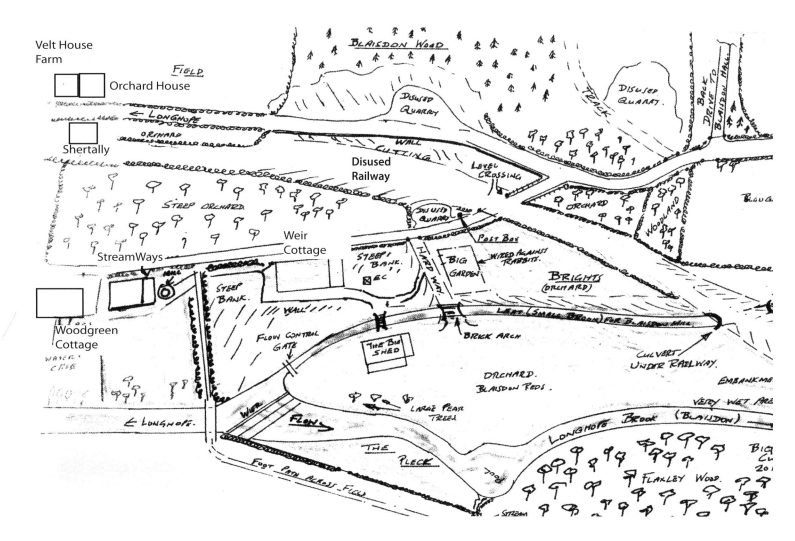

Sketch of Woodgreen.
(Not to scale)
(B. Jones)

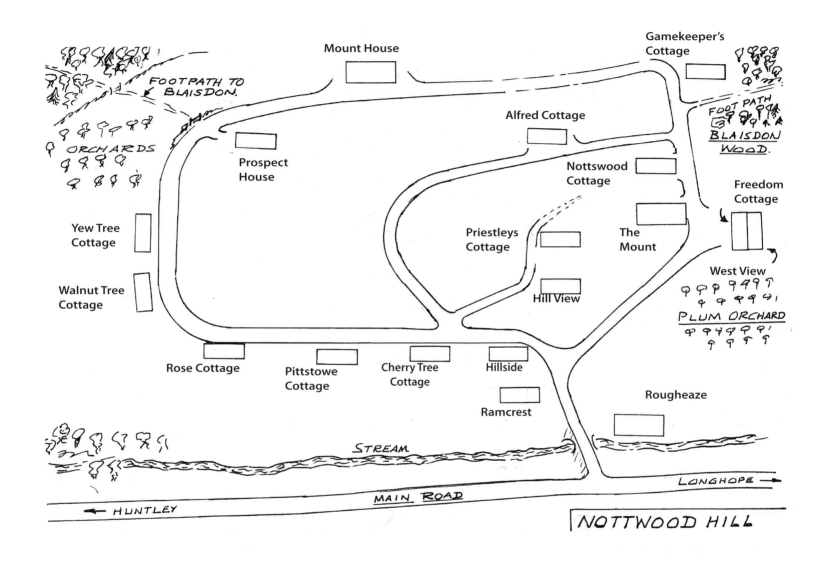

Map of Nottwood Hill.
(Not to scale)
(B. Jones)

BLAISDON HALT

Ian & Eleanor Waters with a Blaisdon Halt sign
at The Dean Heritage Railway.

When passenger services along the Gloucester to Hereford line ceased in October 1964, it caused a seismic shift in an established way of life within the small community of Blaisdon. Since the Halt opened in 1926, it had been the main route of departure and entry into the village. *Humphrey Phelps*, local author and farmer, reflects on the nature and extent of this change:

"Blaisdon Halt was on the Hereford-Ross-Gloucester line, which opened on 1st June 1855. It was a broad-gauge single track running from Hereford to Grange Court station, where it joined the South Wales line. It was twenty-two and a half miles long with four viaducts over the River Wye and with tunnels at Lea, Fawley, Ballingham and Dinedor. In 1869 the line was changed to standard gauge.

Blaisdon Halt opened on 4th November 1929 and despite its name it was actually in Westbury parish but it was indisputably Blaisdon's station. For those who never knew or used the Halt it is difficult to convey what it meant to Blaisdon and with what affection it was held. It was the gateway to Ross and Gloucester and far beyond by buying a ticket in the little office where parcels were left for local people. Some used the line occasionally, some regularly, weekly or daily. During most of the lifetime of the Halt hardly anyone had a car; the trains were the only means of transport for many.

Those who worked in Gloucester boarded an early train, those who attended the cattle markets at Gloucester went down to the Halt to catch a later train. Those bound for work, business, shopping or pleasure went and stood on the little platform awaiting a train. The Gloucester bound train came huffing and puffing with a fine show of smoke as it came under the bridge. On Friday mornings a dozen or more local housewives caught the 11:15am to Gloucester. This was more than a shopping expedition; it was an enjoyable social occasion. Here, made manifest was the camaraderie of the village, the Halt and the train.

Above:
Site of Blaisdon Halt from bridge in 2012.

Top Left:
View of path of line from Blaisdon towards Longhope from bridge in 2012.

Right:
Cedric Etherington as the businessman waiting for the train that will never come; the disused platform already returning to nature.

Locomotive 7815 leaving Blaisdon Halt heading towards Longhope.
25th July 1964.
(J Goss)

What bliss it was in those days to arrive at the platform and the little tin waiting room and travel sedately to town, especially for those housewives who travelled joyfully ~ and eventually returned, laden with full shopping baskets and gossip.

On six days a week there were seven trains in either direction, fourteen trains on every weekday. We told the time by these trains. The first of the day was the time to rise, the last that it was time to go to bed. And in between the time for lunch, the time to get the cows in for milking, and so on. The sound of the trains also foretold the weather. When we on the south side of the Hereford line heard them loud and clear we knew it would be fine weather. But those at Blaisdon to the north knew rain was on the way when the sound was clear as the wind blowing n the opposite direction.

The siding came before the Halt, it opened in November 1906, perhaps it was then or at a later date the weighbridge was added. I have fond memories of loading or unloading cattle at the sidings, of loading or unloading corn, corn sold or corn bought, big boxes of Blaisdon plums, feedingstuffs, sugar beet or fertiliser such as basic slag. The bags of slag in the open truck were often wet or dusty. In a wind the black, dusty slag got everywhere; in our eyes, on our hands, faces and clothes -1 have no fond memories of this. Charlie Martin was often at the siding unloading coal - besides the adjacent small farm, he also had a coal round. Mrs Sharkey was the porter during the 1940s. For a few weeks she used to play a piano accordion on the platform to greet passengers alighting from a train. A most distinguished, one-time porter eventually became Governor General of Bengal - Fred became Sir Frederick Burrows. On his appointment as Governor General, he remarked 'I know nothing about hunting and shooting but I know a lot about shunting and hooting'.

A woman who lived quite close to the Halt had a propensity for quarrelling which necessitated frequent changes in her will and time to time she'd stand by her garden gate to ask a passenger to witness her will. Two of her many tasks were laying-out corpses and neutering cats. Of the latter she said it made cats better mousers because then that was the only pleasure they could get.

When the line came under threat we held protest meetings and marches, distributed leaflets in the district, on the trains and all over Ross. Cedric Etherington was a staunch supporter of the campaign. On one doorstep of some terraced houses he knocked an empty milk bottle over, which tumbled and clattered down the long flight of steps. Didn't that bottle make a noise which echoed all along the street, you'd scarcely credit one bottle could make such a noise. Cedric rushed away, years later I reminded him and he said, 'Yes, didn't I run.'

But it was a lost cause. Blaisdon Halt closed after 38 years. Life was never the same afterwards and I still mourn the loss."

Another Blaisdon Halt sign seen at Dean Forest Railway.

BRIDGE HOUSE

Bridge House had been occcupied for many years by the Martin family (Volume 2). They were followed by Mr and Mrs Baker and then Alec and Betty Cross with their son, David. Richard (Dick) and **Dorothy Roberts** lived at Bridge House from December 1980 to February 1987.

"During our stay in Blaisdon we were made very welcome right from the start. We spent most of our spare time caring for Bridge House and the garden. My two grandsons just loved coming to stay. They were three and five at the time (now thirty two and thirty four) and we had

Above: Bridge House in 2012, nestled behind trees.
Below: Bridge House with Dorothy Roberts' grandchildren,
John & Michael. (1982)

many walks up May Hill, which they used to enjoy. I remember the Blaisdon Fete and the boys spending all afternoon on the bouncy castle!

I have happy memories at Christmas time when the Blaisdon carol singers would all come inside Bridge House and sing carols and were then justly rewarded with a little sustenance!

I can remember the time when, after a long period of wet weather, a certain farmer's cows invaded our garden and did the lawn no good at all! We were told to expect things like that when you live in the country.

I have two beautiful paintings on silk, which were done

by Mrs Ivy Davis, and I treasure these with fond memories of her.

I really associate Blaisdon with 'plums'. We had quite a lot of plum trees at Bridge House and in a good year you just could not give them away as everyone had loads too. They are delicious plums and I have missed them ever since. In the autumn of last year I received a parcel of two jars of Blaisdon plum jam from Sue Booth. I was so pleased and I really appreciated the thought. I feel it typifies the spirit of Blaisdon village. One of the villagers (I can't remember his name) gave us a tray as a leaving present to remind us of our time in Blaisdon. I also have a couple of recipes given to me by Lynne Hogg, which I still use.

We had a stream at the bottom of our orchard, which in very wet weather used to flood. Some houses used to suffer badly from flooding but fortunately Bridge House was just far enough away that the flood did not trouble us, although the lower end of the orchard was often under water.

In March 2011 I was eighty and my family gave me a party at an hotel in Lydney when all my family got together for a weekend. On the Sunday my son took me back to Blaisdon to reminisce. I was taking lots of photos of Bridge House when the owners came out and invited me in to look round. It was so kind of them and it brought back many happy memories of our life there. We were then invited into Sue and Peter Booth's cottage for a very welcome cup of tea. We had a good old natter about the years we were living there and caught up on family news.

I have just remembered about a Nativity Play put on up

at Blaisdon Hall and they wanted someone from each household to have a part. Dick was the representative from Bridge House, playing one of the 3 Wise Men, though I can't remember which one!

We left Blaisdon in 1987 to come to Yorkshire to be nearer our daughter and her family. My husband, Dick, had retired in 1984. Dick died in 1992, while I continue to live near my family."

2

1

3

This Page:
2 views from the
bedroom window of
Bridge House.
(c1980s)

Opposite:
1. Dorothy Roberts with
Annabel. (1986)
2. Dick Roberts with
Annabel, Michael &
John.
(1986)
3. Dick Roberts in
nativity play costume.
(1985)

Left:
Richard Guy.
Below:
Jean & Coreen Guy.
Eleanor Waters in
background.

When Dorothy and Dick Roberts left Blaisdon, Bridge House was bought by Richard and Jean Guy who lived there with their children, Lauren, James and Corinne, until moving to Cheltenham in 1995 when the house passed to ***Jack Alcock and Jennifer Griffiths***:

Fate and a war in foreign climes were the catalyst for the first meeting of RAF pilot Wg Cdr Jack Alcock and military journalist Jennifer Griffiths. She was living in an Army Officers' Headquarters Mess in Aldershot, on standby to report on the first Gulf War in Iraq in 1991. Purely coincidentally, Jack was allocated a place on a military course and accommodation in the same Mess, where they met fleetingly. She did not know then that it was to change her life.

Within days, Jennifer had flown under cover of darkness in a military transport plane to the remote Tent City in Saudi Arabia, close to the Iraq border. She was the only civilian female, sleeping on a camp bed, sharing a tent with two female soldiers and living alongside several thousand young soldiers. Her role was to produce daily news reports for the Army's 'Soldier' magazine on various army activities throughout the region, dressed in combat uniform and accompanied by a designated civilian male photographer, because women do not drive in Saudi.

Prior to her deployment, Jennifer completed a course in nuclear, biological and chemical warfare training, and had wondered how she would remember all the evasion techniques, should the alarm be sounded. When it did happen, she said her recall was perfect and happily it was a false alarm!

During her desert stint Jennifer and Jack wrote to each other every day and when she arrived back weeks later in the UK, he was there to greet her off the flight at RAF Brize Norton. Jack said: 'After embracing me, she said she was longing for a hot soak in the bath as a treat instead of the open air showers of Tent City. I was happy to arrange it,' he said.

Jennifer, who worked as a journalist for all three of the Armed Forces, said: 'It was a fascinating and exciting career. During the Gulf War I could not have been better looked after by the soldiers in Tent City. I consider it a great privilege to have known them.'

For several years she and Jack shared a home in Fringford, Oxfordshire, from which Jennifer commuted every day to various military bases in the UK. On her appointment to RAF Innsworth they decided to settle in Gloucestershire, and were fortunate enough to find the home of their dreams, Blaisdon's Bridge House, in 1995. 'Within 20 minutes of first seeing the house, our purchase was agreed.

On settling in, we were met with kindness and help from the village, and remain as happy as ever.'

Left:
Jack Alcock & Jennifer Griffiths
at a Morgan Car event.

Moving on to Jack's background, he was brought up in Lincolnshire during the Second World War, where his parents ran a small village pub, The Barley Sheaf, close to RAF Conningsby, one of the RAF's major bomber bases. The Sheaf was frequented by many of the bomber aircrew when not on bomber operations but not for long. Losses of ten per cent were common and the crews flew up to four missions a week. His clearest recollection of the war years was seeing a large part of the RAF's first, one thousand-strong, bomber raids on Germany, forming up directly over his home, before they set course.

It was that impressive sight and sound that inspired him as a young schoolboy towards a career as an RAF pilot and eventually, to command a squadron of large aircraft. However, parental objections could not be overcome and, on leaving grammar school he started training as a civil engineer. But as soon as he was twenty-one and free from parental objections, he knocked on the RAF's door. They gave him a four-day series of interviews and medical tests, and then offered him pilot training.

Following a two-year course, he was posted to a Hunter Squadron to be a fighter pilot. Three years later he started a lifetime series of moves of aeroplane types, roles and locations. Beside worldwide flights his jobs required him to live in 30 different houses, including homes in Thailand, Singapore, Malta and California, where he was on loan to the US admiral who commanded the Pacific Fleet Naval Air Forces. He certainly never lacked variety and was never bored!

For Jack the highlight of his Service career was when he was appointed to plan and conduct the conversion of the RAF's Shackleton crews to the then brand-new Nimrod aircraft. For many of the aircrew, this was a major step forward, bringing them into the jet era. The conversion went well, on time and without incident. For this achievement, Jack was awarded the Queen's Commendation for Valuable Service in the Air, promoted and given command of a Nimrod Squadron. The schoolboy's dream was complete. After 36 years of RAF service, it came time to move on.

It was then he first met Jennifer, and realised within a few days their mutual attraction was serious. As a civilian, Jack set up as an aviation consultant, selling aircraft worldwide for a Bavarian company. His success was marked when he was elected a Fellow of the The Royal Aeronautical Society for his overall achievement in aviation.

For the last ten years he has enjoyed serving as a Governor of Dene Magna School. He continues as a member and former President of the Rotary Club of The Royal Forest of Dean.

The couple continue to enjoy life in Blaisdon, Jennifer with her adored dog and cats, and Jack with his Morgan Sports Car.

BROOK COTTAGE

Peter and Sue Booth moved to Blaisdon in 1969 and since then have lived in Brook Cottage. Their two sons, Francis (Frank) and Edward (Ed), were born in 1975 and 1977 respectively. Work has now taken the boys away from Blaisdon.

Peter and Sue bought the house from Mr and Mrs Beard. Like several other houses in the parish, the house has undergone name changes.
It was called Bridge Cottage when Mr and Mrs Annis (Volume 2) lived there. Mr and Mrs Beard renamed the cottage Brooklyn, possibly combining the brook with the name of their daughter. Pete and Sue lived with the name for some time but then renamed it Brook Cottage.

They have also made substantial alterations and extended the cottage considerably over the years, often using the services of the late Clive Smurthwaite. A much respected local builder from Northwood Green, Clive worked on nearly every house in the village at some time or other.

The cottage has the Longhope Brook running along one side. It is well stocked with trout and also provides an excellent habitat for aquatic wildlife including herons, ducks, kingfishers and dippers.

Above:
Brook Cottage in 2012.

Left:
Peter Booth & Fido in 1982.

11

Top:
Ed, Peter, Sue & Frank Booth.
(2009)

Below;
The Booth family with Fido.
(1990)

YSTON COTTAGE

Syston Cottage sits across the road from Brook Cottage. The Longhope Brook borders one side of the property though at rather more distance than its neighbour opposite. The oldest part of the building is timber framed and the modern extensions have been built during the latter part of the 20th century. Nigel and Lynne Hogg moved to Syston Cottage and Blaisdon in 1975. **Nigel Hogg** continues:

Syston Cottage in the snow. (1982)

"Syston Cottage, then known as Stanley Cottage, was sold from the Blaisdon Estate for £105 to Arthur Lane, railway checker, in February 1934. Arthur, in turn, sold it for £350 to Walter Lane, watchmaker, in 1935. When Walter died in 1948, ownership of what had by then become known as Syston Cottage, passed to his widow, Alice Lane. She continued to live there until 1965, when she sold it to Keith and Diana Boseley. They sold in 1967 to William Page, who also owned the Mill next door. In 1968 he sold the cottage on to John and Cecelia Newman, who lived there until March 1975, when we arrived on the scene. At that point, Syston Cottage was then a two up/two down half-timbered cottage supposedly dating back to 1643, with a small single storey kitchen/bathroom extension. It also had an oil-fired boiler that required hitting with a large stick to get it started. This boiler 'blew up' a year or so later, emitting large quantities of black smoke and soot, never to go again!

The cottage is now significantly larger, but the old part still contains an inglenook fireplace, which Lynne discovered whilst using our best screwdriver to remove cement and wallpaper from the wall behind a Parkray fire. It had apparently not been uncovered since the 1920s. The beams and character features in the original building have been retained wherever possible.

We decided on Syston Cottage after visiting the Red Hart just before Christmas 1974, where we experienced a John Dunbar bread, cheese and onion lunch. The other people in the bar were, I believe, Albert Pithouse and Foster Yemm, who were drinking cider served by Elsie Hogg, heated in a pan on the fire and mulled with a poker. This seemed to us to indicate a good old fashioned style of life that we would like to share! We reckoned we would be in

13

Blaisdon for about 5 or 6 years before work moved us on. We are still here!

As soon as we arrived we had two visitors, Dick Hawker and Grace Jones, who made us very welcome and gave us lots of essential local information. We also found we had some unwelcome guests, death watch beetles, which tap-tap-tapped constantly. It was somewhat unnerving at the time but in the end we dealt with them by stripping the whole cottage, roof and all, treating it and building an extension at the same time! During the disruption we joined the ranks of several villagers who, from time to time, were most generously allowed by Dick and Hilary Hawker to take up temporary lodgings in the Stud Farm flat.

Nigel, Andrew & Lynne Hogg
with Brandy.
(1987)

Our son Andrew was born in 1976, soon after the extension was complete. We were very touched to find a teddy bear on our doorstep, which had been delivered by Albert Pithouse. It seems he gave one to a number of children born in the village around that time. What a kind man he was! The bear was, of course, named Albert and it is still treasured by Andrew after 36 years.

Our main memories of Blaisdon life centre round plum picking for Ron Walton (we only picked about 500lbs a year, but it seemed a lot to us as, unlike the 'professionals', we always kept one hand firmly attached to the tree or ladder!), various Jubilee celebrations, a couple of very successful Plum Festivals, the church, the Parish Council (I was a member for around 27 years), the Red Hart, village

Nigel & Lynne Hogg
with the latest addition to the household,
Bonzo Bob, born 20th May 2012. (I. Waters)

'O come all ye faithful', 'Away in a manger', 'O little town of Bethlehem' and 'Once in royal David's city'. In those days we serenaded many older people who had worked in the same village and lived in the same home virtually all their lives. It was a real social occasion for them and they particularly enjoyed chatting to Roger whilst we performed. Nowadays many houses are occupied by people who have more experience of the wider world and who see our arrival on their doorstep as a pleasant element of their Christmas celebrations rather than as a significant social event.

The arrival of songbirds like Jean Waters and Jill Rodgett in the 1980s was timely, as things changed a bit and we were encouraged by them to experiment with a number of new renderings, with varying degrees of success. Now our repertoire is extensive! Yes, we have been asked not to sing on a few occasions (it will wake the children!) but mostly we are welcomed with open arms and often given hospitality, including home-made plum wine, mince pies and other delicious fare. I believe Roger has been carol singing since the mid 1960s, so it looks as if there is an excuse looming for another Blaisdon celebration - a 50th anniversary party!

fetes, harvest suppers (especially the 'entertainment' that came with them) and the friends, past and present, that we have made in the village.

And then there was carol singing! We were approached by Roger Keyse in December 1975 to join the merry band and this has been an annual event for us ever since. Each year Roger leads us all over the surrounding villages including Popes Hill, Flaxley, Nottwood Hill, and of course, Blaisdon - a journey that takes about a week to complete. All proceeds go to The Children's Society. Before the 1980s the repertoire was somewhat limited but we were good at

There have been many changes in our time. The Red Hart has gone from a small bar and a chemical loo to a much larger bar with integral dining facilities and a car park. One thing that hasn't changed is the friendliness of the staff - from Frank and Elsie Hogg, John Dunbar and Iris, David and Eileen Burton, Guy and Louise Wilkins, to the

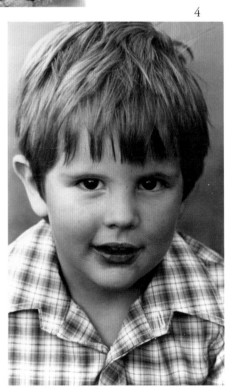

1. Brandy, Nigel, Lynne & Andrew
on holiday in 1985.

2. Andrew in Brightlands school
uniform. (1982)

3. Brandy in serious mode.

4. Andrew. (1982)

most recent landlord, Sharon Hookings. Long may we have such good publicans in the village!

Village fetes too are different. They used to take place in June down the street from the village hall, as far as The Blaisdon Nursery, with stalls etc in most of the front gardens. Vic and Enid Woodman's strawberries - for the teas - and their home grown fuchsias were for a long time the stars of the show. Now the fete is held in August in the village hall and the pub field but the stalls etc continue to echo its long standing character, which makes it work so well. We still manage to produce plums, from Stuart and Sue Gent's orchard, for sale at the fete, even though Ron Walton's distribution operation is long since gone and plums are no longer commercially produced in Blaisdon. One change we find rather sad. We miss the sound and presence of 'ding-dong' Hazel's ice cream van!

Despite all the changes, Blaisdon still has the same magical charms for us that it had when we first arrived. The community still pulls together, the village gossip is just as intriguing (some say 'The Archers' are modelled on Blaisdon life!) and the countryside remains as beautiful and colourful as ever. We are very lucky."

Nigel and Lynne's son, **Andrew Hogg** describes his life, growing up in Blaisdon:

"Born in Gloucestershire Royal Hospital and brought up in Blaisdon, all my memories of growing up are related to the village in some way or another.

Around 1980, my first memory, rather than those imagined from photographs, is of peering over the rear seat of Mum's

Andrew Hogg with Albert Bear.
Given to him by Albert Pithouse.
(2012)

T reg. red Renault 4 at a white, furry Golden Retriever called Brandy, who we had collected from Longhope. He was to be a close companion throughout my childhood along, briefly, with Foggy the cat. During this period of my life, I had to wear shorts. The Renault was equipped with black plastic seats that would suck up the heat of the sun and burn everyone's legs when Mum drove us on group outings, such as to Ross Swimming pool or Cinderford's Double View. I couldn't wait for the time when I could graduate to long trousers.

My friends comprised Frank and Ed Booth, James

Foster and later on James Guy, whose family had moved into Bridge House. We formed a pretty solid gang who ruthlessly roamed the woods to the rear of Syston Cottage, exploring, finding badger sets, making dens, climbing trees and generally getting filthy, grazed and tired. We'd be allowed out in the morning and return in the afternoon, ready for a hot bath. If at least one of us hadn't fallen in the brook, then we probably hadn't made it out of the house. We even managed to canoe along the brook at one point. To this day I still can't seem to retrieve a stick without getting side-tracked into doing something else that ultimately leads to a filled welly.

Other adventures involved setting up tents in one another's gardens and making camp fires. Poor Brandy would be compulsorily enrolled as guard dog in my garden. Fido, Frank and Ed's dog, took on the same role when we were 'across the road'.

Plum picking would be a late summer event, with constant reminders not to eat too many (had unfortunate dietary consequences), a careful avoidance of 'wigglies' that may have been inside and pleas not to trample squashed plums throughout the house. Occasionally selling them out of the drive for only 5p a pound at least kept me outdoors. I can thank the humble Blaisdon Plum for getting me my first celebrity kiss - from the newly crowned plum queen, as reported in the Citizen in 1992 (later in life I got a kiss from Vanessa Feltz but it wasn't such a fond memory).

As well as the plum festivals there were always village events taking place throughout the year. As a youngster my fond memories were more of swinging on the railings outside the village hall, wondering who was under that

Father Christmas beard, great excitement at putting up seemingly miles of homemade bunting, marvelling at Auntie Lilla's rolled butter balls and baskets and of being nervous at being roped into the Blaisdon Hall nativity play as a King. As it happened it was a bit part with no lines, Scott Brickel was the important King.

The village church, St. Michael and All Angels, featured heavily in my life. I was a part of the Blaisdon Bell Ringing team who rung the first round in the tower for some time, trained and led by John Gibson. Being little I was on treble (the lightest bell).

John Magee was the vicar who I remember best. He was just the kindest man. To keep the children involved and interested at church, everyone tended to have a job. Mine was to help Auntie Lilla determine how many wafers were required for communion. The church also had a Christingle service each year where I would help poke raisins and walnuts onto cocktail sticks and then into oranges and we would delight the congregation with our group musical and choral talent. There were a lot of recorders involved I recall.

I went to school at Brightlands in Newnham. Once I was invited to Blaisdon Church with the school choir for a carol concert. This was a highlight in the school calendar, as afterwards we were treated to a get-together at Ceri and Sheila Evans' house where there were good snacks, crisps and all the things we weren't normally allowed. Also there was a huge Christmas Tree in the hall.

Christmas inevitably meant carol singing and as one of the younger ones, I would get to hold the money tin and try and sweeten the customers with a solo of Away in a Manger or, on occasions, a duet with Ruth Jones. I dispute allegations that they ever paid us to leave!

Other key characters I remember are Cedric Etherington and Frank Baylis (Snr). Dad would often give Mr. Baylis a lift into Gloucester and I was always curious as to why he didn't ever wear any socks – I still don't really know why but he used to give me First Day covers which I proudly collected in a file.

In the late 1990s, Snuffles the cat adopted us and stayed with us until he died. In 1997 we acquired some chickens as a retirement gift to Dad. One of them managed to live for nearly 9 years. They were all lovely pets in their own peculiar ways.

For my 17th Birthday I was given a C reg. Vauxhall Nova, previously owned by Mum. I spent quite a lot of time trying to clear a space for it in the garage. However, it seemed that the only way to get the garage properly cleared was to host a party. Syston Cottage, with a few rusty mowers and other 'features' on display, hosted my 18th, 21st and 30th birthday parties

and my Sten do (Stag and Hen). The Red Hart always acted as a reliable temporary diversion, allowing Mum and Dad a chance to survey the damage before the hordes descended once again.

For the moment I am living away from Blaisdon but still refer to the village as home and still enjoy getting back, with Fuzzy my wife, to catch up on the critical local news: Where is the Uno Trophy? What's best on the pub menu? When's that pothole going to be repaired? Why don't you get another dog? and critically, now my Nova has a new home, Why can you still not get a car in the garage? Maybe it's time for another party?"

At Andrew & Fuzzy's wedding:
Top: Lynne & Nigel Hogg.
Left: Andrew & Fuzzy Hogg.
Above: Andrew's prized Nova.

Above:
Longhope Brook and snowdrops in the garden of Syston Cottage.

ILL HOUSE

The Martin family (Vol.2) continued to live in the Old Mill until they moved to Gloucester in 1967. Since then it has been divided into two houses, the left side being called Mill House and the right continuing as the Old Mill. Mill House has undergone several changes of ownership since the 1960s. Ken and Pat Hodgkinson lived there for some years with Pat's parents next door, in the Old Mill. Mill House was later bought by Peter Brooks, a Captain in commercial shipping.

Above: Mill House in 2012.
Below: Daphne Chappell.

They were followed by John and Daphne Chappell, who brought a large collection of snowdrops with them, discovering and developing many more, each one slightly different from the others. They even producing one they named after the house, Galanthus Pride of the Mill. This is described as an early flowering hybrid that has darkly marked inner segments and thick, rounded outer segments. Another couple, Nigel and Marian followed before Mill House was bought by **Waddy Warr**.

"In 1997, I moved my stud of Connemara and Welsh ponies to Blaisdon. My daughter Nicola and her husband Rupert had bought Tan House Farm and the ten acres over the road were offered to me. I had sold my farm at English Bicknor and had nowhere to live, so rented a bungalow in Huntley for a year hoping somewhere in Blaisdon would come on the market. I knocked on a few doors and amazingly the cottage, which actually adjoined my fields, was on offer to someone subject to survey. It did not pass, so I asked Rupert to do a basic inspection and did a very quick deal on the house. Meanwhile, for three months I lived in the cottage end of Spout Farm with my elder daughter Erica. We moved into The Mill House in March 1997.

It was somewhat dark and draughty but fairly dry and had a history. The garden was large with a lovely, huge, leaking pond and a space adjacent to my field for a stable yard. Quickly the ground was levelled, stables, hay store and feed room built and a space left for the lorry. I pulled down the dilapidated garage and put up a largish conservatory. I virtually lived in this room except for midwinter.

Erica eventually moved into Tan Cottage (the former farmhouse of Tan House Farm and I took on bed and breakfast (summer only) and continued to breed ponies. Bits of the house were reinstated and double-glazed cottage style windows kept it snug. Then in July 2007 came the Flood! It rained non-stop for a week and the main village road was a torrent of water. It came at the Mill House from front and back, and ended at the third step of the staircase! Stalwart members of the village climbed through the windows to move the furniture upstairs and the insurance company took a year before they helped financially and work could begin to put things back together.

Helena, Viki, Kyriakos & Theo Simonidis.

During this time Nicola and I had the bright idea of taking out the hall wall to enlarge the sitting room. Why had I not done this before? Eureka! I now loved the cottage as never before. But age creeps up on one slowly and inevitably. The garden seemed to get bigger; the ponies actually became fewer due to old age and there were fewer foals. Energy diminishes and the offer by Nicola of The Old Tannery became more attractive, and so in January 2012 I moved. The Mill House and eight acres still belong to me, the house and three acres now being tenanted.

Rudgeway Stud was started in 1956. Riding ponies, Welsh and Connemara ponies have moved about with me. The Connemara stallion Oxenholm Matador came with me to Blaisdon, a prolific winner in the show ring, both in-hand and ridden, and sire of top ponies throughout this country. Three of his offspring from my broodmare Oaklands Silver Orchid have been exported to USA, Denmark and Eire. Orchid, now aged twenty-one has just had her thirteenth foal, (by Nicola's dressage horse) a really beautiful colt. Matador was put down aged 32 and is buried with his favourite Welsh mare (aged 29) in his field, in Blaisdon."

The Simonidis family recently moved into Mill House. *Helena and Kyriakos Simonidis* continue:

"We have recently moved to Blaisdon from Greece. Kyriakos has also lived in Italy. and Helena is originally from the US. The kids, Theo and Viki, very much enjoy going to the local school, having already made many new friends. We enjoy living in the Mill House, it certainly is full of character. The village has beyond a doubt embraced the whole family and made us feel very welcome and part of the local community. Moving from one country to another can be quite stressful, and so having good neighbours has proven helpful and a godsend, at times."

OLD MILL

The Old Mill was occupied by Pat Hodgkinson's parents, Mr and Mrs Philip Horton. When they left the house was sold to **Joan Knowlman (nee Shepherd)** who lived in The Old Mill between 1977 and 1983:

"I had been living in New York for the few years beforehand, so when I moved to Blaisdon, 'culture shock' wasn't in it. I joined the WI and that's been a good part of my life ever since. We were flooded 2 or 3 times, when the water together with what seemed like most of other people's gardens, came through my back

Above:
The Old Mill in the snow.
Below:
The Old Mill decorated for the wedding of Joan &Brian Knowlman.
(1983)

door, which was in my bedroom. It then went through the ceiling and into the kitchen below, before leaving through the front door when the water level subsided. I got £25 from the EU if I remember rightly to help with repairs. A boy friend made me a mammoth and excellent drain in the garden, which just needs to be kept clear. The building has changed since my time, with the roof space being utilized and the back path and steps to the garden and the rear being constructed. I kept chickens in a wardrobe turned on its side, which everyone except me thought was very strange.

In 1983 my life changed when I married Brian. My wedding day was great fun, made all the more special by our neighbours. Lynne and Nigel Hogg provided a wedding breakfast served in the Old Mill. The house was dressed by our neighbours and Nigel even dressed up as a butler to serve the repast! I then moved away from Blaisdon to live in Somerset, though I still own the Old Mill, renting it to Jules and Ian."

Above Left:
Brian & Joan Knowlman are served their wedding breakfast by Nigel & Andrew Hogg.

Above Right:
The happy couple walk down from Blaisdon Church.
(1983)

Jules De Bharra, Ian Richardson, Megan Sharp & Maddy Sharp came to Blaisdon in 2000:

"We moved in to Old Mill in January 2000. I was 33, Ian was 36, Meg was 12 and Maddy 9. We've been here 12½ years. We were living in Newnham on Severn, which is where I met Ian in '98. The house hadn't been lived in for a few years and we asked Joan to put central heating in, as the house was cold and damp. The garden was a bit of a mess but we cleared the rockery in the front and made flowerbeds. We decorated the inside & pulled the larder down in the kitchen to give us more room. Ian and I were married on 1st July 2000. We both love the house very much.

The girls soon made friends in the village and enjoyed roaming about the fields and streams. Meg went to Dene Magna up the road and eventually Maddy joined her. There are 2 huge Sycamore trees on the edge of the leat in the back garden. We made a tree house in one and later put up rope swings for the girls. They played for hours and gave us performances of synchronised swinging.

The neighbours were flooded early 2000. We pitched up in the early hours after being woken by Sue & Peter Booth who asked Ian to move his truck from over the drain cover, so they could lift it to let more water from the road go down the drain. Ian was a little disorientated at 5 in the morning, but he went down and put his wellies on. He took a torch and shone it in the road as he could hear rushing water, he couldn't believe the road had turned into a river. He stepped out and the water filled his wellies! He managed

Jules De Bharra at her 40th Fancy Dress Birthday
under a rose arch built by Ian.
Below:
Old Mill with Jules' vegetable garden.

to get to the truck, but found it hard to concentrate & drive it. He drove it quite a way up the road before the water was shallower. We were all up then and went and helped our neighbours empty their flooded kitchen. Maddy worked hard with a dustpan, scooping water into a bucket. The children were happy as school was cancelled the next day!

We were flooded again in 2007. The water was so high in the driveway to The Mill House, that my knickers got wet wading round to rescue Mrs Warr's furniture and effects, which I could see floating through her window. As I was helping her, I looked out of the window towards our porch and saw shoes floating about. At this point I climbed out of Mrs Warr's sitting room window and tried to rescue our shoes and carpets. We got off lightly, and just had to wash and dry carpets. People from the village came down to offer support, which was great.

One memory of a Blaisdon fete was Megan and Maddy helping with the stocks. They managed to persuade Guy the landlord at the time to get wet and people were queuing up to throw sponges. During the 2011 fete, the pub pig escaped and was running around the stalls. It took a deal of catching.

We've really enjoyed living in Blaisdon. It is such a beautiful, quiet spot with lovely people. We especially love our neighbours Lynne and Nigel, who are the warmest, most generous neighbours you could wish for. We've looked after their chickens when they've been away, watered each other's plants and generally kept an eye on things. They invariably bring us back some goodies from wherever they've been.

When we first arrived, Lynne & Nigel Hogg had a spectacularly cantankerous cockerel, called Rex. Fantastic as he was we had mixed feelings when he finally fell off his perch. He was very reliable as an early morning wake up call and we were looking forward to many peaceful lie-ins from then on. Imagine our surprise when one of the widows from his harem took it upon herself to fill the gap, with a noble but less operatic attempt at the dawn chorus. We were woken by a strangulated cock-a-doodle-doo from then onwards until her demise, which

Above:
Ian Richardson at Jules 40th birthday party,
as a tax return.
Below:
Ian serving dinner across the oak table he built.

occurred when we were looking after the hens. We were not responsible we promise. We have spoken to many chicken keepers since and no one has heard of this phenomenon before.

We cut down a large conifer in the driveway in 2010. It was 40ft high. This gave a lot more light to the Old Mill. We also made vegetable beds in 2009 in the front garden in the shape of a torque. I have also planted a herb garden in the front bed.

Ian and I ride a tandem and have spent many happy sunny days riding out from the house round all the beautiful lanes that radiate from Blaisdon. We get as far as Ashleworth, usually to the Boat Inn for a pint before cycling home. Maddy joined Westbury Young Farmers Club and very quickly took on responsibilities such as secretary 2009-2010. They had a very successful few years, winning the county rally 5 times in a row. Maddy now lives in Rodley but remains very attached to Blaisdon and the Forest of Dean in general. Meg is away working in London. She felt she needed to leave but has the benefit of being able to come back often to soak up the countryside. Meg really misses the closeness of nature after being in

Jules De Bharra & Ian Richardson
outside the Old Mill.(2012). The house sign was carved by Ian.

London for 4 years and hankers for the great outdoors much more than she ever did."

Megan Sharp adds:

"As one of a small group of similar aged kids living in Blaisdon, we had a brilliant time picking conkers, swimming in garden pools, apple fights (not strictly allowed), following the stream as far as we could, discovering hidden tunnels, building dens, exploring the woods on the hill, sledging etc. It's a beautiful place to grow up, peaceful and safe. At times we found it a bit far from our school friends living in Mitcheldean and Cinderford but looking back now, I feel like it couldn't have been a more perfect place to grow up."

THE  ORGE

Roger Etherington clearly has Blaisdon in his blood, spending his childhood at The Forge with his parents, Cedric and Dinah Etherington, and sister, Elizabeth (Volume 2). As a married man with young children, he lived on the Stud Farm. He returned once more to live at The Forge in 1990 with his now elderly parents. Dinah Etherington died in 1992 and Cedric in 1996.

Above: The Forge
Below: Roger Etherington in his summerhouse.

Cedric continued to play an active part in village life throughout his later years. His efforts to collect local historical information formed the seeds from which was developed the book 'Blaisdon Memories of a Country Parish 1935-64'. His door was the one to which enquiring visitors would be sent if they were researching their relatives from the Blaisdon area. More often than not, he would have some little gem for them and he always made sure he found out how they were connected to the village.

Roger Etherington continues to live in The Forge and passes on his thoughts:

"During the late spring of 1990, I came to live again in the cottage where I spent my childhood. The house itself was little changed. The vegetables and chickens in the garden had been replaced by lawn and flowers. Electricity had long since replaced the oil lamps and a modern stove stood where the old cooking stove had been. Gone too was the copper boiler. In its place was a fridge full of cold drinks and ice cubes. The old tin bath was now permanently left outside behind the wooden stable where horses once waited patiently to be shod. Happily, horses still graze in the meadow opposite the house and the countryside is as wonderful as ever and the church tower clock still measures the passing seasons as it has done for more than a century."

ILL COTTAGE

Above: Hill Cottage in 2012.
Below: Annie & Ernest King at home in Hill Cottage.

Steve and Judith King:

"Hill Cottage was purchased by the King Family of Monkhill Farm, Flaxley, in 1958. Annie & Ernest King moved into the cottage in April that year following the marriage of their son Dennis to Jean Bullock. Following the death of Annie in 1977 Ernest remained at Hill Cottage passing away in 1981 after a spell in hospital.

The house stayed empty until September 1985 when Stephen and Judith (nee Cadogan) moved in following their marriage at Awre Church. They had met through Westbury on Severn Young Farmers.

The house went through some modernisation. It was completely rewired, re-piped, a modern bathroom was installed and the hand pump that serviced the well in the front garden was removed to make way for a new kitchen. The following year the over grown fruit trees at the back were removed to open up the lovely views to Flaxley Wood. Steve continued to work at Monkhill Farm and Judith commuted to Gloucester working in an accounts Dept.

On 8th August 1992 Robert was born, completing the family. He attended Westbury on Severn C. of E. School

from 1996 to 2003, then on to Dene Magna School, Mitcheldean, until 2008. He studied agriculture for 3 years at Hartpury College and is a keen member of Westbury on Severn Young Farmers Club

In 2003 Steve left the family farm taking over the ownership with Judith of Hill Cottage, plus Dick & Oaks Bough field and the adjoining disused railway line, which still has the remains of Blaisdon Halt's platform.

In 2003-2004 oil fired central heating was installed, the original roof replaced adding roofing felt and loft installation making the house much warmer. The majority of the downstairs was damp proofed, new floors laid and the old pantry wall knocked through to the living room to create a dining area leaving the six meat hooks on the ceiling. The kitchen revamped & replaced and a conservatory added to the back of the house together with a patio area.

Steve continues to work locally on a beef farm with Robert following in his footsteps. Judith still commutes to Gloucester for work and Smudge the cat keeps the mice at bay.

We enjoy leaving in Blaisdon for the peace and tranquillity and regularly take advantage of the lovely walks through Blaisdon, Flaxley and Ley Park woods and the surrounding footpaths.

We can't finish this without mentioning what a great pub the Red Hart is and Roger Keyse's tasty tomatoes."

Top:
Judith, Robert & Stephen King.
Below:
Stephen & Judith King
At a Village Hall party in 2012.

AN HOUSE

Tan House.
(2012)

Christopher and Patricia Manners moved to Blaisdon in 1961. Christopher remembers:

"As I write, we have spent 51 years at the Tan House, half a lifetime. The house has seen all of our married life: Our family being born, growing up, going to school and then university; Patricia's and my work and careers; our dinner parties, BBQ's, and celebrations with friends. Through all of this, it has always been there to welcome us back from the various holidays and trips that we have been lucky enough to make.

Undoubtedly village life has changed greatly over that period. Back in the 1960s and 1970s there was much more of a community feel around the village. Most of the houses were lived in by people whose parents had lived there before them, and who had been brought up in the village, unlike now when houses change hands continuously, and there always seem to be new faces around. Perhaps the most obvious sign of this is in the cars. When we arrived in the village, only Captain Back from Blaisdon House and ourselves had a car and villagers on the whole did not go far, perhaps to Gloucester, on the village bus. They depended on the village for their amusement and entertainment. Now however, most houses in the village

have 2 cars parked outside – and villagers travel to find their pleasures.

In those days, Blaisdon Church played a much bigger part in village life. And for several years during the 1960s it put on a Nativity Play, with the congregation, which was considerably larger in those days, very involved playing the various parts, and Patricia providing the music. I can remember some amazing headdresses made by Roger and Hilary Etherington. It was at this time that the once-per-month Family Service started up, under the guidance of our curate, John Magee. John had himself been a pupil at the Salesian School, become a schoolteacher, married a local village girl, Ruth Brewer, and moved back to the village when he retired. He was one of the first men to be ordained as a non-stipendiary priest in the Anglican

Church and a good friend of ours.

Our children, Caroline, Charles and Tom, grew up in the village. As far as I remember it was playing in the garden, rabbits and tortoises in cages, children's tea parties, walks with the dogs, pooh-sticks under the bridge down by Nigel Hogg's house and the sun always shone every summer.

We have always had a dog at the Tan House. Mostly golden Labradors, Fudge, Muffin and Barley, but currently we have Maisie, a gorgeous Cavalier King Charles.

By the time Caroline was 5, the village school had shut down. She went to the Primary School at Minsterworth, followed by Charles and Tom. The school was brilliant with a wonderful Head Mistress, Miss Wallace, who embodied all the best virtues of Scottish education, and a fabulous teacher for the younger children, Mrs Gunn. I remember that every term they had a concert, when every child without exception had to perform in public on their own. 'I'm a little tea pot, short and stout' etc! We firmly believe that any success our children might have had in their lives, dates back to Minsterworth School.

The winter of 1962-3 was very severe – and for 4 days the village was cut off from the outside world by 4 feet of snow. At one point, a group from the village set off on foot with a sledge for Longhope, to get food. On the

The Tan House & Wisteria.

first day of being cut off, each house cleared its drive of snow down to the road. Early next morning, Br. Joe, one of the Lay Brothers at the Salesian School, drove his JCB and snowplough down the village to clear the road. So, when the villagers emerged, they found all the snow had been dumped back on their drive, which was now blocked again, causing a certain amount of frustration!

In the 1960s Patricia and Mrs Back started the WI in the village, which ran for 40 years before closing down.

One of the pleasures of our kitchen is the ever-changing variety of animals in the field behind such as cows, sheep and horses. On one occasion, we came down to breakfast to find a huge Hereford Bull up against, and framed in, the window!

When she was 8, Caroline, and Thursa Lilley, used to go off to Northwood Green every Saturday – to learn embroidery from Noreen Littleton, who also did the most beautifully written and illustrated prayers on cards, which you can still get at Gloucester Cathedral.

In about 1970, we started our annual 'Wisteria Coffee Morning.' The Tan House has a spectacular wisteria growing by the front door, and we used this as an excuse to have a coffee morning for charity, generally for Christian Aid, but one year we had a very successful one for the hospice that we visited in South Africa, which raised £500 and bought them a generator.

1

2

3

4

5

The Manners Family:
1. Charles
2. Charles, C. Smith, Caroline & at the
front, Tom.
3. & 4. Caroline.
5. Tom.

1. Patricia Manners with
Tom & Chris.
2. & 3. Christopher Manners
with Salmon.
4. Massie enjoying spring in the
Tan House Garden.

It was about then that Patricia started music and dancing classes in the Village Hall and children from far and wide came. Another venture for children, in which she was involved, were the children's summer opera camps. Over a period of 17 years, for a week each summer, about 60 children gathered together to rehearse an opera, camping under canvas, and then put on two performances for parents, relations and friends. One year it was in Blaisdon, because Patricia had suffered a car accident and could not drive far, the opera being 'Pirates of Penzance' by Gilbert & Sullivan. The camp was in Dick Hawker's field behind the Tan House. And the rehearsals and performances took place in the gym of the Salesian School at Blaisdon Hall. Patricia did all the music and Christopher did the lighting, as well as being the Camp Commandant when under canvas. It was a struggle to keep girls in girl's tents and boys in boy's ones! The performances were such a success that the following year we took it to The Fringe at the Edinburgh Festival, where again the cast excelled and at the same time had a really fun time. They played to audiences of 250, which when you think that there were over 750 different shows available each week is not bad.

Having the Salesian School in the village was a huge bonus to us and to all other villagers. We made really good friends with the Father Rector and the Head Master, as well as many other members of the staff and quite a few of the boys. For a number of years, Patricia played the piano for their annual pantomime.

Also in 1970, Christopher moved to the Group Head Office in Worcester and then left in 1973 to start his own company on the Gloucester Trading Estate. He sold out in 1985, and became a Marketing Consultant, tying up in 1998 with a colleague in St Petersburg, Russia, to provide consultancy and start a joint food ingredient company. Meantime, Patricia was self-employed, teaching piano to countless children and as a relationship counsellor.

We both got involved in outside activities. Christopher was on the Council of a school, a non-executive director of the Severn NHS Trust, and a JP and member of their Advisory Committee. Patricia was a Relate Counsellor for 29 years, on the Board of the Gloucester Prison, an ACCM Selector (vicar picking) and the national Board of Ministry, and as a Director of the Aston Theological Training School. She was also heavily involved, from time to time, in putting on and organising various major concerts in Gloucester Cathedral, Tewkesbury Abbey, and London, to raise money for charity.

The Tan House has been the scene for numerous celebrations. 1985 saw our Silver Wedding, with a lunch in a pavilion on the lawn. 1993 was Caroline's wedding, when she married Pierre. The marriage took place in the benefice church at Westbury-on-Severn, as the Blaisdon Church was too small. The wedding took place at 4.00 pm, and being just before Christmas it was dark. There was no electric lighting used in the church but candles, 300 of them, a lovely warm glow! The reception was in a large marquee in Dick Hawker's field behind the house. I do remember that the week before was very wet, and part of the matting in the marquee was completely waterlogged but it did not stop all enjoying themselves. 2010 was our Golden Wedding and again we had a pavilion on the lawn with local friends who had had an influence on our lives over the years, to drinks the evening before and friends and relations from further away to lunch the next day.

Suddenly, having been very wrapped up in the Tan House for so long, our children were grown up, left school, and fled the nest. They all did a gap year before going to university. Caroline went to Venezuela on a research expedition, Charles to Australia to work on an oil exploration unit, and Tom to Kenya to teach in a school in Nairobi. All three went to Durham University and we got to know the road from Blaisdon to Durham very well.

In 1986 we doubled the size of the Drawing Room and built an en-suite bathroom above it. A bigger drawing room meant that we could have small concerts in it, with about 40 people. Singers who performed included Jean Waters, on several occasions, who lived in the village, and other friends and always with Patricia accompanying on her piano. The music was of high quality, and much appreciated.

The Salesian School up at Blaisdon Hall did a wonderful job caring for and teaching the boys who were lucky enough to be sent there by various Local Authorities. However, sadly, with the passage of time numbers dropped as the Local Authorities found themselves short of cash. When we came there were 65 boys, but by 1995 it was down to 19 and the Father Rector took the decision to close.

Just before the doors closed, and the remaining boys went off to other schools, the staff decided to take them to Disney World in France, so they would have something to remember. The village had various fund-raising events to help finance the adventure and off they set. When they got to the hotel the night before their day at Disney World, they learnt that due to the very cold weather and ice, most of the rides were shut, and had been for several days. The then Head Master, who was with them, told us that when he went to bed that night, he prayed to The Lord, saying, 'Lord, the lives of these kids are being turned upside down, and their only bright light is the adventure tomorrow, so please ensure all the rides are running.' And lo and behold, next morning the sun was shining, it was warmer and Disney World had all of the rides operative! Such is the power of prayer?

The only thing that springs to mind during the time of the next owner of Blaisdon Hall, Hartpury College, is the Pop Concert. Presumably to raise money, Hartpury allowed a pop concert to take place the weekend after Glastonbury on the fields below the house. The police had roadblocks on all roads into the village, to prevent crowds coming before Friday, and villagers were issued with passes to get into the village. A police command post was set up in the village hall. On the Friday people poured in and the music started on Saturday morning. Tan House was the nearest house to the stage, and in direct route. We could not hear the music, other than as a background noise but the beat, boom, boom, boom, was very clear and objectionable. The police carried out a good job but life in the village was disrupted until Sunday night. Fortunately it was not repeated.

Who knows what life will be like at the time of the next Blaisdon saga? Two things are certain. One is that life in the village will have changed again, as it has done during the period of this book. And the second is that, by then, someone else will be living in, and enjoying, the Tan House."

The Manners family celebrating Christopher's 70th birthday.
Patricia & Christopher, Centre with from the left,
Back row: Eleanor, Charles, Alex, Sally, Pierre, Caroline & Tom holding Freddie.
Front row: Matilda, Lucy, Alice, Angus, Ralph with Will in front.

AN HOUSE SINGERS

Tan House Singers (2012),
Conductor Janet Upton.
(N. Funston)

Christopher Manners writes of the Tan House Singers:

"Patricia formed the choir 'The Tan House Singers' in 1983. About a dozen local enthusiasts got together to sing and make music. Initially they rehearsed in the hall of the Tan House, hence their name.

Gradually their numbers increased, as did their skills ,ambitions and reputation, to the point that in 1997 rehearsals had to be transferred to the Blaisdon Village Hall, where they still meet. Their repertoire widened, to embrace Madrigals, Folk Songs, and music for weddings, as well as major choral works by all the well-known and famous composers. Many of the concerts given were fund-raising for charities.

In 1992 The Tan House Singers carried out what they grandly call 'their first Foreign Tour,' to Holland, with concerts in Amsterdam and The Hague. In 2000 and 2001 they had tours to St Malo. This culminated in a tour to the very beautiful City of Chartres in 2002. They celebrated their 20th anniversary with a concert at Blackfriars Priory in Gloucester. The choir is still thriving, goes from strength - to - strength, and will be celebrating their 30th anniversary next year, in 2013.

Since the very beginning, Patricia has been, and still is, the accompanist on the piano, singing when she is not playing, in addition to being their organiser and driving force and Christopher is the choir's 'longest serving groupie' having been to just about every concert they have given. If you ask a choir member, they will tell you that they take their music very seriously but they also have great fun, laughter and friendship, which is really what amateur music is all about."

Conductors of the Tan House Choir.

Ian Dollins	James Mustard
Adrian Hutton	Benjamin Nicholas
Richard Mynors	Oliver Mason
Adrian Partington	Ralf Blasi
Andrew Sacket	James Atherton
Janet Upton	

1

2

3

4

1.Patricia Manners with soloists, Eleanor Waters
(Oboe), left & Keira Hazen (Violin).
2. Tan House Singers in Amsterdam,
conductor, Adrian Hutton, front left.
3.Patricia Manners (N. Funston)
4. Tan House Singers. Jean Waters, solo soprano,
centre.

St. Malo Tour

1. Choir rehearsal with conductor, James Mustard.

2. time off for a clifftop walk, from the left,
Jean Waters, Jeremy Barnes, Joe Willison, Patricia Manners,
Mary Barnes, Christopher Manners, Ken Watson.

3. Followed by a well earned drink, from the left,
Mary & Jeremy Barnes, Joe Willison, Christopher Manners,
Ken Watson, Tom Fenton, Jean Waters, Patricia Manners.

Pictures to the left: The choir enjoying a sociable lunch.

AN HOUSE FARM

Ron and Mary Walton (Volume 2) had bought the land and buildings that formed Tan House Farm in the 1950s. They continued to live in Blaisdon, having built Tan House Cottage next to the farm buildings in the late 1960s. On retirement, they sold the farm including their home to Nicola and Rupert Klaiber.

Tan House Farm
with stabling to the left.

Nicki Klaiber continues:

"In the autumn of 1995 Rupert and I purchased Tan House Farm with almost thirty two acres of farmland, the house and associated farm buildings. We moved into the house with our two young children, Phillipa, then three, and Alex, eighteen months. We purchased the farm with the hopes that we would get planning permission to convert the Grade II listed timber clad barn within the yard to a family dwelling. It took two years to obtain the planning required. But finally in 1998 it was converted and we moved into our new home. We retained the Tan House Farm name and named the house next door Tan House Cottage.

The same year my father, Richard Warr, purchased the bungalow from us. It was his intention to move closer to the family and his grandchildren for his retirement.

Unfortunately, he sadly died shortly after moving and therefore never fulfilled his wish.

My sister, Erica and I inherited the bungalow, which she later moved into. In 2004 Rupert moved to Newent and then Gloucester. Phillipa, Alex and I remained in Blaisdon. Unable to continue maintaining the whole farm, I sold nearly ten acres of fields that run along the length of the nearby brook to a neighbour, Nigel Hogg. This now left the farm with approximately twelve acres

Eventually I obtained planning permission to convert the Old Tannery, a Grade II Listed brick barn. This was with the intention of doing holiday letting. It was converted in 2011/2012. However, just as it was nearing completing it was decided that it would be better if my mother moved into it and sell or let her own property, The Mill House.

The children had a wonderful childhood playing, as they should, in the fields woods and swimming in the brook on summer days. On the rare occasion we had heavy snow they, along with the other children in the village, would sledge on Blaisdon bank or on the hill behind the Church."

1. Removing the roadside barns in front of what is now the Tan House Farm house c1998.
2. Phillipa Klaiber. (2012)
3. Waddy Warr, Alex & Nicola Klaiber working on Waddy's new garden.
4. Nicola Klaiber on Oxenholme Matador (Matt).

OLD TANNERY

The Old Tannery, sits alongside the road, opposite The Tan House and adjacent to the barn conversion that is Tan House Farm. Nicola Klaiber has also had the Old Tannery barn converted into an attractive dwelling that makes the most of its timber-framed structure. Her mother, Waddy Warr moved into the house on completion of the building works, early in 2012.

1

2

3

4

5

1. The Old Tannery.
2. Waddy relaxing outside her new home.
3. Waddy enjoying her new garden.
4. Exterior view of The Old Tannery.
5. Interior of The Old Tannery, showing large internal beams.

AN COTTAGE

Ron and Mary Walton lived in Tan Cottage from when it was built until they retired and sold it along with their land. Richard Warr bought the cottage from Rupert and Nicola Klaiber when they bought the farm in 1995. Unfortunately, he was only in the bungalow for a short time before he passed away. His daughter, **Erica Warr** continues:

Above:
Tan Cottage.
Below:
Erica Warr.

"I came to Blaisdon from Cornwall in Febuary 1997 and moved into Spout Farm House, where my mother was living. After a month we both moved to The Mill House, where I lived for six years.

I moved into Tan Cottage in April 2003. My partner, Martin Bilby, has lived here since August 2008. Since owning the bungalow some of the windows were replaced in 2006 and others in 2012. A new front door was put in in 2011. Part of the front lawn was laid with stone in 2009 and we replaced the back lawn with decking in the same year. The greenhouse on the side was replaced with a shed in 2011. I am a chef at South Herefordshire Golf Club and my partner, Martin, works at Messier Dowty in Gloucester"

 OLMELEA

Above;:
Holmelea.
Below:
Karen & Brian Pearce.

Brian and Rita Pearce moved to Blaisdon in 1967. Their daughter, Karen was born in 1971. Brian is a keen filmmaker, having produced films of life in Blaisdon during the years he has lived in the village as well as recordings around the Forest of Dean. He shares his love of model trains with the younger and older boys around the village. Ian Waters recalls spending many hours discussing the merits of different model engines and Brian helping him to get them to work when his Dad had produced another second-hand bargain!

Brian is something of an inventor but his greatest love is clocks. Many vintage and antique clocks have had the benefit of his expert hands, restoring them to prime condition. He built a garage alongside Holmelea that also houses his workshops.

Sadly, Rita has passed away but Brian continues to live at Holmlea, working on his latest project and enjoying life in Blaisdon.

BLAISDON NURSERIES

Roger Keyse worked with his father, George Keyse (Volume 2) at Blaisdon Nurseries until his father's death in 1982. He continued the family business until his own retirement in 2011. He tells of these years:

"In the days when my father and I were running the nursery together, we operated a rotation system, with chrysanthemums, tomatoes and lettuce. The chrysanthemums were grown outside in ten inch pots, while the tomatoes were in the glasshouses. When the tomatoes were finished around September, the chrysanthemums were brought inside and the spare ground was used for winter lettuce.

Above:
Blaisdon Nurseries with Annexe to left.
Below:
Ada Keyse.

I continued this after my dad died but pressures from outside gradually made the operation non-profit-making. Newer varieties of chrysanthemums were developed that could be grown in the ground and improved transport brought in flowers from abroad. Similarly, cheap imports of tomatoes from sunnier climbs made home grown ones uneconomical.

Perhaps the final nails in the coffin were the demise of the local auction markets at Grange Court, Gloucester and Cheltenham, together with the rise of the supermarkets. However, with people becoming concerned about the health issues relating to how their food is grown plus the cost to the environment of transporting food long distances instead of growing locally, perhaps things are swinging back to favour local producers. However, it is not possible for a small nursery to rely on passing trade down a small country lane.

I also grew other vegetables and flowers, providing a small business of floral bouquets and wreaths for funerals. Christmas wreaths have also been much in demand and I have won many awards in competitions for them in the past.

Alongside the nursery business, I also rented the grazing on Blaisdon Hall's land for many years, running sheep on it, until the Salesians sold the estate. I continued to have sheep until the foot and mouth epidemic in 2001. Although not infected, the sheep had to be put down for animal welfare reasons, as I was unable to move them onto fresh pasture due to the restrictions in place around Blaisdon at the time. After losing my flock, I just couldn't face starting again and possibly facing the same heartbreaking scenario in the future. It was a big part of my life for many years, more a lifestyle than a job. On some days, I would dip over six hundred sheep in a day.

I had married Ann in 1978 and we set up home in Blakeney, where she comes from. Claire was born in 1979 Mum died in 1998 and soon after, Ann, Claire and I moved back home to Blaisdon.

I have always tried to play an active part in the village, being Lay-Chairman of the PCC since the 1970s and sometime Chairman of the Village Hall Committee. I have also been the Sunday newspaper delivery boy for Blaisdon since 1956!

One of the things I have most enjoyed is leading the carol singing around Blaisdon, Flaxley and Popes Hill. This was started by Rev. Bick in the early 1960s. When he left in 1973, I continued to organise it. Over the week before Christmas, a sturdy group of singers would climb in the back of Dick Hawker's and later, Pete Adams', Land Rovers. Whatever the weather, we would trek along the dark lanes to remote houses bringing our own bit of festive cheer. Woe betide us if we missed any of our regulars out. They would be on the telephone the next day! The collections have always been for The Children's Society and over the years we have raised £40,000.

In 2011 I retired and Ann and I moved into our new house. We converted the old apple and fruit store, which was on the opposite side of the drive to the main House, into a new home for us. One of the 'finds' during the building work was the garden's old sharpening stone. This very large sandstone has been moulded by many years of grinding tools on it. It is now used as a garden bench outside our cottage.

Perhaps the biggest change to the village in my lifetime was Blaisdon Hall passing into private hands. After generations of villagers had enjoyed access to the grounds, understandably, this came to an end when the Hall was sold."

Claire Keyse and Richard Jones together with children Ella, 3, and George, 1, moved into Blaisdon Nurseries

1. & 2. The nurseries in summer &
winter.

Roger Keyse:

3. At work in the nurseries.

4. Aged 14.

5. Enjoying himself.

6. After a haircurcut for charity.

1. Ann & Claire Keyse.
2. Ann & Roger Keyse.
3. Ann Keyse haymaking.
4. Claire, Ann, Julie & Aubrey Keyse.
5. Roger Keyse's 60th birthday party with
Claire Keyse & Richard Jones.

in 2011, when Claire's parents moved into the converted annexe next door. Richard works as a Nuclear Scientist for EDF energy in Gloucester and Claire for AstraZenica in Avonmouth as a Quality Assurance Analyst. **Claire Keyse** though has known the house and village all her life:

"After renovating the annexe, which was a derelict outbuilding used in the past to store apples and other fruit, to live in in 2006, our expanding family needed more room. So, we moved onto the main house and are completely renovating it including an extension, which was built in 2010! This year we have finally had the kitchen installed and the Bathroom will be our next project. Every other room in the house has had new ceilings, been re-plastered, re-wired and plumbed, as well as a new staircase and layout upstairs!

Although not a resident of Blaisdon until I was an adult, it has always been a large part of my life due to it being my father's place of work and my Nan's home. Virtually every Sunday afternoon without fail was spent here during my childhood in the 1980s and 90s, so here are a few

Top:
Visiting Travellers with their traditional home pictured in front of the large barn next to Blaisdon Nurseries.

Centre:
Lamb feeding time for local children At Blaisdon Nurseries.

seasonal memories of the village:

Spring.

Spring was always marked for me by the blooming of the bright yellow daffodils along all of the lanes and in the village. I remember feeling very proud of the fact that my dad and granddad were mostly responsible for bringing these bright cheery colours into the otherwise gloomy early days of the year.

Spring was also a time of excitement at the Nurseries – lambing season! I used to relish the days spent here during this time. They were full of the excitement of seeing new baby lambs born, who were so cute to me! I would walk the fields with my dad expectantly looking for telltale signs of an impending birth! We often had lambs to bottle-feed and nothing was more wondrous to me than bringing a cold newborn lamb in from the harsh outdoors to warm it by my Nan's fire and bottle-feed it glucose and formula.

Summer.

The lambs weren't the only new

arrivals here. A litter of kittens from my Nan's cats were also a yearly occurrence. Anyone who knew me at the time will know that I was somewhat obsessed with the gorgeous little fur balls and would spend hours nursing the tiny little things to the point that my mum complained that not one of my tops was free from the scagged threads pulled by a kittens claws!

Sheepshearing season was also notable. I remember the busy days rounding up the sheep, my dad (and sometimes helpers) expertly and quickly shearing the sheep's coat off then rolling up the oily wool. I was fascinated to watch this go on and remember running back and forth from the yard to the house supplying the workers with cool drinks! During the summer holidays the outdoor pool at Blaisdon Hall was open for locals and campers and I was eager to use it every day possible. I loved it, despite the freezing water! I learnt to swim in this pool with my dad and spent many hours and days having lots of fun there. After, we would go back to my Nan's for tea and sandwiches with tomatoes from the greenhouse. They were absolutely delicious!

Autumn.

Late summer/autumn was the time that the Blaisdon Plum would ripen. Having fields lined with the fruiting trees made for a busy time! My dad would be up a ladder picking plums while my mother and I would be picking up the fallen ones from the grass. I loved them. However I still to this day will always break open a plum to inspect for any 'inhabitants' before eating having being caught out as a child!

Many days spent here would involve me making mud pies,

my favourite game, while my mum and dad went about their work. Afternoon tea with my Nan was usually a jam sandwich. She made jams with all of the nursery produce, strawberry, gooseberry, plum, but my absolute favourite was raspberry. Luckily for me my mother has taken on the jam making and still keeps me stocked with delicious homemade 'Blaisdon Nursery' Raspberry Jam.

Blaisdon Nurseries always had a supply of pumpkins for Halloween – some enormous ones grown by my dad! Carving scary-faced pumpkins here is a fond memory, as is the pumpkin pie my Nan would make from the offcuts!

Winter.

Another time of year that my life revolved around Blaisdon as a child was Christmas – so much excitement and build up to the big day came from the annual week of carol singing organised by my dad and others to raise money for the Children's Society. I would be keen to be here for every night to join in. Large groups of us back then would all scramble in the back of a Land Rover to go around the local area singing at doors and more often than not we were invited inside for drinks and homemade mince pies fresh out of the oven. It was magical and the hospitality so often put on for us was absolutely first class. They are very happy memories from these days, such fun and such generosity exhibited by the locals."

Roger Keyse,
with newly hatched chick.

1

2

3

4

1. Claire Keyse being awarded her degree.
2. Ella & George Jones.
3. Richard & George Jones.
4. Roger Keyse & Ella Jones.
5. Claire Keyse & George Jones.

5

SUNNYSIDE

Robert & Margaret Pickering (Volume 2) lived in Sunnyside until Margaret passed away and Robert's increased frailty resulted in a move to a nearby care home. The new family moving into Sunnyside were ***Claire and Chris Woolham*** with their boys, Clayton and Callan:

"Originally from Derbyshire, we moved to this property in January 2000 from Huntley, a few miles down the road, miles apart in terms of family life style! From a house in an estate with a pocket-handkerchief garden to a house which, although semi-detached, was full of space and gave a young family room to grow! We have no regrets and would find it very difficult to move on. From spending weekends escaping and finding things to do to being so content at home we don't make much effort to go out!

The house had a lovely homely feel although it had been empty for over a year. It was obvious that the last owners had loved the house from the 54 years they spent here. A lot of work was required to make it habitable for modern life, including electrics upstairs where previously there was one bakelite 2-pin plug for a lamp in each room! It was exciting bringing the home back to life. It was great seeing the seasons change in the garden and the plants the previous owners had nurtured.

The boys loved the garden space. They could play in safety

Sunneyside in 2012.

and we installed some play equipment, which helped with their friends from Huntley who loved to visit and with the local children. We thought that they would find the move difficult but they enjoyed it.

Over the years we have built above the flat roofed extension that existed, giving the boys more bedroom space and we have continued to add to the plants in the garden along with building ornamental fishponds. The garden has given and continues to give us great pleasure. Although we now have to admit we have run out of room for the trees we love to plant!

The surrounding countryside has been great to explore; there are some fantastic walks and views. We discovered orchids in several places, elfin cups and much more. There is a wide range of wildlife to see and country lanes to cycle. It has been good to speak to villagers who have lived here a long time and to hear the history of the houses in the village; it stretches the imagination to think of a train running near the bottom of the village.

Blaisdon is a tranquil oasis in a busy modern society. It is a great place to come home to at the end of a working day. It has all of the advantages of rural life while all amenities are accessible if wanted; life is as quiet or a busy as you want it to be, thoughts that are shared by the boys. The downside is that the broadband service is so poor! Sports wise they compete in local football, hockey and golf and socially there are great opportunities with the Young Farmers

The local secondary school, Dene Magna, was a great school where both boys did extremely well and Clayton has gone on in further education to Loughborough University, while Callan has taken a year out to decide what sort of career he might like to pursue and currently works for a DIY store in Gloucester (I see a winter of decorating!)"

Above:
Claire & Chris Woolham, with sons, Clayton & Callum.
(2012)

Left:
The garden and ponds at Sunnyside.
(2012)

THE COTTAGE

Above;
The Cottage with its magnolia in bloom.(2012)
Top right:
The Cottage, later in the year

After the death of Jack Copner in 1968 (Volume 2), The Cottage was home to Mrs Ivor Jones (Volume 2) from Streamways, Woodgreen. She spent the rest of her days in The Cottage. One of the 'charming' aspects of old country life is that although her name was Enid, she was known by the whole village as Mrs Ivor, differentiating her from Mrs Bill, also Jones, who lived next door.

The Cottage is currently occupied by Kevin and Kate Packham.

The Cottage's front garden is dominated by one of the most spectacular magnolias in the area.

WESTERN VIEW

After the death of Mrs Evelyn Jones (Volume 2) in 1995, Western View was sold to Brendan Quinlan and then, soon after, to **Ian and Tracey** Batham:

"In the autumn of 1996 we had spent many days searching the villages of Gloucestershire trying to escape a two bed starter home with a growing family in rapidly expanding Quedgeley.

We were a young family, Ian and Tracey, Hollie, our first, was two and Sam was only just born. We came upon Western View and decided to get a viewing; it was

Western View:
Above in 2012
Below in 2001, before the building of the extension.

unoccupied cold, dark, smelled funny, had unpainted walls and smashed windows, it had a downstairs bathroom with an old tin bath and nowhere to park your car. Not much going for it, but what we recognized was that it did have massive potential and a quaint dovecote with doves on the back wall.

We decided to buy it from a fellow called Brendan Quinlan and moved in on the 17th February 1997. We found out the funny smell was the boiler leaking fuel, so our first weekend was spent with no hot water or heating.

The first villager we met was Rosemary Wagstaff who welcomed us to the village and brought around a list of all the local amenities, doctors, dentists, and the like. She

Left:
Ian Batham with from left,
Callum aged 2, Sam 4 & Hollie, 7.
Above:
The Batham family in 2012, from left:
Sam, Cal, Ian, Hollie & Tracey

also noticed that an old horse shoe was leant against the wall the wrong way round. She turned it the right way up and said she didn't want us to have any bad luck. We also noticed that the doves had disappeared; I eventually found out that they were a nuisance and two very close neighbours late at night had caught them and relocated them to another village.

Our first project was to create a parking area, as it was quite dangerous getting the kids in and out of the car in the road. We drew up some plans and started digging, blissfully unaware of the need for planning permission. I found I needed it when, while at work Tracey phoned in tears, mortified, saying we had been served an enforcement

notice. We got the relevant paper work and it was all sorted in the end.

Sam was christened in Blaisdon church. On the morning of the christening there was a knock at the door. It was Roger Keyse, from Blaisdon Nurseries, opposite. He asked if I would like to go with him to get the font water for the church. We went to St Anthony's Well, the spring at Gunn's Mill, Flaxley and collected the water. I did this for a second time when our third child, Callum, who was born in January 1999, was christened. It made it very special, knowing the water collected was to be blessed and used to anoint your child. We will treasure those memories forever.

Having three children meant we really needed to expand the size of the house so Lee Barrett our adjoining neighbour and I decided to apply for joint planning permission. We recognized that we wanted to retain the character of the cottages and keep the outline of the cottages symmetrical. Our part of the project was completed in 2006. An upstairs bathroom and extra bedrooms were added. We were really pleased with the result and how it all looks quite original. We also added an above ground swimming pool that year and as time goes on we seem to use it less and less. I think we are the only cottage in the row to still have an outside toilet.

Above;
Garden showing the outside toilet.
(Dec. 2004)
Right:
Callum and hose.
(2004)
Below:
Ian & Tracey in the pool.
(2006)
Far Right:
Trick or Treat?
Halloween, 2007.

One of the great assets to living in Blaisdon is the access to the countryside. Often we join the Selwyn family from Claremont and spend a Sunday afternoon walking around Nottwood Hill and the woods behind the hall; we have to then stop for a customary pint at the Red Hart as a treat.

The Batham & Selwyn Families.
Above:
Mulled wine & Mince pies, Christmas 2011.
From the back, left to right
Callum.
Harriet, Hollie, Tracey.
Andy, Archie, Izzie, Sam & Liam.

Left:
Ian & Tracey Batham, Harriet & Andy Selwyn

The Batham Family:
Summer & winter
in the fields
above Blaisdon Church.

Ian also spends a lot of time running around the country lanes. I always look towards the village on the way back and you recognize the beauty of the village when you look at it from a distance, picking up the church nestled on the hillside and the Hall looking all proud and the big evergreen tree at the side of Blaisdon house.

Sometimes the countryside comes to you. One evening we were sat at the top of the garden and a young badger came to visit. He looked us up and down and then decided to sunbathe in the field behind the house.

Looking through my selected photos for the book I realize the importance of the big field behind the Church. We have spent many happy hours up there. It is a field you can do everything in. Gaze at stunning views of the Severn Valley, picnic, sledge and run and jump through the long grass. It is a place to rest and wonder at the joys of life and how lucky you are to live in such a lovely place.

Our favourite time is spring and early summer the village teams with life the hedgerows are gorgeous covered with daffodils and wild flowers, the swallows and house martins return, you can't beat just sitting in the garden and listening to the birds singing their hearts out.

It is the things that people don't think so much about makes village life so good; the way the community comes together. We still remember those villagers that gave their lives in the World Wars. Every year on Remembrance Day we have a service at the memorial. As an ex Royal Marine, I feel a link to those men who died and am very proud to take part in that service.

One of the best things has been the school bus picking the kids up outside the house. What a lot of time and palaver that has saved; it has been a joy watching the kids through the years running up the path desperate to get home as if the first through the door got a medal, or a choice of biscuit when they got to the tin."

Hollie Batham,
Dene Magna Prom. 2011.

Rainbow over Western View.
(2010)

HALT COTTAGE

Brian Jones lived at Streamways, Woodgreen as a child. He came back to live in Blaisdon in 1970:

"I bought Halt Cottage in 1970 at the suggestion of my father Bill Jones (Volume 2), who lived next door at Western View. The cottage was bought by Mr Butler when Blaisdon Estate was sold off. He named it Halt Cottage as he planned to come to a halt there. However, his wife did not like the house and refused to move. He and later his son, George, rented the cottage out to a succession of people including the Salesian order at Blaisdon Hall. My sister, Nancy lived there for a while. Another resident was a Mrs Nailer. One day, while I

Above: Halt Cottage in Spring 2012.

Below: Halt Cottage, right, & Western View, prior to alterations carried out in the 1990s.

was having Sunday lunch with my parents at Western View, there was a large explosion next door. We rushed round to find the kitchen in a real mess. Mrs Nailer had tried to clean the chimney by soaking rags in petrol and pushing them up the chimney, followed by a lit match! Eventually, in 1970, George Butler decided to sell the house.

Initially, I was not planning to live there but 1971 turned out to be a special year in more ways than one, as I married Grace. Our daughter, Rachel was born the following year.

After father's death in 1974, my mother continued to

63

Above:
Rachel Jones outside Halt Cottage.
Right:
Grace & Brian Jones at Waterford Crystal, Ireland.
(1996)

live next door until she too died in 1995. Grace's mother also lived with us for 2 years in the 1990s until poor health necessitated her move to a nursing home.

We made few changes to the house, other than create a driveway to the side and removing a large privet hedge at the front, thus joining the gardens of Western View and Halt Cottage at the front.

Both Grace and I loved living in Blaisdon, where there was always something going on. However, the need to have a bungalow and to be nearer to a Health Centre and other facilities resulted in us moving to Cinderford in August 1995."

Local builder, **Lee Barrett** moved into Halt Cottage in 1996:

"I had been looking for a house to modernise as a project, when I saw the sale particulars for Halt Cottage, it seemed to fit the bill and was in what appeared to be a nice area. So, my then partner, Alissa Ballinger, and I moved from Barrington near Bourton-on-the-Water to Blaisdon. At the time I expected to modernise and possibly extend the cottage before selling and moving on.

What I did not anticipate was falling in love with the village and the whole Forest of Dean area. So, in the end, we stayed in Halt Cottage till 2009, when we moved to nearby Popes Hill for a larger house for the growing family. We are now my partner, Joanne Handcock, boys, Danny, Callum and Louie, and me. The boys are now 20, 19 and 10 respectively and all loved growing up in Blaisdon.

Top: Joanne Handcock, Louie & Lee Barrett.
Left: Programme for Ball organised by Lee.
Above: Lee sledging with Callum and Tim Clements pushing.

1

2

3

4

5

1. From left: Callum, Louie & Danny.
2. Joanne & Lee, compare 'Bumps.'
Jo has just told Lee she is pegnant!
3. Danny, left, & Callum in biker gear.
4. Lee Barrett.
5. Christmas presents. Danny, left, & Callum.

During our time in Halt Cottage we extended it from 2 to 4 bedrooms and increased the ground floor also. We now rent the cottage out since we moved to Popes Hill.

When Blaisdon Hall was owned by Hartpury College, I organised some large scale party events there and in Cheltenham, which was both great fun and a great success, though very hard work."

Chris Helm:

"We're Martin Clayton & Chris Helm and we moved to Blaisdon on Martin's birthday on the 4th July 2008.

Martin's originally from Scarborough, North Yorkshire, which is where I met him at Easter in 2004. I'd moved to Yorkshire as a child from North London with my family, eventually ending up in Scarborough in the early eighties. Currently our household extends to Martin's mum Mavis, his dad Geoff having passed away a few years ago. Our cat Mishka, a 'Felix' look-alike intent on ridding Blaisdon of its rodent population and Drake our pin-up black Labrador who if he knew how beautiful he was would be insufferable.

We rent Halt Cottage currently and it's pretty much as it was when we moved in, barring a lick of paint here and there. We've put up some gates to keep the dog safe and that's pretty much all the changes we've made.

We both work in the Information Technology sector and our commute to work varies, though I must admit we'd love there to be another crossing on the River Severn closer by.

Spare time usually has some element of country pursuits and rural craft/skills attached including beekeeping, candle making, woodworking, and experimenting with preserves (particularly from the huge Bramley apple tree which dominates the top of our garden). Martin is very proud of his annual tomato crop, which seems to increase in size and quality each year.

Have we seen changes since we moved here? Yes, changes in the pub (well of management anyway). We've seen neighbours come and go in the short time we've been here, some we stay in touch with. We watched the kids next door grow up fast in the past four years, now it's cars and motorbikes not pedal cycles and not quite so much football in the garden.

It is a lovely quiet village where one feels safe and where neighbours will look out for each other.

We basically love this area, the Forest of Dean, rural landscape and living between two major rivers – we feel we have the best of everything. Local produce is of a high quality and artisan bread making, cheese making, smoked produce, local meat and others are easily found. We are proud to live in a friendly, productive and beautiful rural area."

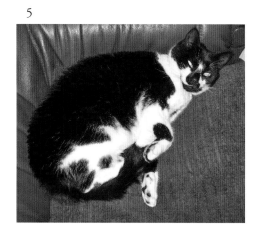

1. Drake & Bryn.
2. Martin Clayton & Drake asleep.
3. Martin Drake & Chris Helm.
4. Drake with prized sock!
5. Mishka.

ETTLESTONES

Although there were many changes to country life during the second half of the 20th century, some of the traditional crafts were and are maintained by those few craftsmen who retain the skills of their forefathers. David Warren was one such man. He and his wife Anne lived at Nettlestones, or Belmont as it was known, from 1936 till his death in 1979. His son, Leslie recounted his memories of family life and growing up in Blaisdon in the last volume. Here **Humphrey Phelps** recalls David Warren's skills as a 'Countryman':

"David Warren (1898-1979) was a man who could turn his hand to any and every job on a farm. In his day the jobs and skills on a farm were many and varied, his especial skills were thatching and hedge laying; at both he was the acknowledged master. A stocky, thickset man about five feet six or seven in height, he could carry with apparent ease four bushel sacks of wheat weighing 2¼ hundredweight up steep granary steps but, as he said, 'You've got to carry them well up on your shoulders; if they slip down on your tail, you're buggered!' His father, a gentle old man with mutton-chop whiskers, had worked on a farm, but when David left the village school he went to work for a baker. He and another boy lived-in at the baker's house. The baker's wife by all accounts was a bit

Nettlestones in 2012.

of a tartar, every day they were given fat, yellow, rancid bacon. 'It was horrible, but we had to have it although it was a job to get it down. When no one was looking we used to slip it into our weskit pockets and dispose of it when we went out on delivery rounds,' said David.

This was during the First World War. The women to whom he delivered bread, often told David that they thought a big boy like him would have been in the army. 'It got that I couldn't stand any more of that talk, so I added to my age and joined the army and after a bit of training I went to France.'

After the war he went to work on a farm. For a time he worked for a hard living, hard drinking man. 'I always got on well with him, he treated me all right but sometimes when he came back roaring drunk he'd cuss and cuss and cuss another chap on the farm who lived-in.' The next farmer for whom he worked was also a hay dealer and supplied hay to collieries in the Forest of Dean.

In the mid-1930s David Warren started to work on my father's farm. One of his first jobs was tackling the overgrown hedges (twenty feet wide and festooned with brambles) on some land recently purchased. He spent all the winter hacking and taming those neglected hedges and laying as many as time allowed before spring brought them into leaf. Less than 10 years later, I had the privilege to assist him with hedge laying (and it was a privilege to work alongside a master craftsman) although my contribution was confined to clearing the old hedge of unwanted growth and lopping willow trees for hedging stakes. Off we set on winter mornings, his tools consisting of axe, hedge bill, billhook and stake beetle, plus some stout hide gloves, in a Hessian sack slung over his shoulder. My hedge bill, axe and fork carried likewise over my shoulder.

David Warren at work.

Once I started to put a bow saw into my sack. David glared at me and said, 'We don't want saws when we're hedging.'

Each stick as he called it, was pleached low to the ground by a couple of swift cuts with his billhook or, if the stick was large, with his axe. All the tops of the sticks were pointed the same way and were held in place by the stakes inclining at a slight angle. The sticks were placed but not woven between the stakes. 'Never bend a live stick,' he used to say. And if ever he saw a hedge where live stakes had been used - that is part of the hedge itself - his attitude was anger and scorn. He made his own stake beetle, (bittle, we called it), a club with a hollow to take the top of the stake which prevented splitting or fraying. 'Some, as don't know any better,' he said, 'do use the back of an axe or a sledge hammer to drive in stakes and then the tops of the stakes look like shaving brushes.' If the hedge was to be hethered - tops of the stakes bound with long, thin wands or sticks - the stakes were placed upright and, in David's words, 'a stick to every stake.'

With thatching his equipment consisted of a long ladder, a homemade hand rake (six inch nails for teeth), kneepads also homemade, hazel pegs saved from year to year and augmented by winter forays into a wood, bolters of the best wheat straw, a bucket and a tank of water to dampen the straw and a pair of sheep shears to trim the eaves of the thatch. When completed his thatching would withstand the wettest and roughest of weather and look what in fact it was, a work of art.

His skills were not confined to farm work. For instance,

he repaired his own boots and on Sunday mornings he became the village barber. During the last war he made his own air raid shelter, fortunately it was never tested by bombs but it did make an excellent place for him to store his potatoes, And during the war he became a special constable and by becoming one, adept at quoits-playing.

To an untutored eye he would have appeared slow, but this apparent slowness was deceptive, it was the seasoned farm worker conserving his energy for long hours of toil. At 9 a.m. he would be unloading sheaves of corn, steadily but unhurriedly and at 9 p.m. or even later he'd still be working at the same pace while those who started with a great bustle would have slackened by midday and be all but done for long before the sun began to sink.

David Warren belonged to an ancient tradition of countrymen. As well as being a skilled and reliable farm worker he was also his own master and had a couple of orchards where he grew apples, pears and plums, made hay and kept a few Hereford cattle. He also had a sense of humour and when things went wrong he was wont to remark, 'It's awful ain't it? But in twelve months time, if we remember it, we'll laugh about it,' By such remarks he reduced the enormity of things sent to try us. Just the same, when some things broke he usually managed 'to fit it up for the time being.'

I knew him well for over forty years and never heard anyone ever speak ill of him. But knowing him well I don't suppose there was ever an occasion for anyone to speak ill of him. He died on 31st October 1979, aged eighty one years. On his tombstone in Blaisdon churchyard, there is this inscription, 'A True And Well Loved Countryman'."

Mike and Rosemary Wagstaff moved into Nettlestones in 1990. *Rosemary Wagstaff* tells their story:

"We first came to Blaisdon at Whitsun 1979, camping at the Stud Farm, which was owned by Dick and Hilary Hawker. They were friends of my sister Susan and allowed the families of my sisters, June and Susan, and my family to camp in the Orchard on Bank Holiday weekends. The first time we came, it rained in stair rods for almost the whole three days, but we would troop down to the Red Hart and hang up our dripping oilskins and dry off over Johnny Dunbar's 'Pie or Ploughman's' and a few beers. The rain did not disguise the attractions of the village or the friendliness of its residents and we subsequently had lots of sunny weekends.

On our fifth bank holiday, Whitsun 1981, we noticed that the top floor flat in the old farmhouse was empty and asked what was going to happen to it. Dick said that he didn't know but they didn't want someone to come for six months and stay for six years. We went back home to Windsor and talked it over and asked the Hawkers that we took it for six months to which Dick and Hilary agreed.

This was the start of ten of the happiest years, coming for weekends and holidays bringing our grown-up children Caroline and Charlie and friends with us. We also brought our Border Collie, Megan. She loved to go for long walks with the Hawkers' Labradors all over the farm fields and woods. In Windsor if she heard the name Blaisdon mentioned she would prick up her ears and put her head on one side and go and stand by the box of things I collected up between visits. We didn't stay for just six months but ten years.

Above:
Megan, Rosemary's Border Collie.

Right:
Mike Wagstaff leading the singing with clockwise from the lower left:
Lynne Hogg, Hilary Hawker, Dorothy Davies, Doug Inger, Iris Rodgett, ?, Mike, Stephen Waters, Ceri Evans, Rosemary Wagstaff, Derek Davies, Jill Rodgett and Louise Hawker.

During these years Caroline had some memorable birthday parties to which she invited lots of her friends to camp but they were always summoned to be at the Red Hart in fancy dress followed by a barbecue at the farm. Passers by the pub were astonished to find a crowd of toga-clad Romans going 'Up Pompeii.' Another year the theme was Brideshead Revisited and yet another was 'A breath of the Orient.' Quite a few of them returned for the Beer Festivals held by the next landlord in the nineties.

We introduced a Wagstaff brand of barbecue either in The Stud Farm garden or in the woodshed, including the standard lamp and a camping gas fire and absolutely no one was allowed indoors in the cold night air but had to wrap up in sleeping bags, duvets and travelling rugs. One very cold and windy night, Dick put hay bales all across the open side of the woodshed and with the lamp and the fire we were quite cosy, to the amazement of one friend's Ancient Aunt. Mike was a great leader of singing, mostly Rugby songs that seemed to be just as well known here and included exactly the same actions. We will not forget his rendering of Old King Cole.

Several times Mike bought tickets for the Middlesex Seven-a-sides at Twickenham and all the Rugby enthusiasts and their wives made the trip up to Windsor by an infamous mini-bus. While the men went to the games I took the Ladies around Windsor.

With Mike nearing retirement, we decided that we would like to live in Blaisdon permanently but at that time there had been no houses for sale in the village for seven years. We were told of a house (Belmont) that had been a holiday let for ten years and we approached the owner directly. He finally agreed to sell it to us and we set about trying to get planning consent for an extension. We employed an architect to draw up plans for an extension but his plans were rejected four times before finally being approved. Eventually we were able to add a bathroom a sitting room and a large brick garage, which would include a workshop for Mike. The house was full of dry rot and an enormous fungus kept appearing on the stairs, in the kitchen and in the outhouses. We had to have the stairs and woodwork downstairs removed and burnt and we went up and downstairs on a ladder for a time. The kitchen was enlarged to include the 'parlour,' the house had to be rewired and new plumbing installed.

When we had a new septic tank fitted, the excavations at the top of the garden revealed a terrific number of old bottles and jars, such as old Marmites, cough mixtures, sauces and poisons etc, but when I returned to collect them they had vanished. I presume the previous owners of the house buried their rubbish before there was a regular bin collection. There was also a huge part of the trunk of a yew tree (shown in the photo of Belmont in Volume 2), which had been felled to make room for the drive some

years before. We paid somebody to take it away because nobody wanted it. An old hedge between Halt cottage and Belmont was cut down at the same time for the same reason. The hedges still remain around most of the garden and may now be about one hundred years old (the house is dated 1908).

Four days after moving in, our daughter Caroline was married in Blaisdon Church and Ceri and Sheila Evans kindly allowed us to put up a marquee in their garden at Blaisdon House for the reception.

Mike had started grass cutting in the churchyard and discovered some overgrown graves, which he subsequently tended. One day he came home grinning to say that one of the newly tended graves now had a bottle on it with a message inside, asking for any visitor to the grave to contact, who else, but Cedric Etherington, who was already researching the village history. Our Church Warden, an elderly lady of ninety who was known to everyone as Aunty Lilla, asked Mike to repair some church fittings, which were stored in the shed beneath the huge laurel bush growing at the north boundary of the churchyard. One was the pulpit door. Another was the old bier used to carry coffins up from the road before the land for the church access road was obtained. Aunty Lilla decreed that it should now come into the church and it hangs on the north wall. The jug which carries the Baptismal water was also cleaned and repaired, so too was a small table which Aunty Lilla needed desperately 'for that night's Evensong.' It was Lilla's habit to give to every baby baptised, an old silver threepenny bit, and when my granddaughter was christened she also gave me minute instructions of where to get a threepenny bit for her. I bought two and still have mine.

1. Rosemary, Caroline & Mike Wagstaff
at Caroline's wedding.

2. Mike & Rosemary Wagstaff
at the toga party.

3. Caroline Wagstaff with
Maddie Wagstaff, left, & Evie Wagstaff.

4. Evie Wagstaff feeding Roger Keyse's lambs.

Above:
Rosemary Wagstaff amongst foxgloves.

Left:
Planting the commemorative tree in memory of
Mike Wagstaff, from the left:
Ceri Evans, Hilary Hawker, Dick Hawker,
Rosemary Wagstaff, Stephen Waters, Sheila Evans,
Lynne Hogg, Eleanor Waters, Jean Waters,
Ian Waters.

Mike then took charge of organising our entry for the Bledisloe Cup for small villages, which we won and have done so several times since. We both sewed Tapestry kneelers for the church, Mike's favourite being the remembrance kneeler, 'We Will Remember Them.' My favourite is the crown commemorating our present Queen but worked some years ago for a previous Jubilee. For many years we joined Roger Keyse's carol singing party. We went to houses in the district other carol singers would not dream of going to. Many people extended hospitality to us and over the years Roger has collected a very great deal of money for children's charities.

Just over a year after we moved and less than a year after he retired, Mike was struck down with a completely unheralded heart attack and died in Gloucester Royal Hospital on 10th September 1991. He is buried in St Michael's churchyard and was carried at his funeral by six friends from the village on the bier he had renovated.

I have now lived on my own for twenty one years - it doesn't seem like it because I have very good friends in the village. My granddaughters, children of Charlie and Heather, my son and his wife, have been regular visitors. Evie first stayed with me when she was only seven months old and Heather was still flying with British Airways. Maddie has been coming since she was a year old even though Heather quickly stopped flying after Evie was born.

I think they like to come to Blaisdon too. They are familiar with sheep, cows, badgers, foxes, squirrels, horses, birds and flowers, which they don't get in High Wycombe. My granddaughters especially like the birds of prey centre at Clifford's Mesne. Caroline comes down very frequently and often brings her friends for a taste of real countryside. When we first came nearly everything was delivered, milk, bread, fish, greengroceries, newspapers and a mobile library, but only the newspapers and mobile library call nowadays.

I took up flower painting after Mike died and went to college in Cheltenham to learn how to do it. This was something I'd always wanted to do. Subsequently the pictures had been assembled and printed onto greeting cards and composition name pictures. These are marketed by my daughter, Caroline, and are sold in the Windsor castle farm shop and the RHS Wisley garden amongst others.

I joined the WI, which was always behind any cake stall or catering undertaking in the village. With diminishing numbers sadly it is now closed and most members have joined Longhope WI. We now have a gardening club in the village with an annual (light-hearted) competition with various entries such as the tallest sunflower and the longest runner bean!

After Mike died, my border collie, Megan, was well aware that something was wrong and for the first and only time in her life she dug a big hole in the garden and into it I planted a Silver Birch, which was Mike's favourite tree. I planted an oak that we brought as a seedling from the oak tree in our Windsor garden and another which grew on Mike's grave but obviously could not be left there. Seedlings of a beech and another Silver Birch, given to me by a school friend of Mike's have also matured and some seedling plum trees have grown up. Koulruteria and a honeysuckle given to me by my 90-year-old uncle have

The Wagstaff family.
From the left:
Charlie, Maddie, Heather, Evie (at the front), Rosemary & Caroline.

now grown up as well. The honeysuckle by my back door was given to me by Mr Bill Jones' son, Brian, who lived next door at Halt Cottage when we moved in. Mr Bill Jones would visit all newcomers to the village bearing a Blaisdon honeysuckle and when we came the smell of honeysuckle on a summer's evening if you walked through the village was absolutely wonderful.

In August the Blaisdon plums ripen and to celebrate we helped with plum festivals. The date of the fete was moved from late June to late August to coincide with the ripened plums, which were picked and sold in huge amounts. I made a church kneeler to mark the plum festivals.

You can tell the passing seasons in the village by looking at the flowers in hedgerows, which come out in turn. There are snowdrops, wild daffodils, primroses, cowslips, plum blossom, dandelions, bluebells, Queens Ann's Lace (cow parsley), wild roses, honeysuckle, blackberries, plums, chestnuts and autumn tints. In the winter there's mistletoe, holly and blackthorn. You can always see the stars here in Blaisdon as there is no street lighting.

Blaisdon is a lovely place to live and I wouldn't want to live anywhere else."

Rosemary was also responsible for instigating an amusing pastime for several village families. Initiated after Mike had bought a flour container of questionable worth at a village auction, raising funds for the church. She decided that it would make an ideal trophy to be awarded to the winner of a game of Uno, a well-known card game. So desirable was the trophy that those involved started to find more and more ingenious ways to pass it on. In time, it has been hidden in pies; used as a container for soup; delivered to hospital as a vase for flowers; turned into a life size dummy; and 'sold' as a new business marketing garden gnomes. When Rosemary retired the Uno Trophy, she was then treated to presents of other items in the same style as first Steve and Jean Waters and then Nigel and Lynne Hogg found other food containers in the range. The final laugh is likely to be Rosemary's though as she has let it be known they will all find new homes, as they feature in her will! Over the years it has given a great deal of pleasure and many amusing memories to all who were involved.

Rosemary Wagstaff
with the coveted Uno Trophy.

CLAREMONT

Claremont in 2012
showing the side extension.

Mr and Mrs Tom Davis (Volume 2) lived in Claremont for over fifty years till their deaths in 1993 (Tom) and 1994 (Ivy). The house was then sold by the family. Current residents of Claremont are the Selwyn family: Andrew (age 45), Harriet (age 40) and their 3 children, Liam, 13, Isobel (Izzie), 11, and Archie 5. ***Harriet Selwyn*** continues:

"We moved to the village in May 1998 from Gloucester. I was born in Blaisdon and wanted to return to raise my own family. I was pregnant with Liam within two months! All three children have grown up in the village, Liam and Izzie were baptised in Blaisdon Church, as I was, being born in Blaisdon in 1972. My father (John McCreery) is buried in Blaisdon church.

Our children have all attended Westbury-on-Severn C. of E. Primary School. The school bus collects them from outside the house and takes them to and from school every day. Liam now attends Dene Magna Secondary School and Izzie will be attending Denmark Road High School for Girls in September.

I ran Westbury-on-Severn Toddler group whilst my youngest was small and worked at Westbury School Playgroup. Andrew is an Installation Analyst for Barclays Bank and is based at Barnwood Data Centre and I am a Teaching Assistant at Mitcheldean Endowed Primary School.

The original cottage had been extended by the previous owners, who added a single storey extension to the rear of the house. Over the years we have subsequently remodelled and added an additional extension to the side as our family grew. This consists of an extra bedroom, ensuite, utility room and entrance hall and we have removed and relocated the staircase. We have also paved the driveway and added a patio and decking area to the garden.

We love the friendliness and community feeling of Blaisdon and we have made some of our best friends here. We spend a lot of time with the Bathams who live in Western View. Over the years we have built our own Blaisdon traditions with them, such as Christmas day drinks in the pub where lots of the villagers gather and our 'six o'clock club' where the two families sit in the pub garden in the Summer for a pint or two, sledging down the hill past the church and the annual 'trick or treating' round the village. A vast difference from the housing estate in Barnwood (where we moved from) where neighbours rarely saw or spoke to each other. We were so excited to receive a lovely 'Welcome to your New Home' card from the Lisseman Family (Dairy Cottage) had been pushed through our door when we first moved in and have found the village so welcoming ever since.

Our children love living in the village and have some great friends. My eldest son loves that he can ride his bike to his friends in Northwood Green and Velthouse Lane."

Top:
The Selwyn Family
From the left:
Liam, Harriet, Isobel, Andrew & Archie.
Right:
Claremont from the front.

Above:
Harriet Selwyn holding Liam & Andrew holding Isobel at Isobel's
christening.
Top Right:
Hollie Batham, Harriet & Archie Selwyn.
Right:
Andrew & Archie Selwyn mowing the front lawn.

SPOUT FARM HOUSE

Janet Royall (Jan) moved to Spout Farm in 1966:

"We moved to Blaisdon from Newnham on Severn. My parents, Basil and Myra Royall (nee Albutt), had the newsagents shop in Newnham but life had got more difficult when Mr Beeching's cuts in 1964 meant that the daily papers no longer arrived by train.

They bought Spout Farm House from Blaisdon Hall for the princely sum of just over £1000 but it was in a pretty poor state. For the first

Above:
Spout Farm House in 2012.
Below:
Spout Farm House prior to any alterations.

few months of the year Mum continued to run the shop whilst Dad renovated the house with a builder from Awre, Cyril Jones. With little money they did a brilliant job but we still find some of Basil's interesting 'innovations'. One thing I am very grateful for is the Rayburn cooker that they installed, which now has pride of place in my new kitchen.

The house was then divided into two parts and my maternal grandmother, Edith, moved into one part as soon as it was habitable. In many ways she was coming back to her roots because her father, John Green, had grown up in Flaxley where he went to school. Edith's second husband, Freddie Blake, had recently died so it was a new beginning for her. We moved sometime during the summer and for us too it meant a new life. Mum was a qualified nursery nurse and Dad decided to take a basic social work course so that they could become house parents in a school for what were then called maladjusted boys and Dad was also the bursar. In many ways this was my first social awakening, knowing of and spending time with boys who were boisterous but not bad, and who often came from difficult families.

I didn't want to move from Newnham. I had passed my eleven-plus, not that I remember taking the exam, and was due to go to Lydney Grammar School with my friends. Unfortunately Blaisdon was in a different catchment area so I had to go to East Dean in Cinderford where I knew no one and it meant getting a bus from the end of the lane. Mum or Dad used to take me to Hinders Corner every morning where I got the service bus together with Ann Walton, and in the evenings I often used to walk down the lane.

Life got easier in 1968 when East Dean and Bells came together in the new Royal Forest of Dean Grammar School at the end of the gorgeous beech avenue in Berry Hill. A school bus then came through the village and in the mornings stopped outside the door. If I was early I would sit and read on the milk stand outside Tom and Ivy Davis's house, next to a milk churn. If I was late the driver would toot the horn and I would come running, toast in hand. In the evenings the bus stopped opposite the war memorial. The bus journey to and from school was usually fun but in winter we all longed for snow at Hinders Corner, which meant that the bus couldn't get up the slope onto the main road.

Top:
Mrs Edith Tranter with Charlie Royall.
Below:
Mrs Tranter, right with Mrs Ivy Davis of Claremont, opposite.

83

Living next to Nana caused tensions from time to time. Unbeknown to me, Mum was ten years older than Dad and, looking back, I think that perhaps caused occasional difficulties between my mercurial father and his mother. Mum was gentle and placid at all times. Edith always lived an independent life, although there was a connecting door between the houses, oddly enough between our bathroom and her landing. Nana was very sociable and liked dressing up. She usually wore a hat and gloves when she went shopping and if I close my eyes I can smell her perfume now. Whilst a stalwart of the WI, living in a village with just a weekly bus service cramped her style, but in 1970 she married her third husband, Eric Tranter. He was a fine man from Derby who, most importantly, could drive and she was again able to 'gad about' or 'go gallivanting' as she used to say.

When we came to Blaisdon, I had a pony for a short time called Prince and I learnt to ride but I was always pretty hopeless. For a couple of years the wallpaper in my bedroom was green with pictures of horses and jumps, and the paintwork was orange; mind boggling but true. I was an avid reader of pony club stories, not that I ever mixed in those circles, interspersed with Mallory Towers and the Chalet School.

I loved school, both East Dean where I soon became firm friends with Vicki Henbest, who had just moved to Longhope and remains one of my closest friends, and Royal Forest. Vicki's parents Bob and Joy (who was later a LibDem Councillor for Blaisdon and Longhope) were also lifelong friends. They were teachers and led what seemed to me to be a very sophisticated life. They read the Guardian and ate exotic food for lunch and dinner. My parents read The Daily Sketch and we had meat and two veg. or a casserole for dinner, then beans on toast or the like for tea. Every Sunday before church, where I was in the choir, we had bread and butter with tinned fruit and ideal milk for tea. I can taste it now. There were always lots of cakes and creamy rice puddings with a wonderful skin thanks to my Mum's skills with the Rayburn.

A couple of nights a week my parents' work meant that they would either be very late home or had on duty all night. On those nights I had tea with Nana and in winter we would make toast in front of the fire. A working Mum meant that doing the washing in the prized twin tub was one of my chores and I soon learnt to cook. Whilst I was taught to iron, that was always Mum's job. On Friday nights when I got home from Guides, Mum was usually in the kitchen, at the ironing board, listening to Friday Night is Music Night. Until April of this year when a collapsing floor meant big changes to my kitchen, I always did my ironing in the same spot.

Janet Royall.

Girl Guides were for a long time the focal point of my social life. We used to meet at the Latchen Room in Longhope on Friday evenings but at weekends there were often guiding activities and in summer there was always a week's camp in Dorset. We really did build rope bridges and dig latrines.

Sometimes I used to go to whist drives in the village hall with Mum as a treat, and then there were harvest suppers every year and the auctions at the pub of all the harvest produce. The village fete was another high day and for many years we had stalls throughout the village. We always used to have the cake stall on our lawn. Later on we had plum festivals, which were wonderful but a lot of work. One year I remember being severely and rightly reprimanded by Sheila Evans who had a line full of newly washed table cloths for use the following day, and I had lit a bonfire, which was wafting black smoke into her garden.

Basil Royall

Christmas meant carol singing with the wonderful Roger Keyse and for a few years, Dad used to drive some of us round in a minibus. These days, to my shame, I rarely go out singing for more than one night but as a teenager it was a badge of honour to go out every night. On Christmas eve, until well into my teens, I had to rest in the afternoon whilst listening to the Festival of Nine Lessons and Carols from Kings so that after carol singing I could go to Midnight Mass with Mum. Walking up and down to church was part of life (sometimes calling in at the post office with groundsel for Mrs Goddard's budgie) but on Christmas Eve it was always magical.

Summers meant playing in barns full of newly stocked hay. Dad used to help Jack and Mary Griffiths with haymaking at Gawlett Farm and often Vicki and I would spend Saturdays with the Palmers at Court Farm in Longhope.

Pocket money had to be earned so there was babysitting for the Manners and the Hawkers throughout the year and fruit picking in the summer months. The season began with Mr Woodman's strawberries, which I picked and sold at a profit to Mum and Dad's colleagues, later on there were always plums followed by blackberries. Blackberrying was a family occupation and still is, for me and my children, and we take our plastic bags to the same spots that I went to with my parents over four decades ago. August and September meant restocking the store cupboard with jams and jellies. Mum did it, I did it and now my son, Ned, does it. As soon as I could drive I used to spend days picking gooseberries and blackcurrants for farmers near Newent.

3 views of Basil Royall's garden at Spout Farm House, with Myra Royall, left.

The Salesians and Blaisdon Hall were part of our lives. Whenever we had visitors we would walk around the Hall grounds and Dad and I did various evening classes there including pottery. Brother Joe and Father Hilton were frequent visitors and Mum used to do b+b for their families.

The garden was Dad's pride and joy. He used to grow hundreds and hundreds of bedding plants from seed, usually seeds that he collected, and he had a beautiful garden each summer. People used to stop their cars and lean over the wall to admire his work. Mum was in charge of the chickens and the vegetable garden. The beans were always brilliant, the potatoes and spinach good, the carrots always had carrot fly and the plums were plenteous.

It was from Blaisdon that in 1973 I went to university in London, but I spent most of my holidays at home. I used to work in the Gloucester Post Office at Christmas (sorting letters did wonders for my geographical knowledge of Britain) and had a variety of jobs in the Easter and summer holidays.

Stuart Hercock (Stu) first came to Blaisdon in 1978 after we had met at a party in London in the autumn of 1977. As a much-loved only child I continued to go home frequently, and Stuart came with me. He was an absolute saint. It took a while for Dad, a working class Tory, to get used to the fact that I had fallen in love with a man who was not only seven years older than me but was an active member of the Labour Party and trade unionist. At that time Stu worked in the House of Commons for the Parliamentary Labour Party which introduced us to a whole new world. Every other weekend we would help with the garden and the orchard or do jobs around the

Jan Royall & Stuart Hercock.

house. Stu soon demonstrated that he was an ace with the spade, the drill and the paintbrush and there was always much to do. Mum and Dad did the decorating and DIY with our help but over the years they had a new roof, a new stairs and some new beams in the attic, a new floor in the sitting room, a new fireplace and central heating was installed in 1985 for Charlie's benefit. Until then winter mornings meant frosted windowpanes and swift runs between warm spots in the house.

On 6 September 1980 Stuart and I got married in Blaisdon church and had our reception at the village hall. Sheila Evans made bouquets for me and my bridesmaids, Vicki and Ruth Stu's niece and goddaughter, and did the flowers in the church, which looked stunning. Trish Manners

The wedding of Stuart Hercock & Jan Royall at Blaisdon Church. (1980)

played the organ. She thought that we walked down the aisle to 'O Tannenbaum' but of course our friends all realized that it was 'The Red Flag'! We all walked down from the church in the sunshine. It is still the best wedding that I have ever been to, a beautiful day and fun. In the evening we had a barn dance outside the hall with bales of hay around the yard for people to sit on. Dad's garden was glorious and I remember doing a jig on the lawn whilst Stu was waiting patiently at the church. We hired lots of the glasses and after clearing up they were dutifully loaded into our car. Stu and I drove to London in the middle of

the night in order to get a flight to Rome the following morning and when we got to Cheltenham remembered the glasses which had to be returned to Gloucester. Time was tight so we went into the police station and persuaded them to look after the glasses until Dad collected them later in the day.

Pop, my name for Nana's husband, Eric, was a life-long smoker and died of lung cancer in 1977. Nana was then seventy nine and in good health until she had a stroke in 1984. That was the year that our first child, Charlie

(Charlotte Rebecca Royall) was born and it was talking to Charlie that helped Nana regain her speech. We were plum picking in the orchard when I had the first twinges of contractions but I wanted our baby to be born in St Thomas's where I had had my antenatal care so we loaded up the car and zoomed up to London. Ned (Edwin Henry Frederick Hercock) was born in 1986 and Harry (Henry Jonathan Hercock) in 1989.

Having grandchildren was a hugely important part of my parents' life. My short-tempered father was a patient, adoring grandfather who would willingly walk up and down the landing with Charlie in the middle of the night when she had colic. Mum was loving and brilliant. Every other Friday evening we used to load up the car and drive home, firstly with one then two and three little people sleeping in the back with an occasional, 'when are we going to get there?'

Nana died in 1986 and Stu and I took over her part of the house, modernising the kitchen, installing a shower and opening up a door between the sitting rooms in the two parts of the house. This meant more space and more independence for us as a family when we were at home but on Saturday and

Above:
Basil Royall with Charlie & Ned.
Below:
Myra Royall with Charlie.

Sunday mornings Stu and I would have a lie in whilst the children popped next door for boiled eggs and soldiers with Mum and Dad. Blaisdon enabled Charlie, Ned and Harry to have a great balance in their lives with the garden, the fields, the forest and bonfires not to mention the bikes and tractors for which there was no room in our London flat.

Mum had osteoporosis and rheumatoid arthritis and gradually Dad became her carer. She had frequent stays in Standish Hospital and was there in 1993 when Dad was admitted with a chest complaint. It was soon diagnosed as lung cancer. He came home for a few weeks, to his grandchildren and his garden but died in Standish in late August. That summer the children all went to a sort of summer school in Northwood Green, as they had done the previous year.

Mum was increasingly frail and finding life difficult but naturally she wanted to stay in Blaisdon. She had a personal alarm, which she used to set off accidentally from time to time, and Roger was always first on the scene. After a couple of months and a couple of falls Billie Ensor came to live with Mum as her carer but she went home every other weekend when we came to Blaisdon.

Mum died in April 1995 by which time we were living in Brussels. We wanted to keep Spout Farm House but didn't want it to be unloved and empty. We decided to keep our part of the house but to rent out Mum's half. We spent lots of our holidays in Blaisdon and had a brilliant party on my fiftieth birthday for village, family and friends. It was a very, very hot day and the champagne was flowing so everybody took part in an amazing fight with water pistols. For two or three years we had tenants, then we did holiday rentals until 2004 when I became Baroness Royall of Blaisdon and we moved back home. I say home, but whilst an important part of our children's lives, our flat in London and then our house in Brussels was understandably their home. They would associate Blaisdon with summer holidays, Christmas, carol singing and walks rather than day-to-day life.

Spout Farm House was again filled with the seeming incessant clatter of builders. The house became a whole again and we filled all the rooms. Stu and my Dad had always said that there must be an inglenook in what had been Nana's sitting room. We decided to put their theory to the test and found not only a beautiful inglenook but a perfect bread oven. Most of the windows were replaced, as many had begun to rot and were very drafty, and the house was repainted.

Two years later, in 2007, Stu masterminded the conversion of the attic into three bedrooms and a bathroom, and my childhood bedroom (later my children's bedroom) became a bathroom enabling the former bathroom with its connecting door to revert to a landing. It is only now as some further building work comes to an end that I really appreciate the many, many months that Stu devoted to

overseeing the work and taking the difficult decisions. I was working in London during the week so didn't have the day-to-day headaches that he had.

We now had the house as we wanted, there was just the kitchen to do, and we had great plans to enjoy it, sometimes just the two of us, sometimes as a family and sometimes with friends. Charlie, Ned and Harry were all at university (Charlie doing geology at Imperial, Ned doing English at Cambridge and Harry doing mechanical engineering at Edinburgh) but they often visited with friends. In 2008 Stu was diagnosed with prostate cancer, a ghastly disease but if diagnosed early can be treated. Tragically Stu's diagnosis was too late and the cancer had spread to his bones. He was immensely brave and we lived life to the full, much of it in Blaisdon, but he died in May 2010. He was determined to be at home for what turned out to be his last Christmas, despite the fact that he had had two major operations in London in the preceding two weeks. The children prepared the house and the food and I collected Stu from hospital, gave him lots of morphine, and zoomed down the motorway.

Earlier this year I embarked on what I think will be the last major change that I make to the house, my kitchen floor was sinking so the need for a new floor seemed a good opportunity to implement plans of which Stu and I had spoken. In 1966 Dad had built a porch outside the back door and this was extended to include a lavatory in 1993. It was now looking tired, likewise the coalhouse and porch outside Nana's back door which was riddled with woodworm. And my kitchen essentially hadn't changed since 1966. I now have a beautiful new kitchen with a dining area looking over the courtyard to catch

1. Stuart Hercock.
2. Stu Hercock, Jan Royall, Basil Royall
& Ned Hercock.
3. Jan Royall & Stu Hercock.
4. Harry Hercock.
5. Stuart Hercock & gardening helpers, Ned
& Harry.
6. Harry Hercock & Charlie Royall.

the morning sun. By this time next year I hope that I will have transformed the back garden into a glorious cottage garden that can be enjoyed from the kitchen. Apart from routine decorating, I don't intend to make any more changes to the house but perhaps the children will have different plans in the future.

It's strange, as I sit at my computer looking out of the window, little appears to have changed apart from the addition of a couple of sheds but Blaisdon and my home have provided a haven, a safe space for both routine and momentous changes in my life. I don't have a great memory but I can see my husband and children, my parents and my grandmother all over the house, I can hear the laughter and the arguments, I can smell the rice pudding and the casseroles, I can feel the love as well as the warmth of the fire as the wind whistles through the windows. I grew up in Blaisdon, I was married here, my husband, parents and grandmother are buried in the churchyard and it is where I hope my children will want to continue to come home, in time with my grandchildren."

> The House Of Lords:
> Baroness Royall of Blaisdon, centre,
> with, from the left,
> Charlie Royall, Harry, Ned & Stuart Hercock.

AIRY COTTAGE

Mr and Mrs Allen and their two sons, Chris and Steve moved into Dairy Cottage in 1965. **Steve Allen** continues:

"We moved to Dairy Cottage in May 1965. Although we were a family of five, only two of us moved initially. My sister Val had long since married and was living in Maidstone; my brother Chris was just finishing school at the Salesian College in Battersea, then on to university and so never lived in Blaisdon; and our father worked in the post office in Battersea and had to wait for a transfer to Gloucester, a process which took two years during which period he visited us at the weekends.

I was a few weeks short of my 14th birthday. Having lived until then in Battersea within walking distance of school it was quite a culture shock, made all the worse by my parents' decision to send me to Whitefriars School in Charlton Kings over twenty miles away, involving a bike ride and two buses each way.

Dairy Cottage was then called Home Farm Bungalow and was owned by the Salesian order. It was tied to the job my mother took as matron at the Blaisdon Hall. She was the first matron they employed.

Above; Dairy Cottage in 2012.

The house looked very different, the front consisting of horizontal wooden slats. Brother Joe Carter laid a cement driveway. After we had been there about a year we moved out while a major refurbishment was carried out.

When we returned to the house the front had been built in brick, a carport attached and it had a modern kitchen. By then the house was certainly called Dairy Cottage. .

My parents moved out of Dairy Cottage in 1971. They had been hoping to buy it from the Salesians, but were unable to do so as the Salesians decided not to sell. They moved to The Haie at Newnham on Severn. My mother continued to work at Blaisdon for another couple of years before taking a job running a children's home in Pembroke. I do recall that we used to get our milk from Mrs Davis

just across the road – it came straight from the cow I believe. I also recall that our garden at Dairy Cottage was full of fruit trees, mostly apple I think although probably also some plum trees.

My mother was the only female the boys had to relate to and some keep in touch with her even to this day."

Other occupants of Dairy Cottage in the years that followed included Barbara Jackson with her husband, Steve and son, Hardin. Barbara was Blaisdon hall's first lady teacher, arriving in early 1973. The family later emigrated to Canada, where Barbara died in 2000, the funeral being attended by Father Sean Murray.

Ron and Margaret Smy lived in Dairy Cottage from 1974 until Blaisdon Hall ceased being a school. During this time he was the school bursar.

Father Aiden Murray also lived in Dairy Cottage for a couple of years in the 1990s.

Top Left: Dairy Cottage pre 1960s extension.
The car is an Austin A40.
Top right & above:
Dairy Cottage, Oct. 1967
showing new extension.

1. Chris outside Dairy Cottage (1965)
2. Mr & Mrs Allen with Steve, aged 14. (1965)
3. Steve Allen in garden of Dairy Cottage with Blaisdon House in the background.
4. Chris outside Dairy Cottage. (1967)
5. Mr & Mrs Smy.

The Lisseman family in Dairy Cottage garden:
Jade, up the tree, Paul, Louise, Bonnie & kneeling, Chelsea.

Paul and Louise Lisseman moved from The Napping in Longhope to Blaisdon in 1997 with their three daughters, Bonnie, Jade and Chelsea, now aged 24, 22 and 21 respectively. *Louise Lisseman* continues:

"I had always been a fan of Blaisdon since I was a teenager, when we used to pick blackcurrants in Blaisdon and then go to the Red Hart and spend all our earnings on rough cider!

In September 1997 we came to the Red Hart with my Dad, Mike Anstey, for a drink and saw the 'For Sale' board go up outside Dairy Cottage. I phoned the agent from the pub and went to view the premises. I loved it immediately, although with only two bedrooms and one reception room, Paul disregarded it as being too small for a family of five. I persuaded him of the potential and we agreed to go ahead with the purchase. I remember Sheila Evans looking over the wall and asking, 'Are you just looking or buying?' Paul said, 'Looking,' and I said, 'Buying!' Sheila said, 'are you a plumber? That is all we need in this village!'

Unfortunately for the village, neither of us were plumbers. Paul was a teacher and I was a college lecturer at the time. Paul is still a teacher, working with special needs children at Heart of the Forest Special School and I am Managing Director of a Training Company called Betaris Training, based initially from our boiler room at Dairy Cottage and now from offices on Highcross Farm in Minsterworth.

We used to cycle with the girls to Blaisdon from Longhope in the weeks leading up to our move to the village. Bonnie, then aged ten years, remembers falling off her bike on Velthouse Lane and cutting her arms, legs and face. Bert and Sheila Daniells gave us help and cleaned her up; very friendly villagers!

There are so many fun parts of living in Blaisdon. When we have snow, all the family love sledging on the hill up behind the church. When the weather is better, there are walks in the woods up around the Hall. We used to call it the fairy walk as it was so magical. Another walk was the bone walk along the old railway track. The girls called it the bone walk as there were always remains down there. We would walk down the village to the Tan House. Mrs Manners kindly let us use the swimming pool in the summer and Jade remembers skateboarding down the village with Emma Boyer. A highlight of the year was carol singing at Christmas round the village with Roger Keyes.

1

2

3

4

5

1. Bonnie, Jade & Chelsea at the front.
2. Chelsea, left, & Jade
3. Workers resting? Louise with her parents.
4. Chelsea, Jade & Bonnie with cousins Harry & Ruby.
5. Chelsea, left, Jade & Bonnie.

The day we moved into Dairy Cottage was chaos, as both Paul and I had to work so my parents and friends did the move for us. Tracey and Ian Batham came to welcome us to the village, as did Sheila and Ceri Evans. Bonnie remembers Sheila and Ceri calling the girls, 'the fairies at the bottom of the garden'. They used to go to Blaisdon Church with Sheila and Ceri on a Sunday to the family service and then make toffee with Ceri afterwards in Blaisdon House kitchen, leaving Sheila to clear up afterwards, no doubt.

The three girls were attending Churcham Primary School when we moved to Blaisdon. They all then attended Dene Magna School and the Royal Forest of Dean College. Bonnie has just achieved an Honours Degree in Early Childhood Studies and Early Years Professional Status at University of Gloucestershire. Bonnie works as a Curriculum Leader at a Nursery in Gloucester. Jade is an Advanced Apprentice in Business and Administration at Betaris Training and Chelsea works in the hospitality/ media industry for Heart Radio Station as a Heart Angel, promoting the radio station.

We made changes to our house, in stages as we could afford it. Each time I got promoted, we did a little more extending. Initially, we put an upstairs floor into one of the bedrooms and then extended the lounge. Later, we added a first floor that included a bedroom and bathroom. Then, we extended the kitchen and patio and, finally we widened the drive to accommodate the 5 cars used by all the family. Every day that I drive home from a hard day's work, I thank my lucky stars that I live in such a beautiful place. We love Blaisdon."

Top:
The Lisseman family with the 25th wedding anniversary bench.
Left:
Tracey Batham, Louise Lisseman & Harriet Selwyn, on a girls' night out at the Red Hart.

RED HART INN

John Dunbar was a pupil at Blaisdon Hall and worked on the Stud Farm (Volume 2) before leaving in 1957 to start his army training:

"After I left the army in 1959, I went to live in Wrexham, North Wales with two of my sisters. I stayed there for three years before returning to Blaisdon in 1962. Elsie and Frank Hogg (Volume 2) very kindly let me lodge at the Red Hart Inn.

Above & Below: Red Hart Inn (2012)

In 1968, Iris, our son Neil, plus myself, moved across the River Severn to a cottage in Frampton-on-Severn, where we remained until 1972. We then returned to Blaisdon

to take over the licence and the running of the Red Hart, as Elsie and Frank had decide to retire. For the first three years, I continued to go out to work and helped with the running of the pub when home.

It was about this time that Whitbread Brewery, our landlords, decided to bring the pub into the 20th century. This was done by installing modern toilets, which until then had only been 'Elsan buckets'. We had a grand opening for the new toilets by inviting local Morris Men to come and do the official opening, done in their inimitable style. A splendid evening was had by all.

It was another three years before alterations were made to the bar and the sitting room. The old layout comprised of a corridor leading from the front door to a stable door

1

2

4

3

1. Neil, John & Kay Dunbar.
In front, Linda holding Hannah.

2. Frank & Elsie Hogg with Neil Dunbar.

3. Neil Dunbar.

4. John & Neil Dunbar.

The interior of the Red Hart before the alterations:
1. The original bar. the table is still in the same position today.
2. View from the bar, darts and quoits can be seen.
3. The sitting room, a small room to the right when entering the pub.
4. The entrance corridor viewed from the back towards the road.
5. The bar, looking towards the fireplace. Again the table is still in use in the pub.

at the back. On either side was a door. On the left was the bar and on the right the sitting room or snug. These walls were taken down to produce one larger room and the bar extended to its present size. This made such an improvement to the pub that it was unrecognisable internally. It was lighter, airier and, in a way, more comfortable. Something else that made a big difference was the car park. Prior to this being made, cars were parked either side of the road making it slightly difficult for traffic to pass through.

With all these improvements to the pub, it made it more 'user-friendly' but, in my humble opinion, it didn't have quite the same atmosphere. But then, everyone to their own opinion! It gave us more room to indulge in pub games and join in the local leagues that were abundant in those days. We had darts teams three times a week, mixed on Mondays, ladies on Tuesdays and men on Thursdays. There was also cribbage on Wednesdays and Sundays saw the pub quiz night. The quiz was, of course, only for the intelligentsia. Believe that if you will!!

The main thing about all of these was that it introduced a lot of people to the Red Hart and it was nice mixing with customers from other pubs and villages. It was surprising how many of these visitors would turn up in the pub later on just for a social drink. My, how pubs have changed since I left the Red Hart.

John & Linda Dunbar in the bar of the Red Hart.

In 1987, there was a big change in my life. This was due to the fact that I had met a 'little blonde' called Linda. We initially met through darts. What a difference she made. When customers came in, they would rather Linda served them their drinks than me. I've never really worked that one out! Linda settled into pub life quite well and also made my life that bit easier, not to mention, happier.

For a couple of years, things continued to run smoothly until the Government dropped a bombshell into the lap of the brewers. In their wisdom, they decreed that all the big brewers could only have 2,000 pubs in their portfolios. This came as a big shock to the brewers but an even bigger shock to the many pub landlords in tenanted pubs. The brewers then approached their tenant landlords of the pubs they were going to sell and asked them if they wanted to buy their pubs.

1

2

3

4

5

6

Some of the 'old locals':
1.Dave Reed, renowned for driving his lorry cab up the steep slope into the car park! (N. Hogg)
2. Albert Pithouse (Volume 2) who spent the last years of his life living at the Red Hart, with his neice.
3. & 4. Foster Yemm with, in 3, John Dunbar & Brian from Yorkshire.
5. Frank Hogg, Albert Bullock & Br. Neil McElwee
6. Julie & Steve Pickersgill & Chris O'Carrol (Green Court).

Very few did because they felt that the brewers had priced the pubs far too high and out of reach of the normal tenant's borrowing capacity. No account was taken of the many years of loyal service given by the landlords either.

It was at this point that we 'squatted', as we had nowhere to go. The regulars took to calling us the squatters, which we felt was a badge of honour. They also suggested that, as we were squatters that the drinks should be cheaper. To do that would have let me down in their eyes because they wouldn't have been able to have a go at us about the high price of beer. Once Whitbread had given us notice, they stopped delivering supplies, so we had no alternative but to seek supplies elsewhere. This was Lydbrook Valley Springs, where we bought the same products that Whitbread supplied but at a cheaper price. Work that one out!

In time, we had to resign ourselves to moving out but not before we had arranged a 'Big Moving Out Bash', organised mainly by our customers. What a night that turned out to be. It seemed as if half the Forest had come to say 'goodbye' and 'thank you'. In the car park a stage had been built for musicians to perform. Many had performed in the Red Hart over the years.

It was a surprise to us when we had a firework display, which finished the evening off. Again this was organised by customers. It was a grand finale to a special evening. Perhaps the bit everyone there will remember was when a firework display spelt the words 'B*****ks to Whitbread', a sentiment echoed by all there. This brought an emotional evening to an end with heart felt cheering from most of the audience. It was a fitting end to our reign as landlord and landlady."

John & Linda's Farewell Bash.

Above:
Linda Dunbar draws a pint.

Top right:
John & Linda Dunbar presented with a painting
of the Red Hart.

Right:
Drawing of the Red Hart.

The Harvest Home at the Red Hart:

A harvest-time sale of local produce donated for the occasion by locals and sold in aid of local charities. The Red Hart used to be packed to the rafters with locals out to spend all their money and outbid their friends on every item. Led by the auctioneer, Jack Waite, with his cries of 'hen fruit' (eggs), 'peace offerings' (flowers) and 'the size of it!' (absolutely anything). Nobody left the pub that night with any money. If the produce hadn't taken everything, then the Harvest Loaf was sure to. It would be sold and resold till it seemed like everybody had bought it at least once! Then it was split and all had a bite to wash down with their last pint.

After a year on the market, Whitbread Brewery sold the Red Hart to David and Eileen Burton in 1991. David started to expand the food side of the pub business as well as taking advantage of the pub no longer being tied to a brewery. This meant that he could source beer from any brewery. At that time, the Campaign for Real Ale (CAMRA) was beginning to bear fruit and after years of dominance by tasteless keg beers, real ale was making a most welcome comeback.

Although there were not the numbers of independent brewers that there are now, David leant his support to this philosophy with an endless stream of visiting real ales making appearances at the pub. (David disliked the term 'guest beer' as he thought it smacked of tenant pubs.) This resulted in CAMRA awarding the Red Hart its Gloucestershire 'pub of the year' in 1994 and 1995. This devotion to providing high quality real ale continues at the Red Hart to this day.

David also ran Blaisdon beer festivals with great success. Without the national network of suppliers that bring local beers to pubs further afield, he had to drive and collect the beers both for the festivals and for the pub. It is a great credit to his determination that the festival presented over forty beers from all over the country. Souvenir glasses were also produced for the tastings.

The call of the sea, where David had spent a lot of his working life proved too great and he and Eileen moved to the south coast in 1996 and the pub was sold to **Guy and Louise Wilkins**, not to mention Spot!

Top: Bavid & Eileen Burton bid farewell to Blaisdon, on the bench they donated to the village.
Left:
David behind the bar.
Below:
Two labels for special commemorative beers at the Red Hart.

CASK BEERS

	Trade price	*Public Bar Price*
Best Bitter	337/- per barrel	1/7 per pint
Cheltenham P.A.	288/- per barrel	1/4 per pint
Stroud XX	288/- per barrel	1/4 per pint
Mild Ale	288/- per barrel	1/4 per pint

KEG BEERS

Whitbread Tankard	(10 gallon casks) 12/8 per gallon	2/- per pint
Flowers Keg	(9 gallon casks) 12/8 per gallon	2/- per pint

DRAUGHT CIDER (GLOUCESTERSHIRE CIDER Co. Ltd.)

Country Dry, Medium Sweet: 216/- per barrel (6/- per gallon)

KINGSTON BLACK

Dry, Medium: 246/- per barrel (6/10 per gallon)

H. P. BULMER and Co. Ltd.

Dry, Medium, Sweet: 216/- per barrel (6/- per gallon)

COUNTRY CIDER

2 Gallon Jar	16/- per jar
1 Gallon Jar	8/- per jar

Deposit Charges

2 Gallon Jar 10/- per jar 1 Gallon Jar 2/6 per jar

BOTTLED BEERS

	Trade price per dozen Bots.	*Trade price per dozen* ½ Bots.	*Public Bar price* Bots	*Public Bar price* ½ Bots.
West Country Ale	—	11/6	—	1/4
Cotswold Ale	—	9/-	—	1/0½
Cheltenham Ale	14/2	7/7	1/9	11d.
All Bright	14/2	7/7	1/9	11d.
Brown Chelt	14/2	7/7	1/9	11d.
Nourishing Stout	14/2	7/7	1/9	11d.

WHITBREAD

	Per Dozen Bots.	*Per Dozen* ½ Bots.		
Pale Ale	19/6	10/10		1/2½
Forest Brown ..	18/-	10/-		1/2
Mackeson ..	24/-	12/6	*Nips*	1/5½
Final Selection ..	—	—	14/5	

			Nips
Guinness	—	12/7	—
Bass and Worthington	—	13/6	10/6
Heineken Lager ..	—	14/-	—
Skol Lager ..	—	14/-	—
Carlsberg Lager ..	—	14/6	—
Tennant's Gold Label	—	—	16/11
Bass No. 1	—	—	18/1

Deposit Charges:—
All bottles 3/- per dozen.
1 dozen cases 3/- each, 2 dozen cases 6/- each.

To meet the requirements of the Acts of Parliament we take every precaution to ensure that our Casks and Bottles shall contain full measure, but exact measure is not guaranteed.

BOTTLED CIDER

	Trade Price Per Dozen Flags.	½ Flags.	½ Bots.	*Public Bar Price* Flags.	½ Flags.	½ Bot.
GLOUCESTERSHIRE CIDER Co. Ltd.						
Dry ..	25/11	—	10/2	2/9	—	1/1
Medium Sweet	23/6	—	9/8	2/6	—	1/-
H. P. BULMER and Co. Ltd.						
Extra Quality	—	—	9/8	—	—	1/-
Woodpecker	23/6	13/10	—	2/6	1/6	—
Dry	25/11	—	—	2/9	—	—
Perry ..	23/6	—	—	2/6	—	—
Strongbow	29/3	—	11/8	3/3	—	—
No. 7 Still Cider	—	—	11/5	—	—	—

FLASKS

Golden Flask and Strongbow ..	5/3 per flask
Vintage Cellar	6/7 per flask
" "	3/8 " ½ "

BOTTLES *Deposit Charges*

Flagons 6/- per dozen, ½ Flagons, 4/- per dozen, ½ Bottles and Nips 3/- per dozen, Flasks, 2/6 each, ½ Flasks 1/- each.
Cases 3/- each 4-Flagon crates 1/- each.

	Bots.	*Nips*	*Bots.*	*Nips*
Pomagne	56/9 doz.	11/2 doz.	7/-	1/5

Deposit 3/- per dozen.

Wines, Spirits, Minerals and Cordials
ARNOLD PERRETT and CO. LIMITED
Lower Tuffley, Gloucester *Telephone* 24054
Branches:
BEWELL STREET, HEREFORD *Telephone* 2426
51, WESTGATE STREET, GLOUCESTER *Telephone* 22901
137, HIGH STREET, CHELTENHAM *Telephone* 23103
7, FOREGATE STREET, WORCESTER *Telephone* 23373
26, BROAD STREET, LEOMINSTER *Telephone* 2002
ALBION SQUARE, CHEPSTOW *Telephone* 2055
REGENT STREET, SWINDON *Telephone* 5607
1, HIGH STREET, STROUD *Telephone* 333

Left: Trade price list 1964. 1/7 per pint equals 8.5p!

Below: List of beers at 1st Blaisdon beer festival. (1994)

Bullmastiff Son of a Bitch	6.4%
Duffryn Clwyd Cysur Bitter	4.0%
Plassey Bitter	4.0%
St Austell Tinners Ale	3.7%
Mill Janners Old Original	4.5%
Thompsons Botwrights Man of War	5.0%
Summerskills Whistle Belly Vengeance	4.7%
RCH PG Steam	3.9%
Foxley Best Bitter	4.0%
Bunce's Benchmark	3.5%
Hop Back Summer Lightning	5.0%
Ringwood Old Thumper	5.8%
Goldfinch Flashman's Clout	4.5%
Shepherd Neame Master Brew Bitter	3.8%
Larkins Best Bitter	4.7%
Pilgrim SPA	3.7%

Kemptown Celebrated Staggering Ale	5.0%
Brewery on Sea Riptide	6.5%
Crouch Vale Woodham IPA	3.5%
Reepham Rapier Pale Ale	4.2%
Mauldon's White Adder	5.3%
Nethergate IPA	3.6%
Freeminer Speculation (Glos)	4.8%
Donningham SBA (Glos)	4.0%
Uley Old Spot (Glos)	5.0%
Stanney Bitter (Glos)	4.5%
Judges Barrister	3.4%
Cannon Royal Arrowhead	3.9%
Bateman XB	3.8%
Enville Ale	4.8%
Rising Sun Rising	3.9%
Titanic Lifeboat	4.0%

Hanby Draw Well	3.9%
Coach House Coachman's Bitter	3.7%
Lions Original Bitter	4.1%
Gooseye Wharfedaie	4.5%
Linfit Lead Boiler	6.6%
Trough Wild Boar	4.0%
Taylor's Landlord	4.3%
Rydale Stabbers	5.0%
Sam Smith OBB	3.8%
Butterknowle Bitter	3.6%
Yates Bitter	3.8%
Hesket Doris's 90th Birthday Ale	4.3%
Harviestoun Original 80/-	4.2%
Orkney Raven Ale	3.8%
Caledonian ERA	4.2%

22·8·1996 – 10·3·2012

LORD SPOT
OF BLAISDON
O.B.E D.O.G

Spotty Wilkins (22 /08/96 - 10/03/12) ran the Red Hart for all of his life with the help of the Wilkins family. He was so successful that he had a special mention in CAMRA's Pub Guide virtually every year he was at the pub. Shortly before his death at the respectable age of sixteen, he gave an exclusive interview for this book:

"I was born the day my family moved into The Red Hart at Blaisdon and it was to be my home for all of my life. At first it all seemed so strange; the pub had so many doors, which one would let me out!! There were so many people to meet, apart from my own family, Guy & Lou (the grown-ups supposedly!) then James, Charlie, Victoria, Johnnie & Emma. I feel that I grew up with the children and did we have some fun! I also worked hard at the pub. I was the main PR man (alongside Guy). I would meet and greet our customers, escort them in and always check if they needed any help finishing their delicious food and beer. I was also very good at seeing them off the premises too!!

The other highlight of my time in Blaisdon was being 'Best Dog' at the wedding of Guy and Louise, being in close attendance throughout the ceremony at the village church and helping eat the food at the reception afterwards.

The Red Hart was always buzzing and I loved it, getting to know all the old familiar faces with some new ones mixed in. It was a great life. Although never officially recognised by those in high office, the locals gave me the unofficial title of Lord Spot of Blaisdon, an honour I deeply cherished.

The Red Hart will always be the heart of Blaisdon and my family and I were only caretakers, but what a wonderful sixteen years we all had."

Spot is buried in his favourite corner of the land adjacent to the Red Hart. He was commemorated with a special bottled brew by Bespoke brewery, Mitcheldean with its own label showing him at his best. In 2012, Guy and Louise decided to relocate to Guy's native Devon, and the pub passed into the capable hands of Sharon Hookings.

Above:
Guy & Louise Wilkins outside the Red Hart.
Top left:
Portrait of Spot by Lyn Dixon.
Left:
Bespoke Brewery's special bottle label commemorating Spot.
Opposite page:
Spot's commemorative plaque in the Red Hart.

Sharon Hookings and Rakesh Kaushik are the present landlords of the Red Hart;

"I first came to Blaisdon in 1999 to work for Guy & Louise at The Red Hart, although I was living in Mitcheldean at the time. The price for a pint of beer was £1.85, minimum wage was introduced in April of that year at the rate of £3.60 per hour. Our resident pig was called Spam; she enjoyed her wallow in the back field and the children enjoyed watching the piglets frolic.

That New Years Eve, the whole country was waiting for the 'millennium bug' to strike, although I don't think it would have had any effect on the Red Hart. We served dinner and put on some music, then at midnight everyone congregated outside to watch the fireworks. I never did find out whose fireworks they were but Guy happily took the credit for them when the customers thanked him for the effort! Needless to say on January 1st the bug did not strike, everybody's computer continued to work normally and life continued as normal. In August 2000 I left the Red Hart to work on board P&O Cruises in the bar department.

Seven years later and I returned with a husband, Kaushik. We stayed with my parents in Longhope whilst re-habilitating ourselves to shore life. About a month after our return in the September my Mum saw an advert for a manager at the Red Hart. I spoke to Guy & Lou and the job was in the bag.

The Red Hart was much busier than it had been in 1999. In fact on sunny Saturdays the kitchen would get so overwhelmed, Guy had built a barbecue on the back patio to ease the pressure in the kitchen. Along with the barbecue, Guy added an outside bar called the Bazaar bar. I think it should have been the Bizarre Bar but Guy was always hopeless at spelling! I think most of the children in the village have worked on our barbecue nights collecting plates or helping in the kitchen washing pots.

I had learnt well from Guy and when we had a hen party come for dinner by coincidence on the same night as the Cotswold Morris Men performance, I took all the credit for organising it for the girls!

During the following years Guy & Louise stepped back more and more and eventually we moved into the Red Hart in January 2011, and Guy & Lou moved to Devon, returning to give me a break once a month.

Finally in April 2012 Guy & Lou retired from the Red Hart and my husband and I have taken on the pub. Kaushik continues to run his business, Simply Desserts, from his base in Mitcheldean. In the future we hope to maintain the village pub atmosphere that we have already, and to continue to serve great food and ale.

Guy's pig Esmerelda is providing our pork at the moment, her daughter princess Fiona will become our breeding sow when Esmerelda retires later this year. As well as our pork we use our own plums, apples & pears. It has even been known for Guy to forage for wild garlic, wild horseradish and blackberries.

By the way, as I write this in 2012 the current price of a pint is £3.10, and minimum wage is £6.19 per hour. Compare this to the 1964 price list of 1s7d, about 8p.

Well, that's forty eight years of inflation but the beer is much better now!

The Red Hart supports Westbury-on-Severn Young Farmers Club who meet most Mondays and every year and holds a bonfire and fireworks night on November 5th in our field. We have had the privilege of watching the youngsters grow and continue their custom with us, some of the young farmers from 1999 are now bringing their children to the pub, and their children are the young farmers of today."

Fran Smart of *Westbury-On-Severn Young Farmers* continues:

"Although we call ourselves Westbury-on-Severn Young Farmers, the Red Hart is where a lot of our social events happen. We have an annual bonfire and firework night, though Guy would never take on the role he was named for! We usually raise in the region of £1500 at the bonfire each year this then gets split between 2 local charity's, Great Oaks Hospice every year and the second charity we change each year to a local charity that has helped our members or their families! The pub hosts our Christmas meal and, throughout the year, the Red Hart also hosts a variety of other events and we are supported in everything we do there."

Right:
Sharon Hookings & Rakesh Kaushik
outside the Red Hart.

BLAISDON HOUSE

Captain and Mrs Back (Volume 2) lived at Blaisdon House, formerly known as the Old Rectory, through most of the 1960s and early 1970s. In 1977 Mr & Mrs Prytherch left Blaisdon House after about five years in residency and were followed by Ceri & Sheila Evans with their sons Ben and Sam. ***Sheila Evans*** continues:

"We arrived in April and the first village event which we attended was the celebration of the Queen's Silver Jubilee at Blaisdon Hall.

The village had great community spirit in those days and everyone knew everyone else. It was a village of friends who enjoyed working together for the good of the village, its church, its village hall and the general well being of all who lived in Blaisdon, as we looked out for each other.

Whoever organised events never really had to take charge as everyone found their jobs and delivered with energy and good humour. These were always the happiest of times and although many were tiring, it seemed to us that we always had more fun than anyone who had just bought tickets! The Evans family got involved in village life at every level and enjoyed feeling like the 'new kids on the block' as this was a village with many retired and quite elderly

Blaisdon House.
(2012)

inhabitants and very few children. Vic and Enid Woodman lived next door and had the most wonderful pick-your-own strawberries and raspberries and a great garden. Their fuchsias were known far and wide and much sought after. On fete days a long queue would form outside their gate to buy some of the hundred or so beautiful specimens before we were sold out. The plants usually made more money than the rest of the fete put together!

The village fete used to take place down the road with everyone putting their stall outside their homes. The fetes began at 2pm and the first year we lived in Blaisdon we were quite anxious as at about 12.30pm there was no sign of any activity. Within minutes stalls were set up and bunting raised before the fuchsia queue arrived soon after 1pm. The fetes were fun and supported the church and village hall and by 4.30pm all had disappeared, tables gone, signs down and bunting put away. It was the perfect example of everyone doing their bit and in their own way with a little friendly competition on who had raised the most for their beloved village!

No one interfered with others or controlled them, it was a place where everyone could and did live in peace with each other as all trusted that everyone had the wellbeing of the greater picture in view and was a wonderful place to live."

Mention needs to be made of the exceptional contribution Ceri and Sheila have made to village life in the past thirty five years. Their modesty prevents them telling their own story but they have been at the heart of almost all events and fundraising activity that has occurred in Blaisdon during that time, including the three day Plum Festivals and a Nativity Play that involved somebody from every house in the village. Everybody enjoyed their cheese and wine auctions and Ceri always managed to get virtually everything sold at way above its face value, raising much needed funds for Blaisdon church.

Ceri and Sheila's contribution extends beyond the village to the wider community of the Forest of Dean and Gloucestershire. The lists are endless but their efforts are perhaps most widely recognised with Sheila founding the much needed Great Oaks, Dean Forest Hospice and Ceri serving as Deputy Lord Lieutenant for Gloucestershire from 2000 and as High Sheriff 2010-11. He is the third person from Blaisdon to be honoured with this ancient office following Peter Stubs in 1900 and Colin McIver in 1915.

1

4

1. Ben Evans.
2. Ceri Evans in the High Sheriff uniform & Sheila Evans.
3. Sam & Claire Evans on their wedding day.
4. & 5. Ceri in more relaxed mode.
6. The Stratton & Evans families at the wedding of Claire & Sam.

3

5

6

1. Barbecue at Blaisdon House, clockwise from left:
Doug Inger, Gordon Gower, Andrew Rodgett, Sam Evans, ?, ?, Mike Wagstaff, ?, ?,
Jean Waters, Jill Rodgett, Maria Gower, Glenys Gower. (1984)
2. Ceri & Sheila Evans.
3. The garden at Blaisdon House, design by Julian Dowle.
4. BBQ at Blaisdon House, clockwise from the left:
Maria Gower, Glenys Gower, Ceri & Sheila Evans, Doug Inger, Gordon Gower. (1984)
5. Blaisdon House.
6. Sheila Evans with Nicky Kear.

PARKWOOD

Above: Parkwood.

Steve Waters (Spring Cottage) writes about Vic and Enid Woodman:

On 28th August 1962, an auction was held by Bruton, Knowles & Co. to sell Stud Farm on behalf of the Salesian Order. A second lot was made available, 1½ acres adjoining the Old Rectory, Blaisdon (now Blaisdon House). Outline permission had been granted for the erection of two houses on the plot. Bidding was fierce apparently, with Captain Back of the Old Rectory keen to obtain the land. However, it was Vic Woodman who purchased the land for a reported £1,000.

After serving during the Second World War in Burma, Vic and his wife Enid eventually came to Gloucester. Here he worked as the Head Librarian for Gloucester City Library. While there he had books published, 'Gloucester As It Was' (with A. Kent) and 'Wills Proved in Gloucestershire Peculiar Courts' (with M. Dickinson). He also edited a further book entitled 'Library Resources in S.W. England & the Channel Isles' as well as contributing to Gloucestershire volumes of the 'Victoria History Of England'.

On retirement, Vic and Enid decided to move into the countryside and looked for somewhere to build their retirement home and leave enough land for them to grow fruit and vegetables on a semi-commercial basis. The plot in Blaisdon fulfilled this need nicely, though as Vic said later, the price pushed him to his limit and after building the house he had nothing to spare.

As the building of the house drew to a close, Vic announced to local Albert Pithouse (Volume 2) that he was looking forward to being the first person to sleep in the house. Albert took a perverse delight in telling him that he had been beaten to it as Albert had slept there when he couldn't be bothered to walk from the pub back to the top of Nottwood Hill!

Once in the house, Vic and Enid began to turn their land to growing crops, mainly strawberries and raspberries.

Parkwood.

'Pick-your-own' was a fairly new concept at the time but it proved a success, with their fruit becoming well known and people travelling from far and wide to pick it. Over time Vic added to the land by buying the orchards from Mrs Griffiths at Hillcrest (Old Post Office) in 1972 and a small plot opposite Farview.

Fruit growing was not their only plant-related interest. Enid grew fuschias and produced them in abundance for the village fetes that she and Vic supported wholeheartedly. In time these became in such demand, that on fete day a queue would form at the gate of Parkwood some time before the opening time with people desperate not to miss

out. Their plant stall usually made more on fete day than the rest of the stalls put together!

Vic's family was originally from nearby Northwood Green, so he knew the Red Hart well. Here on weekend lunchtimes, he would have his bottle of light ale, always sitting in the first window seat on the left of the bar. He would be joined by neighbours and friends such as Dick Hawker and Ceri Evans and later, Steve Waters and Mike Wagstaff. They would watch with a little amusement as he rolled and smoked his cigarettes, each one so tightly rolled there was more paper than tobacco. Indeed, most of the tobacco seemed to end up on his jumper. Luckily, he was

3

2

5

4

1. Vic enjoying a drink in the Red Hart.
2. Vic Woodman.
3. Blaisdon fete: Enid Woodman, centre, with Lilla Smith & Evelyn Jones, selling plants outside Parkwood.
4. Blaisdon fete: plants outside Parkwood.
5. Vic's dog Tess had her own gate into Parkwood. Here she meets a young Ian Waters.

no longer around when smoking in pubs was banned!

In time, Vic decided that age meant that he could not continue fruit growing on the same scale. As he gradually decreased the land devoted to it. He sold the small piece of land opposite Farview to Steve and Jean Waters. He and Enid did keep one other job going right through their time in Blaisdon. They maintained the war memorial throughout the year, planting the verge around it and taking water up on their buggy every week in the summer. Perhaps Vic's wartime experiences had something to do with this devotion but he never spoke of his wartime service. It was not till the 1980s that he was persuaded by Rosemary and Mike Wagstaff (Nettlestones) to collect the medals he was due.

As their land ceased to be used to produce fruit, Vic and Enid decided that one of their other interests could now be explored. They set to with the help of neighbours David Brown and Dick Hawker to lay out and build a grass tennis court, complete with the right sort of grass and surrounding fence. Needless to say, their neighbours thought this was great idea and also a great excuse for a garden party for the grand opening. This was done with great ceremony, Vic cutting the ribbon and playing the first game with Enid, before everybody else had a turn. Over the following years, Vic and Enid were hosts to every young and old budding Wimbledon star in the village, making their tennis court available to all who asked.

Vic continued to enjoy village life until his death in 2002 at the age of eighty five. Enid moved away to live with relatives but after she died aged eighty seven in 2005, was brought back to Blaisdon church to be buried with Vic.

Parkwood was sold when Enid left Blaisdon to Bob and Lynne Scott with daughter Bethany. It was later sold to Henry Tombs and for the last time to Mr A. Walding. Planning permission to build a larger home on the site has seen Parkwood demolished in 2012 with building work is likely to be completed in 2013.

Left:
Vic & Enid Woodman open the tennis court.

Below:
The Brown family help prepare the ground for the tennis court.
(P. Brown)

The tennis court opening party.

1. Vic Woodman, facing the camera, with, from the left:
Ben & Sam Evans,
Rosemary Wagstaff, Ceri Evans,
Hilary Hawker, Steve Waters,
Grace Jones, Sheila Evans,
Dick Hawker, Lynne Hogg,
Enid Woodman & Nigel Hogg.
(M. Wagstaff)

2. Vic Woodman.

3. Ceri Evans on butler duties.

4. Enid Woodman.

THE ILLAGE HALL

In November 1964, Captain Terence Back of Blaisdon House (Volume 2) reported to a parish meeting the consequences of the village school closing earlier in the year. An Act of Parliament in 1955 had directed that the trusteeship of all C. of E. schools should be vested in the Diocesan education Committee (D.E.C.) instead of the vicar and churchwardens. Before this was carried out, each parish had been asked to give consent or voice objections. When a school subsequently closed the D.E.C. had to sell the property and the Ministry of Education approve the price, i.e. the school could not be given away.

The Village Hall & to the left, School House.
(2012)

The D.E.C. offered Blaisdon the chance to purchase the school for use as a village hall for £500. The Community Council in Gloucester indicated it was prepared to provide a grant towards the purchase and another towards furnishing and maintenance, provided the committee charged with running the hall would be representative of all village interests.

"Blaisdon had been fortunate," Captain Back continued to say "In that it had been allowed to use the school as a village hall for the previous 70 years without being called to pay for its upkeep. We are now being offered a first class hall for what is really a nominal sum."

The well-attended meeting then decided without dissent that the purchase should be agreed. Captain Back informed the meeting that, after allowing for grants, the

village had to raise £155. A most generous anonymous gift of £75 had been received. It was suggested that if all 40 houses in the village each contributed £2, the target would be reached. Every house did indeed make this donation. Running costs for the hall were estimated at £46pa and it was suggested by the Rector, Rev. Bick that funds from the village fete could be used for this.

By the next village meeting in January 1965, a Village Hall Committee had been set up with Captain Back as Chairman and Treasurer, Mr Robert Pickering as vice-Chairman and Mrs M. Keating as Secretary. Other founding committee members were Mr C. Manners, Mr G. Keyse (Parish Counsellor), Mr Small (Independent), Mrs S. Daniell (Parish), Mrs Warren (P.C.C.), Mrs E. Jones (Parish) and Mrs Hyatt (WI). Such was the confidence in the venture that a further seven villagers were appointed onto a separate Entertainments Committee.

The village then set about raising the funds to purchase the school building. Although the sums seem tiny in 2012, the average weekly wage for an agricultural worker in 1964 was £9. 9s. 0d. (£9.45) (Dept. of Employment and Productivity 1981, Lund 1982). A £2 donation from each house was not an insignificant sum to many in what was still a village dominated by people who worked in the immediate rural locality.

In the summer of 1965 a special fete raised £55 to add to the household donations already collected and in a letter to the Secretary of State in the Dept. of Education and Science, Captain Back was able to report that funds collected amounted to £315.

After some delay with the grant being withdrawn then reinstated after Captain Back's letter above, the purchase for the agreed £500 was completed on 21st March 1966 with Captain Back and Mr Pickering signing on behalf of the Village Hall Committee. The village hall was to be 'held on trust for the purposes of a village hall for the inhabitants of Blaisdon and the neighbourhood without distinction of sex or of political, religious or other opinions and, in particular for use for meetings, lectures and classes and for other forms of recreation and leisure time occupation with the objective of improving the lives of the inhabitants'. Very laudable objectives that ring true some fifty seven years later.

The village set about using its village hall with some gusto. Meetings report art classes, barn dances, whist drives, harvest suppers, Sunday school, yoga classes, handicraft classes and much more. In 1967, Counsellor George Keyse (Blaisdon Nurseries) was instrumental in getting rates removed from the village hall. In 1968, Captain Back stood down as Chairman and was ably replaced by Mr R. Pickering. A Lilac tree and Peony bush were given as a mark of the village's appreciation of Captain Back's service.

Since that time, the village hall has been used by generations of local people of all ages. Everything from christenings to funeral wakes, from children's parties to retirement celebrations with plenty of wedding lunches, dinners and parties. Everybody who has lived in the village has reason to be thankful for the foresight of those villagers in 1964.

Today, the village hall is in the careful stewardship of a committee led by Stuart Gent and all being well, it will continue to serve the community for many more years.

Jean Waters reminisces about Harvest Suppers at the village hall;

"One of the highlights of the village hall calendar is the annual Harvest Supper. For many years it followed the same format, with a dedicated groups of ladies providing a ham or beef salad with hot jacket potatoes, followed by apple pie and custard and cheese and biscuits. Everyone had to bring their own cutlery and almost every year we forgot. It was then I appreciated living next door to the village hall, as we could nip back to Spring Cottage and collect the forgotten tools! Working away from home for several years meant I was slightly peripheral to the proceedings but like many other ladies in the village, I contributed to the puddings (subversively introducing crumble instead of pie) and at the end of evening, the washing up. This latter activity was surprisingly popular but getting a group of ladies together in the kitchen was a great way to catch up on gossip, critique the evening's turnout and assess the standard of that year's entertainment. Whilst we set the world and the dishes to rights, the men cleared the tables away and snuck off to the pub.

The entertainment was an integral part of Harvest Supper and was always enormous fun. Sometimes it was homespun and sometimes 'bought in'. Whether it was a puppet show where the over enthusiastic puppeteer took domestic violence to a new level for poor Judy and rendered Punch senseless from Police aggression, or a small group of village men presenting new meaning to the term 'belly dancing', laughter was ever present. No offer of skills seemed to be turned away and on more than one occasion, Vic Woodman entertained us with his accordion, as did Frank Baylis with his monologues. Ladies including Joyce

Inger, Jean Waters and Pam Feddon brought comedy songs, complete with costumes, to the fore and a dubious collection of rather masculine 'Spice Girls' swept us all into convulsive laughter. Patricia Manners directed some of the younger village children in lovely musical endeavours which delighted us all and on occasions, local celebrity, Dick Bryce would show us just how his songs of the Forest should be sung. No matter what was presented, once supper was over, the chairs would be pulled back and everyone settled down to enjoy that year's offering. It was a great chance for everyone to enjoy the camaraderie the village offered, to eat well, relax and make merry.

Nothing should remain the same for ever and once we reached the 21st century, new blood took over the running of the Supper and we have been treated to hot food and varied puddings and with the updated kitchen containing full sets of cutlery, we no longer have to remember to bring our own. Thanks to Jean Adams, the Harvest Loaf, which once featured in the Harvest Homes at the pub, has been brought back to be auctioned at the supper , with the great difference that it is now beautifully edible. We still have the entertainment post supper and the laughter and camaraderie remains. So too does the washing up. Some things never change!"

Frank Baylis Jnr gives his famous rendition of Stanley Holloway's monologues.

1

Harvest Supper peformances:

1. Patricia Manners with Ian & Eleanor Waters (front) & Francesca & Lara Rodgett.
2. Joyce Inger, soprano.
3. Eleanor Waters, oboe.
4. Jean Waters, soprano.

5. & 6. Dancing Heads,
Dick Hawker, Steve Waters,
Ceri Evans, Doug Inger
& Vic Woodman.

2

3

4

5

6

1. The Spice Girls:
Scary (Doug Inger), Sporty (Nigel Hogg), Posh (Dick Hawker), Baby (Lee Barrett).
The Audience:
2. Evelyn Jones & Ada Keyse.
3. Hilary Hawker & Margaret Pickering.
4. A village harvest gathering.
5. Dick Hawker & Ceri Evans.
6. Frank & Dorothy Baylis.
7. Bob & Margaret Pickering, Lilla Smith.

SCHOOL HOUSE

When the school was sold to be used as a Village Hall, the Head's house was sold separately to local resident Ron Walton.

Joyce and David Lilley lived at School House in Blaisdon for 46 years:

"In 1965 we moved into the School House when David started working for Ron Walton of Tan House Farm. David worked for Ron until he, Ron, retired and sold the farm in 1997. The work varied with the seasons. In the late summer, he took plums and damsons

An Aerial View of School House & Blaisdon Village Hall.
Also showing:
Parkwood to the right.
Land to the rear bought by Vic Woodman from Mrs Griffiths.
The garage to the left is on land now part of Spring Cottage.

An example of David Lilley's hedge laying.

to Manchester and Liverpool and to Robinsons in Bristol for jam. Later, cider fruit would go to Shepton Mallet. Towards Christmas, trees, holly and mistletoe would go to Leeds, Liverpool and Manchester. Just as well that he had passed his driving test in August 1965 at the first attempt. It is amazing to think that his lessons were only £1 an hour! All this driving was on top of the routine farm work of haymaking in the summer and lambing and raising beef cattle in the winter. Since he stopped working for Ron, David has continued working in and around Blaisdon, becoming a much sought-after gardener. His hedge laying can be seen in various places around the village. David also won awards for growing Chrysanthemums.

Top Right:
David Lilley presents a cheque for over £1300 to the
Rheumatology Ward, Standish Hospital.
(1990)
Others:
Chrysanthemums grown by David Lilley and a 1st prize award.
(1992)

David and I arrived in Blaisdon on Saturday 13th March 1965, with our children, Thursa, aged three years, and Christopher, ten weeks old. It was a beautiful spring day, which was just as well as our furniture was on the back of a flat bed lorry. Cecil Beard, who lived at the bottom of the village, helped David move the furniture indoors. Two days later, David commenced employment with Ron Walton of Tan House farm, a job that was to last almost thirty one years.

The weather continued to be good and most afternoons that summer I was able to take the children for a walk, going in turn up towards the main road or down through the village. The ladies of the village, notably Mrs Elsie Hogg, Mrs Bill Jones and Mrs A. Keyes would often come out for a chat to see how we were settling in and also taking a great interest in Thursa and Christopher's progress. They were just like mothers to me.

The village school had closed in July 1964. About six children attended Westbury-on-Severn Infants and Junior School. The only children in the village who were a similar age to ours were Caroline and Charles Manners. When Thursa started school in January 1967, I found out that six of the children attending the school lived at Woodgreen.

Mrs M. Board from Brickhouse farm and Mrs M. Hatch from Glaymar organised a yearly whist drive in aid of Cancer Research. David went along and accompanied these ladies and Mrs I. Davis to their whist drives in Northwood Green, Westbury, Minsterworth and Huntley, plus a monthly one at the police club in Gloucester.

In 1968/9 David started running a whist drive at the

Joyce Lilley outside Blaisdon Hall

village hall on the first Monday of every month, all monies raised went to the village hall funds. These continued until 1986. David was also a keen darts player with the Red Hart team.

Among our neighbours were Mrs Small and her husband, Alan, who lived in a caravan in Mrs Goddard's orchard behind the Post Office. She was a teacher at the village school and had a daughter Catherine. In 1967, I was persuaded by Mrs Small to go along to see a demonstration by Pat and Martin, hairdressers from Mitcheldean, put on for the WI. I hadn't joined when we moved but there was no charge to go to the rest of the year's meetings so I joined up and remained a member until the Blaisdon WI closed in 2009. During that time I was Secretary three

to our very special neighbours and friends in the village, especially Lynne, Sue and Sheila. They were always on hand to help with washing, cleaning and cooking. He also found time to run the London Marathon, raising funds for the local rheumatology ward.

Father Christmas with
Left: Jack.
Centre: Tom.
Right: Dan plus Ned and Sue Booth.

times and President twice. We were a small but friendly group and had great fun over the years. Some of us still go to WI in Longhope.

In 1974, I went to work at Blaisdon Hall, then still a school run by the Salesians. I worked there until rheumatoid arthritis forced me to stop in 1984. In 1982, I fell in the heavy snow we had that year, breaking my arm, when going for some cigarettes. Proof that smoking is bad for your health! I stopped smoking but not for a few more years.

As my arthritis worsened, David was able to continue working, thanks

Below:
Chris Lilley, Thursa Lilley, Evan Smith, Joyce & David Lilley.

Thursa and Christopher were married to Evan and Donna and, in time, we had grandchildren, Daniel, Thomas, Jack, Ashley and Kieran. We had a Christmas tradition of meeting at the Red Hart on Boxing Day lunchtime, then going home for lunch. Later, Father Christmas would pay a visit, bringing presents for the younger members. By that time he had talked to so many people, he had lost his voice so was never able to say anything!

Perhaps the highlight of recent years for us was being invited by the Queen to a Garden Party at Buckingham Palace, in recognition of service to

David & Joyce Lilley:
1. At their wedding.
2. At their farewell party, Blaisdon.
3. At Thursa's wedding.
4. 25th wedding anniversary with bridesmaids, Jean Hobby, Wendy Causier, Sandra Neale.
5. At their farewell party, Blaisdon.
6. In London for the Garden Party
7. David's 70th birthday, Eastbourne.

the community. Lynne and Nigel Hogg made the trip special by ferrying us there and back and arranging pretty well every aspect of the trip, which included a theatre visit to see Mamma Mia. On the day itself everybody was dressed up to the nines but the heavens opened and there was a torrential downpour. It didn't dampen the spirits of anybody there and the Royal Family made their way around the party with umbrellas carefully positioned over them. It was certainly a special day for us.

Having had many happy times in Blaisdon, we realised that we needed a home more suited to our advancing years and sadly, in 2011, we left School House for an apartment in Mitcheldean. We were treated to a wonderful sendoff with most of the village turning out for a party in our honour. It was a lovely way to leave Blaisdon, though in truth we don't feel we have left, as we still see all our friends from the village and return to join in with all the village events."

Thursa Smith (nee Lilley) was 3 when she came to Blaisdon and lived with her parents at School House until her marriage to Evan in 1983. Her memories are

David & Joyce Lilley at their 50th wedding anniversary with grandsons, Ashley, Tom Keiran, Jack, Daniel holding great grandson Holly.

of the many people who made up the village during her childhood:

"Some of my earliest memories are of being taken on Dad's pushbike, which had a small saddle on the crossbar. We would sometimes meet the Longhope policeman who also patrolled Blaisdon, also on a bike. Mum would take Chris and me up to the old reservoir in the woods. Iris Dunbar (nee Hogg) would also come along bringing her son, Neil. We would make fishing rods and nets from broken twigs and cut off tights, though the big fish always seemed to get away! Chris and I would be taken to the hay making fields for tea. This was a great treat, though we didn't realise that if we hadn't gone, we wouldn't have seen Dad for days at a time. Hay making meant working from dawn to dusk and beyond, every day to get everything done before the weather broke. Lambing was also a very busy time for Dad and we often had a lamb in front of the fire. When I was older, I would help Dad skin a dead lamb and put its skin on an orphaned lamb so the sheep would accept the replacement. Dad worked for Mr Walton. It annoyed me at the time that he never got my name right, always calling me Thursala, though it sounds rather funny now.

There always seemed to be people about in the village, whatever the time of day. Mr Bill Jones was always out and about pruning, weeding and cutting grass. Everywhere seemed to benefit from his green fingers. Each week we would be treated to Frank, our singing butcher, entertaining us as he prepared his joints of meat.

Mrs Bill Jones, Mrs Keyse and Mrs Elsie Hogg always seemed to be together and there was always a lot of laughter between them. I'd have loved to know what the jokes were. Perhaps it was the antics we children were getting up to. They also seemed to operate to their own time. It didn't matter what time something started, such as WI, they were always late and never seemed to apologise. Perhaps it was years of seeing village men-folk operating on 'Blaisdon Time' when returning from the Red Hart!

We would always look out for Tom Green walking up from the pub with his dog, Rover, and his bottle of GL cider in his jacket pocket. We'd help him drink it during the afternoon, watching him peel potatoes and cutting them into very thin chips that would be called French Fries today. He'd cook them in a pan full of lard but they tasted fantastic. Mr Green would baby-sit for us. Mum discovered that he had taken us to the pub where we'd had coke and chocolate, two things weren't allowed at home. Mum thought she could stop that by putting us to bed before he came but it didn't work. He just got Chris and me up and put on our day clothes, dirty or not, over the top of our pyjamas and then took us to the pub! There was always laughter and music coming from the pub and

we would listen to the characters we now think of with such affection, Albert Pithouse, David Read and Tommy Brain. In the winter they would warm their cider in a saucepan over the open fire. Another character we loved was Curly or Lawrence Stanton. He would ride his bike down into Blaisdon and, as we liked him, we named one of our rabbits after him. Another thing we looked forward to seeing was the visits of the Morris Men and The Hunt with their hounds.

Margaret Green would take me into Gloucester on the bus. We would go into Chelsea Girl. I thought I was so grown up. Mrs Pickering was a lovely lady. I realise now that she had a single-minded attitude to children. I once did a fashion show for Mrs Pitt who had a clothes shop in Newent. I modelled a bikini, which Mrs Pickering thought was very inappropriate. Just down the road from Mrs Pickering's house was The Tanhouse. You always heard the piano being played, as Mrs Manners would be teaching when she wasn't playing or having a choir rehearsal. Across the road, at The Forge, lived Mrs Etherington who delivered the Citizen. I always seemed to meet Mr Pickering on his way to or from the bus on the main road.

Next door to us were Mr and Mrs Woodman. Their smallholding produced wonderful strawberries and other soft fruit. I would earn pocket money picking fruit for them. Just one or two didn't quite make the basket though! Just behind us was the Post Office. We had a hole in the hedge so we could slip through into her orchard and feed her chickens or go round the house to the shop. Her house always seemed very dark and I know now that it smelt very damp.

1. Chris Lilley. (1965)

2. Chris Lilley at his christening with grandmother, Emily Hobby.

3. Thursa Lilley, aged 3.

4. Chris & Thursa Lilley aged 3 & 5 respectively.

5. Chris & Donna Lilley.

6. Evan & Thursa Smith at their wedding.

(1983)

As I got older, I was able to baby-sit for the Hoggs and Booths down at the bottom end of the village. I'd get £5 for a night, which seemed like a lot of money then.

Trips out were always an exciting treat. Mrs Prytherck took me to see a Beatrix Potter ballet in Bath, which seemed such a long way away. I sat on the edge of my seat throughout; it was so magical. Mr and Mrs Barlow took me to see Jesus Christ Superstar in Bristol. We stayed at Mrs Manners' mother's house. It felt like a carbon copy of The Tanhouse. Caroline Manners and I also went to Brownies together and to Miss Littleton in Northwood Green for embroidery classes. I also remember singing Lord Of The Dance with Anne Walton and Ann Scott. Mrs Scott was the infant teacher at Westbury School, which reminds me of how Chris and I were put on the Westbury Schools Bus from day 1 at 7.40 in the mornings.

Carol singing with Roger Keyse was always great fun, especially when invited into people's houses. There, even the younger members of the company would be offered refreshment. I remember coming home when I was nine or ten, swaying into the living room and telling Mum what a wonderful evening I'd had. Needless to say, I was packed off to bed before dad got home. I went to see the pantomimes at Blaisdon Hall. They did Sleeping Beauty and Ali Ba Ba. There was Sunday School with Hilary Etherington, held in the village Hall and, later, in her house down on Stud Farm. Once. we went to visit a children's home taking toys we no longer needed. Years later, I went for a job interview and upon entering this massive hall and seeing the large staircase, recognised it as the same place we had been to. It was Watton House, near Tewkesbury.

Mr John Magee gave me my first reference, for a job at a residential home in Tewkesbury. I earned £120 a week with £20 going on board and lodging for living-in. We would meet Mrs Ruth Magee on the bus into Gloucester. I loved hearing her stories, especially about how she worked with the barge children on the canals.

It was Mr Magee who married Evan and me at Blaisdon Church on 23rd July 1983. He was such a lovely man with a soft voice. He helped make the day very special for us, as did the rest of Blaisdon. Mum made my dress, three bridesmaids' dresses and a pageboy outfit from material that cost about £100 in total. Sheila Evans did the floral bouquets for the bridesmaids and me. Sue Booth and Lynne Hogg went around the village collecting flowers from the gardens to decorate the church in pink and white. Then there was Mrs Woodman washing the floor and Mrs Smith removing moss from the path so my dress wouldn't get stained. Finally, it seemed like the entire village was inside the church for the service.

Generally, I just remember everyone in the village was always busy doing something, gathering for different events. There was a real buzz of life with its characters that made Blaisdon such a special village. I am so pleased I was able to share this with my children before, as is the nature of things, people passed on or moved away and the village moved on with new folk now creating their own legacy. Christmas was always a special time in Blaisdon and it was lovely to bring the boys to Blaisdon so they could share Christmas with their grandparents and the Booth family. They loved Pete Booth dressing up as Father Christmas and we always seemed to pick up a few extras for tea after our traditional trip to the Red Hart."

John & Jill
Tutton

After David and Joyce Lilley moved to Mitcheldean, the Walton family sold School House to *John and Jill Tutton*:

"We are originally from Raynes Park in London and moved to the Forest of Dean area in 1977, when we moved here from London. We lived in Bream for two years before moving to Blakeney and lived there for thirty two years!

We met at a local youth group and have been married for forty years. We have two lovely children, Lucy and Stephen. Lucy works for Oxfam and Stephen for the Probation Service. They both live in Bristol. We are both retired; John worked for Social Services and Jill was a teacher.

Our passion is the Arts and Crafts Movement and that is what attracted us to School House. We feel we are moving into an Arts and Crafts house in a lovely village community, the very essence of the arts and crafts movement.

The house is currently undergoing a major renovation. We are taking the interior back to the original brick walls and starting again. We are discovering some lovely features such as a very nice fire surround. Luckily, we have a very willing and skilled craftsman in our son, Stephen, who is spending many days helping us in the renovations."

SPRING COTTAGE

Emily Townsend (Volume 2) sold Spring Cottage in 1965 to Lucy Thackwray, previously of Iden, Rye in Sussex for £2,900. She in turn sold it in 1973 to Philip and Richenda Williams from Mitcheldean, for £10,000. In 1978 Philip Williams sold to Michael and Heather Crawshaw for

Above: Spring Cottage in its recent form. (2002)
Below: Spring Cottage after 1st extension. (c1985)

£18,380 and they in turn passed the cottage to Deborah Saunders for £28,500 in 1979. Two years later, in 1981, Stephen and Jean Waters bought Spring Cottage for £37,000. It is quite interesting to see how house prices moved over these sixteen years, given that the property remained unaltered through this period. The only attempt at upgrading the property had occurred in 1961 when Mrs Townsend had sold part of the garden to Mr Bill Jones of Western View in order to have the small single story extension built that housed the kitchen, bathroom and toilet.

1. Inglenook with bread oven to right.
2. Jean & Steve waters in front of Spring Cottage c1982. The 1961 extension is to the right of the inglenook & chimney stack.
3. Spring Cottage, winter 1981-2.
4. Spring Cottage from the road c 1982.
5. The back of Spring Cottage showing the 1961 extension. (1982)

Dentist and Doctor, **Stephen and Jean Waters** moved into Spring Cottage in 1981. Steve had started working in Cotteswold House Dental Practice in Gloucester that March, while Jean was still working in Liverpool. They would meet at weekends and search for a house:

"House hunting had been going on for some weeks. One Saturday, we had viewed a house in Longhope and were following the map to Westbury-on-Severn along Velthouse Lane. As we stopped at the junction in Blaisdon we were greeted by the sight of a beautiful timber framed cottage. 'Why can't houses like that come on the market,' we sighed, as we drove on. Sometimes wishes are granted and in the newspaper two days later, an advert for Spring Cottage appeared. We viewed it the next weekend in the pouring rain, though it didn't stop us falling in love with the cottage. It is said that people decide on a house purchase within seconds of entering a house. I think Jean had decided before she had got out of the car. The aubretia cascading over the wall was sufficient, despite the rain! A price was quickly agreed and we moved in on the 1st June 1981.

Within minutes of arriving at Spring Cottage, we were greeted by some of our new neighbours, Lilla Smith and

Above:
'Burglars' caught on camara are, from the left,
Joyce & Doug Inger, Lynne Hogg, Ceri & Sheila Evans,
Dick Hawker & Rosemary Wagstaff.
Below:
The Uno trophy caught in bed with a companion!

Grace Jones. Mrs Griffiths, from the Old Post Office (Hillcrest) followed, when despite her severe arthritis, she arrived at our door to refresh us, carrying a tray complete with her best china and teapot. This was our introduction to the very friendly village that was Blaisdon, though some interest may have been due to the two large removal wagons blocking the lane. Fortunately given the size of Spring Cottage, we were a small part load in just one of the wagons.

We were soon invited round to neighbours for drinks, barbecues, parties etc. Indeed when some neighbours held a party to thank those who had helped earlier that year when they flooded, our invitation was on the understanding we would help next time! It took another twenty five years, but we did!

Neighbours soon became friends and over the following twenty two years, Spring Cottage saw its fair share of parties and general fun: Red Nose Days were celebrated and funds raised via penalties for being rude about the red food being served (they were not Delia Smith's best recipes); a Millennium Party that saw over thirty people sitting down in a 15x10 foot square room; and a wedding anniversary

1

2

3

4

5

6

7

1. Red Nose party from left:
Lynne Hogg, Doug Inger, Nigel Hogg, Steve & Jean Waters,
Hilary Hawker, Rosemary Wagstaff, Ceri Evans,
Jennifer Griffiths, Sheila Evans, Dick Hawker.
2. Millenium party. from left:
Eileen Waters, Gail Jones, Doug Inger, Jan Royall, Keith
Watkins, Roger Jones, Julia Watkins, ?, Pete Adams. (1999)
3. The Waters family on millenium eve. (1999)
4. Puds a speciality at Spring Cottage! (1984)
5. Halloween party, Ian front left & Eleanor back.
6. Christmas. Steve & Jean with from the left:
Tom, Ian, Eileen & Martin Waters, Keith & Julia Watkins.
In front: Graeme & Jordan Watkins, Eleanor & Pat Waters.
7. Jean, Eleanor & Ian, grandparents, Florence & Luke Toft.

celebrated with a weekend break-in that featured the 'burglars' leaving an Uno Trophy in our bed! The joke was enhanced when we had a film in the camera developed some weeks later and we found the perpetrators had left evidence of their presence in the form of photographs taken on our camera!

In the mid 1980s the village still had quite a few older folk who had lived in the area all of their lives. Alongside these were the incomers such as ourselves. We were always made to feel welcome and everybody joined in village events and worked together, whether it was to raise funds for the Church or Village Hall, or to win the prized Bledisloe Cup. Time may give us rose-tinted spectacles, but we hope that those folk who are no longer with us looked on us as favourably and fondly as we did on them.

At that time the cottage consisted of the original timber framed building plus a poorly built lean-to extension that housed a kitchen plus small bathroom. This was the only part of the building that had water and there was no central heating other than a couple of aged and inefficient night storage heaters. Unlike the original cottage, which was very sound, the extension had a severe damp and mould problem, caused, as we found when it was demolished, by it neither having a cavity between the inner and outer layers of bricks nor a damp proof course. We were to find out how inefficient the storage heaters were in the very severe winter of 1981-2. With the temperature at at record -23 degrees centigrade, snow thick on the ground and the village cut off, we took a chicken out of the freezer. Despite having it in the sitting room, 2 days later it still had not defrosted! The large inglenook fireplace was no help as lighting this filled the entire cottage with smoke!

Luckily neighbours Angela and Keith Foster took pity on us and had us over to Parkside for Sunday lunch.

During our years at Spring Cottage, we undertook two sets of building extensions. The first, in 1984, was to replace the existing single storey lean-to with a two-storey extension, giving us a modern kitchen, an upstairs bathroom and a third bedroom. We also had dormer windows put in upstairs and much needed central heating. A small loo was placed in the old cottage, which, because of its position, had to have a macerator attached. This was rapidly named the 'Grundle Box' by Lynne Hogg, due to the noise it made and audible to all downstairs! The problem of the inglenook was finally solved and it became a functional fireplace again.

All this thankfully happened during a warm and dry summer. During the time the house was not easily lived in, Dick Hawker kindly let us live in an old caravan down on Stud Farm. While there we experienced all the joys of farm life: newspapers delivered to the bed by Roger Keyse; waking at inordinately early hours to the sound of Dick and David Brown rhythmically pounding on the feed silo to restart the flow of cattle feed; finding the dustbin crushed by the milk lorry; and lovely farm fresh milk every day. We have lovely memories of joining the weekend members of the 1984 Stud farm commune (Rosemary & Mike Wagstaff) when they arrived car weary from their weekly journey from Windsor. Deck chairs came out of the boot of their car , the drinks were poured and we sat in the yard in the evening sun before they had even entered the upper flat! The sun shone a lot that summer and we all made the most of it..

The Waters Family:
1. Ian.
2. Ian's christening day with John Magee.(1989)
3. Steve & Jean.
4. Ian's christening day. (1989)
5. Eleanor & Ian. (2008)
6. Eleanor with Brandy. (1986)
7. Budding Gardeners!
8. Some years later!

A few years later and with a growing family, we added a further extension providing a large lounge, utility room, shower room and two more bedrooms. This later work was undertaken by local builder, Clive Smurthwaite, who has left his mark on most buildings in the village. We were also able to build a garage to replace the wooden one erected by Brian Jones and his father. They had bought part of Spring Cottage's land in the 1960s but Brian had kindly sold it to us when he got vehicle access at his own house.

The final changes were to the garden. Jean is a very keen gardener, but with a very busy job plus two growing children, we decided we needed professional help in a major redesign including incorporating the recently re-acquired land. Julian Dowle, the well-known garden designer from Newent, provided all that we needed and Jean was able to plant many of her favourite old roses alongside other features such as a wisteria covered pergola and pond.

In December 1985, Eleanor was born, arriving just too late to appear as the baby Jesus in the village nativity play. Steve was therefore forced to represent Spring Cottage and was typecast, (so others said), as the Grumpy Shepherd. He was hard pressed to make it back from the hospital in Cheltenham to the village for his starring role!

Eleanor spoke very clearly from an early age, a fact that caused much amusement around the village. Aged two or three in church one Sunday, she heard John Magee mention Jesus during his sermon. 'Where's Jesus,' interrupted the voice from the front pew where she always insisted we sat. After a pause, she announced to all, 'There's Jesus, on a stick!' She had seen the crucifix on the wall behind John!

John, bless him, was never fazed by anything and took it all in his stride, as he did on the occasions that our cat, Crum, followed us into church.

Ian was born in February 1989, giving us, as Aunt Lilla said, a pigeon-pair. Like Eleanor, he was christened by John Magee in Blaisdon Church. Ian too had his moments in church, usually caused by the Thomas The Tank Engine models that went everywhere with him and would occupy an entire pew during services. From an early age he and his sister enjoyed all the delights of country living, tramping across the fields, damming streams, feeding the calves and watching the milking down at Stud Farm. They were 'village children' knowing and being known by everyone.

After school at Brightlands, Newnham, Eleanor was a chorister at Llandaff Cathedral School, and then went to Monmouth Haberdasher's School for Girls. Birmingham University followed with a degree in Nursing and 2012 finds her approaching the end of her Medicine degree at Dundee, thus following in her mother's footsteps as a doctor. Her early musical abilities have continued, reaching Diploma standard on the oboe.

Ian moved from Brightlands when it closed, to Cheltenham College, Junior School, before going to Shiplake College, Henley-on-Thames. He became a proficient hockey player and also enjoyed his rugby, though he proved very injury prone and seems to have visited every A&E in the South of England! Luckily there was no lasting damage and he went on to get a degree in Geography at Birmingham. He is currently putting this knowledge to 'good use' by visiting as many countries as possible before embarking on a career.

Crum, our cat, lived until she was thirteen, when she, like several other cats we subsequently had, fell victim to the increasing traffic along Blaisdon Lane. We also had other pets, including two Kune-Kune pigs. These lived nearby, in our small orchard, when their previous owner realised he didn't want his smart lawn in Painswick brown side up! They quickly became village favourites, which was just as well as they were great escape artists. Once they even managed to visit the Red Hart before we realised they were out. Being a very friendly breed, they enjoyed the constant stream of Blaisdon folk visiting them with tasty vegetable titbits and giving them a good rub under their ears. Eleanor and Ian could even get them to sit for an apple.

Eleanor had a special nanny for the first two years of her life in the shape of Lynne Hogg, capably helped by Brandy, Lynne's Retriever. Danielle Price then joined our extended

Far left: Ian & Eleanor with Patsy, left, & Reggie. our two Kune Kune pigs.
Left: Ian & Crum.
Top: Jean & Eleanor with Crum.
Above: Left, Jean with Patsy & right, being shown the art of cattle rearing by David Brown on Stud Farm c1984.

1. Danielle Price holding Grace with, in front, Robert Price, Ian & Eleanor Waters.
2. Eleanor & Ian Waters with Grace, Frances & Robert Price.
3. Eleanor Waters at Danielle Price's wedding.
4. John & Danielle Price at their wedding with 'their' children, Eleanor & Ian Waters.
5. Danielle Price & Eleanor Waters.

family and looked after Eleanor and Ian for over nine years. When she started she was 19 but seemed to have a 30 year old head on her shoulders and this proved to be the case with the many scrapes our children, especially Ian, got into. She also had two of her own children, Robert and Grace, during the time she was in Blaisdon, Frances coming along after she moved to Ringmer in Sussex because of husband John's work. The children grew up together and still keep in contact with Ian and Eleanor often going to stay with the Price family.

Sadly, Danielle died suddenly in 2011 at the age of forty one, leaving so many people devastated by the loss of her but none more so than John, Robert, Grace and Frances. Her Facebook memorial page had over 650 people leaving messages of condolence. John and the children continue to live in Ringmer. All of them, but especially Danielle, have a very special place in our hearts. Their time at Streamways, Woodgreen makes them eligible for inclusion in this book but even if this were not so, they would be in these pages as they were such an important part of this family's time in Blaisdon.

We finally left Spring Cottage in November 2003, having fallen in love with The Temple in Longhope, with its large garden and big airy rooms, so completely different from Spring Cottage. As this is not much further than the other end of Velthouse Lane, we do not feel that we have really left the village. Indeed, we still own the small orchard plot adjacent to Sharon and continue to attend both the church and the pub. With so many of our friends close by we scarcely feel that we have left the village and it will always be in our hearts."

Eleanor Waters writes of her childhood in Blaisdon:

"Growing up in Blaisdon was so very special. There was always something to do and adventures to be had. I was and still am, great friends with Lara Rodgett (Stanley House). We would bike to each other's house and then go off into the fields and woods around Blaisdon. We would be climbing trees, playing in the quarry down Velthouse Lane, collecting conkers from the tree along the drive up to Blaisdon Hall and building a den to put them in. Wherever we went, we would always meet somebody who knew us, so I don't think our parents ever worried about us being out. We were village children and I think, the whole village knew and cared for us.

When mum and dad took us around the Sculpture Trail in the Forest of Dean, one of the sculptures we saw was a wigwam built of wooden branches and twigs. Not to be outdone, we set about and built our own mini-wigwams to go alongside it. My contribution to local art!

The family always went to harvest suppers in the village hall. The entertainment was always fun, especially when provided by members of the village. I will never forget the 'Spice Girls', especially Old Spice! (Ceri Evans)

Mum has always been very musical with a lovely soprano voice, so I was brought up with music either being played or performed and was often taken to her concerts, which instilled a strong musical interest of my own. I went to Llandaff Cathedral School as a founder girl chorister and learned to play oboe, violin and piano. My voice is mezzo-soprano and I remember a highlight was singing a duet in the church with mum.

When I was little, there were many aircraft coming over the village very fast and very low and they terrified me. It was the time of the first Gulf War and the RAF undertook a lot of low level flying exercises. I can remember being at Lynne and Nigel's house (Syston Cottage) out in the garden and running as fast as I could to get inside as I was so scared of the loud planes coming over. This was cured, so dad tells me, when we went to RAF Lyneham on a flight open day and had the chance to sit in one of their jets. We have the picture to prove it.

One day, I came home from school to find Patsy and Reggie, our pigs, had escaped by lifting an extra wide five bar gate off its hinges! So in school uniform and a pair

Eleanor Waters 'pilot' in her jet fighter!

of wellies, I set off with apples to entice them back into the orchard!! They followed me like the obedient pigs they were. They were so well trained that they would sit like dogs for an apple offered by Ian or me.

Danielle Price looked after Ian and me for 9½ years. She would pick us up from our first school, Brightlands in Newnham on Severn, and take us down to the River Severn for ice creams. She would take me swimming and I would cling on for dear life, as when I was little, I was just a little scared of swimming!! I just remember Danielle always being there when I was growing up. She was like an extra parent but became more like a big sister, one I could always turn to for advice and support when I needed it. It's so sad to think she is not with us anymore but she was such a special person, her spirit will always be with Ian and me."

Ian Waters writes about growing up in Blaisdon:

"Growing up in Blaisdon seemed to be one long playtime. There was always something to do, whether it was with Mum and Dad, with Danielle our nanny, or one of the other neighbours who occasionally looked after us when we were young. Then there were friends such as Lara and Francesca Rodgett or pals from school. It always seemed to be a big adventure going out into the fields and woods around us.

A favourite walk with mum and dad was up past the church, through the field above it, which in those days was planted with blackcurrant bushes, and into the woods. There the old reservoir was a great, if muddy, attraction and we would always return covered in mud and soaked through.

Playing in the brook with El. (Eleanor) was always fun. Mum used to take us down through the Stud Farm to the brook for a damming expedition and picnic. I remember having to show my older cousin, Graeme, how to climb over a five bar gate as, being a townie, he had never met such a big obstacle and was quite upset as he didn't know how to get over it. Sometimes, Smudge the dog would appear and join us playing in our games. Perhaps our biggest (mis)adventure in the brook was going up to our necks in the water when Andrew Hogg was looking after us!

We grew up drinking farm fresh milk from Stud Farm and we would go down to collect it fresh everyday. Louise Hawker would take me out on the quad bike when we went walking the dogs.

Once dad and Ceri Evans took me up the church tower, which was quite an adventure as I wasn't big enough to stretch across the gap over the bells. They had to pass me over from one to the other. When we were up there we saw people had scratched their names in the lead flashing, so we added ours!

Danielle Price was our nanny and she looked after Eleanor from age two and me from when I was born until I was nearly ten. During her time in Blaisdon, she had two children, Rob and Grace, who were like our brother and sister. Her third child Frances was born after she moved to Ringmer in Sussex and she and John asked us to be Godparents. El. and I used to go and stay with them in Ringmer and are still very much in contact with the Price family.

We always looked on Danielle as part of our family and it was so sad to lose her, first when she moved away to Ringmer, near Brighton, and then when she died last year,

aged only forty one. She will always be with us in spirit as we will never lose the memories of the time we spent with her.

Another person who we think of as family and is certainly an honorary Blaisdonite is Roland Smith. He's known round the village as the runner, something he does everyday round the local lanes when he is visiting us. As a close friend of my parents since their university days in Liverpool, I have known him all my life and he has always been good company. When I was younger, he would involve us in experiments in the kitchen. How many other people have made DNA in their mum's kitchen??

Left: Ian Waters & Roland Smith with Rudolf's red nose.
Right: Roland Smith arrives at Spring cottage after a good run.

Even though we have now moved just outside the parish of Blaisdon and I have been away, first to school in Shiplake, Oxon, and then to Birmingham University, I still feel Blaisdon is a special part of my life, as it is to the rest of the family too."

The Waters family:
Jean, Ian, Eleanor & Stephen.

Following Jean and Steve Waters' move to the other end of Velthouse Lane, the cottage passed to Michael and Lynne Hawker, then in 2012, **Roger and Kate Millis** moved in:

"We moved in to Spring Cottage in May 2012 having spent several months in prolonged negotiations to buy it. We had moved from a Victorian terrace house in St Paul's, Cheltenham where we had lived for 7 years previously, via a short let in the Dymock area. Having decided that Cheltenham was becoming a little bit noisy and crowded for us we looked at a number of areas west of Gloucester but immediately liked Blaisdon even when we first visited the empty house on the coldest day of winter 2011/12. Apart from the pub, one of Blaisdon's other benefits is that whilst it is a suitable distance from Gloucester to enable commuting. It is also close to areas of the Forest where we can enjoy mountain biking, climbing, fishing and walking.

When we bought it the house was habitable but a little run down, with some of its prime features removed. We hope to be able to update and cosmetically improve this beautiful house over the next few years. The garden was also a little neglected and it has taken a few months of jungle warfare just to get back to the bare bones of its underlying structure. There are certainly plenty of projects to keep us going!

Roger was brought up in Northampton but has lived in Gloucestershire for about thirteen years and works in Gloucester as the Fleet Fire Safety Manager for the nuclear power company, EDF. Kate was brought up in Kempley and attended Newent Community School before joining the Royal Navy. Having spent several years as a navigator she then returned to University to qualify as a doctor and

currently works for the RN as a Medical Officer. Some of her family remain local and farm in the Kilcot area. We got married in March of this year and do not currently have any children."

Above: Roger & Kate Millis
on their wedding day.
Right: Roger & Kate Millis.
Below: Spring Cottage (c2003)

THE  OLD POST OFFICE

Mrs Annie Goddard (Volume 2) continued to live at the Post Office until moving to Mitcheldean in 1971. She sold the house for £4,100 to Mrs Mary Griffiths of Gawlett Farm. Mrs Griffiths' husband, John, having died, she sold Gawlett Farm and moved into the Old Post Office, renaming it Hillcrest.

Mrs Griffith's niece, **Mary Evans**, recounts how, in earlier times, she lived with her Aunt and Uncle at Gawlett Farm:

"When I was seven, my mother sadly died in childbirth, leaving my father with seven children to look after. Arrangements were made for an uncle whom I had never seen or met to pick me up and take me to Gawlett Farm. So, I came to live with Uncle Jack and Aunty Mary.

I thought I was going to the other side of the world. As we approached, the house looked very large and austere. On a recent visit with my husband, Colin, sixty years after leaving, memories came flooding back.

I remember being picked up by a lady with a horse and cart. Together with other children, I was taken to the small stone school in Blaisdon. During the war years, whilst we were in school, an aeroplane came down in a field nearby.

The Old Post office in 1995.

We all wanted to see it but, of course, we were not allowed.

In winter, when the snow was deep, I would be sent several miles on the old cob horse to fetch a supply of bread and huge lumps of meat from the baker and butcher respectively, returning home with the supplies slung over the horse in sacks. Another vivid memory is of the vast orchards of plum trees on Gawlett Farm. The plums were sold to make jam and large lorries would arrive to take the tons of plums away.

A mile or so away was a boys' home and I remember the long wooden tables in the dining hall, at which sometimes I would be sat and given a meal with them. Some of the boys on leaving did quite well, becoming carpenters, bricklayers etc with skills they had been taught at Blaisdon Hall.

Mrs Mary Griffiths, left, with Colin Evans & daughters, Ann & Wendy.
(1972-3)

wedding cake for the marriage of Susie Lewis, the daughter of Robert and Dorothy Lewis (Volume 2). When he returned it was with the news that the war in Europe was over. This was a moment for real celebration."

While Mrs Griffiths was at Hillcrest, the house underwent some modernisation, the roof being raised and the outside being rendered. In October 1972 the orchard behind the house running down past the Village Hall towards Parkwood was sold to Vic and Enid Woodman, where they incorporated it into their fruit growing enterprise. Mrs Griffiths lived at Hillcrest till her death on 5th February 1983 and is buried in Flaxley churchyard. The house remained empty until sold the following year.

A young Mary Griffiths.

At certain times of year the boys would put on concerts to which we locals would be invited. This was a real treat. Being a Catholic home, every Friday, several boys would be sent to Blaisdon Halt to pick up a huge box of fish, which they would take back to the Hall on a wooden cart.

One day, when walking from Flaxley church, I passed Sir Lance Crawley-Boevey. For some reason, Sir Lance contacted my uncle, complaining that I had ignored him!

My Uncle Jack went to Gloucester one day to pick up a

Right: Hillcrest, as it then was, on 7th May 1984 with Pat, Elizabeth & Catherine.
Taken to compare with old photo, above left, taken in 1904 (see Volume 2).

John Higgins and his family moved to Blaisdon in 1984:

"We moved to Blaisdon from Temple Cloud, a village in North Somerset, on 1st May 1984. I was aged 41, Patricia, 33, and our daughters Elizabeth, 4, and Catherine, 10 months.

I had been working as an administrator in Southmead hospital and was appointed to a post with Gloucester Health Authority, based at Rikenel in Gloucester. I started work there in June 1983. Catherine was born in July. For a while I commuted from Somerset but then the Health Authority let us have a house in Longford Lane, Gloucester, whilst we looked for a permanent home. Our initial idea was to live in Cheltenham, which we knew a little and liked very much, but we could not find what we wanted there at the right price. A colleague asked if we had considered the Forest of Dean.

Now I must admit that I did not know exactly where the Forest of Dean was. I thought that all the land to the west of Gloucester and north of the Severn was Wales! We drove out one weekend and it was immediately clear that this was somewhere that we would like to live and where the house prices were more to our liking. We looked in Soudley, the Pludds, Berry Hill and Elton and then we saw that Lear and Lear, Estate Agents, had a house on their books in a village called Blaisdon. The price was a bit too high for us and I said that we should not even look at it but Pat insisted so on 5th November we drove into Blaisdon for the first time.

The house was called Hillcrest, although it was not on the crest of a hill and had been empty for some time. It looked a bit forlorn. I left Pat to look around inside with the estate agent and I wandered around the garden with Elizabeth. I fell for it. The setting was wonderful; it was

1

The Higgins Family:

1. In the garden for the first time. (1984)

2. Elizabeth, Pat & Catherine on Catherine's christening day. (1985)

3. Elizabeth's first day at school. (1984)

4. Elizabeth with new hair-do. (1988)

5. Pat & Catherine take Elizabeth to meet the school bus, David Ben & Robert Brown are seen in the distance. (1985)

6. Catherine. (1984)

7. Elizabeth & Catherine before the flower beds came. (1987)

2

3

6

4

5

7

the sort of place we would have chosen for a holiday. The idea of living there seemed too good to be true. The garden seemed huge compared to the gardens we had owned previously. I thought I would feel like the lord of the manor. I wanted it. Pat was not so sure. The rooms were a good size but clearly a lot of work was needed to make it into a comfortable home.

We went away to think about it. On the following weekend we went back for another look, this time without the agent. As we were looking around the garden a figure appeared at the front gate, a slightly built old man with a Lancashire accent. He introduced himself as Frank Baylis. He said that he was a churchwarden and asked if we would like to see the church. We followed him up to St Michael's where he showed us around. I particularly remember him pointing out the carvings on the pillars, which were done by an apprentice stonemason. It was a very attractive little church.

Everything about the village appealed to us and we decided to make an offer. After a bit

Above:
John Higgins, having laid new flat roof. (2000)
Below: Old Post Office from the back
showing the old Bramley apple tree. (2000)

of haggling a price was agreed. It took us a long time to sell our own house so it was not until 2nd May 1984 that we moved in. We immediately changed the name to The Old Post Office, to the delight of Cedric Etherington (Volume 2), the local historian.

We contacted the vicar about getting Elizabeth baptised and his deputy, John Magee came to see us. I had never met him before and thought he might ask why we had not had her baptised sooner. When I answered the door he put out his hand and said, 'I believe I am to have the honour of baptising your daughter'. A Christian gentleman if ever there was one. The following year he also baptised our younger daughter, Catherine.

During the summer of 1984 the village organised a Plum Festival, a fete named after the famous Blaisdon plums. Everybody worked hard to make it a success. My contribution was to devise a Treasure Hunt; a walk around the village and up to the Hall, with cryptic clues. It was won by Louise Hawker from Stud Farm. Does she remember, I wonder?

When Elizabeth started at Westbury School, in Mrs Bennett's class, I would take her over to the crossroads next to the Lodge before I went to work and wait there for the school bus with David Brown and his two older children. David and I were governors of the school for a few years. Catherine started at Westbury School in 1988. Later that year we transferred both girls to Newnham School.

At that time the Salesians were at Blaisdon Hall, which was a school, and they allowed the villagers to walk through the grounds. It was a very pleasant walk from the Lodge, past the school, through the avenue of conifers and back along Velthouse Lane. There were splendid views of the River Severn and the Cotswold hills behind. It was ideal for taking visitors after a good meal. We have always enjoyed walking and occasionally cycling with the children in the Forest.

The Higgins Family at the Old Post office,
John, Elizabeth, Pat &Catherine.
(1984)

old. It continues to produce about a ton of apples every year. We created flowerbeds, planted fruit trees and kept the lawn under control. It began to look colourful, especially in the late spring.

Pat, encouraged by Margaret Pickering, became a member of the WI. She later served as Vice-President and then President. In 1987 Pat started learning to ring the church bells, taught by Victor Gibson of Westbury. She enjoyed it immensely and is still ringing.

In June 1986 we made our first change to the fabric of the house; an extension to the front which gave us a small porch and a more conveniently positioned front door. We replaced the windows in 1989 and I fitted a new kitchen, which took me several months, in 1990. In 1992 we made our biggest change to the house; an extension giving us another full-sized room, a shower room with toilet and a small utility room. This changed the external appearance of the house completely. The extension was designed and built by Clive Smurthwaite from Northwood Green, who did a number of jobs for us over the years. In June 1995 we had a summerhouse erected at the end of the garden to celebrate our 25th wedding anniversary.

We set about the garden, starting by clearing a large rubbish heap, which, according to Dave Lilley, our next-door neighbour had been there for at least twenty years. There were two major trees: a yew tree which we estimated was about 300 years old and a large and ancient Bramley apple tree, then probably about 60 years

Social events at that time included parties at neighbours' houses, annual village fetes and Family Service at St Michael's once a month where John Magee's sermons were always forceful and thought provoking. In December 1994, when John died, he was mourned by everyone, regardless of religious belief. We were also saddened when Bob and Margaret Pickering left the village in April 2000 and the following year Margaret died, another great loss to the village and to us.

Pat had left work when Elizabeth was born in 1979 and returned when Catherine went to school in 1988. In the meantime she did some voluntary work at the Citizens' Advice Bureau and the local Community Health Council. She was also clerk to the Parish Council for many years. After a number of part-time jobs she was started work with Gloucestershire County Council , in the Shire Hall, in June 1989. She worked there until her retirement in December 2007. I had retired in April 2003.

John & Pat Higgins in Venice.

a temporary job, washed dishes for six months at the Severn Bore Pub. Later that year she was recruited by the new Tesco store where she worked there from its opening day until she left home. Catherine's first paid employment was next-door, 'babysitting' Eleanor and Ian Waters. She has since said several times that this was the most enjoyable job she ever had; sitting watching TV with a couple of amiable children and getting paid for it. In September 1998 Elizabeth went to Leeds University. Catherine, still at school, took a part-time job at Roseby's in Gloucester. On leaving school in 2001 Catherine had a 'year out', working at the Gloucestershire Record Office. She went to Durham University in September 2002. For the start of her second year there we bought a house near Durham where she lived with a friend for a year. Elizabeth then joined them and lived there until 2006, so by this time both daughters had permanently left Blaisdon. They both still love the house and the village and are very pleased to come back.

There was a bonfire in the field opposite the church to celebrate the 50th anniversary of VE Day, on 8th May 1995.
Elizabeth started at Denmark Road High School in September 1991. In 1997 Elizabeth, now 17, and wanting

In April 1998 an exceptionally large cat was seen crossing Blaisdon Lane near the church. The Blaisdon Beast?! My witness was a sober, church-going young woman with good eyesight, a colleague at the Health Authority!

We debated what we should do to see the millennium in. We went to a party on Popes Hill on 31st December 1999 but left before midnight and sprinted back to Blaisdon. We walked up to the church and sat on a bench in the churchyard, underneath the tower, where we drank wine and listened to the church clock striking twelve. Then we watched and listened to the fireworks all around. The next morning Pat and her fellow bell ringers rang in the new millennium.

We also love Blaisdon and have no plans to leave. There have of course been a lot of changes over the 28 years we have lived here but it is still essentially the same place. The things that attracted us in the first place; the garden, the fine setting, the proximity to the countryside are all still there. On the downside; the road is much busier, there are a lot more lights at night, and the orchards with the smell of plums in the autumn have gone, a lot of the old neighbours have gone too, the Salesian brothers have long gone. Most of the villagers are commuters, as we were; only a handful work on the land. But it is still a very fine place to live and we have never regretted coming here."

John and Pat's daughters have fond memories of growing up in Blaisdon. First, **_Elizabeth Higgins_**:

"When I was about seven years old Mr Etherington (Volume 2), renowned as Gloucestershire's oldest paper boy, paused on his round to talk to my mother about the history of the village and of our house. Catherine and I always loved his stories about the village. This one was a Christmas story from, I believe, the end of the nineteenth century. On Boxing Day a group of men, presumably to get away from their families, met in an old wooden hut in

Ley Park to play cards and drink beer.

The day wore on and everybody was having a good time. It being winter they were heating the hut with an oil stove. One of the men - well-oiled himself presumably - knocked the stove over by accident, starting a blaze that set fire to the hut and caused the poor fellow severe burns. These were the days before A&E or the Air Ambulance, so his friends just carried him back home and left his wife to do the best she could. He lived in the cottage that became the post office, which much later became our house. A few days later he died, at home.

That was the story. Whether it was true or not I don't know but I was utterly horrified. Anyone dying like that would surely not lie quietly in his grave but would leave a ghost to haunt the place where he suffered and died, namely our house! For a long time I knew no peace. I would awake in the night thinking that I could smell singeing flesh; all the little noises that an old house makes in the night became the groans of the dying man. I dreaded walking into a room and finding a card session in full swing. I would not go to the toilet without someone, even if it was just my little sister, standing outside the door to protect me against the smouldering terror.

In time my fears subsided but I find that even as I write this account I get something of the old feeling. I don't think I'll go back to Blaisdon for a while."

Now, younger sister, **_Catherine Higgins_**:

"In a career that so far stretches over 12 years and 4 countries, I can safely say that I have never had a job that afforded such opportunities for fun and responsibility as baby-sitting the children of Blaisdon in the late 1990s. Nor have I ever had such an easy commute as the stroll round the corner to my next-door neighbours.

My first baby-sitting assignment came in 1997 when, at the age of fourteen, I was deemed responsible enough to baby-sit for my neighbours' seven year old son. As none of my friends had yet taken on the proud mantle of baby-sitter, I based most of my knowledge of this noble profession on information I had gleaned from American TV shows. So it was with some excitement and trepidation I headed round to Spring Cottage that first night.

Pat, Catherine, Elizabeth & John Magee.
(1984)

Having been assured that I had full fridge and biscuit cupboard privileges, I proudly took charge of one Ian Waters, age seven. Fortunately he was an amenable child, happy to watch Casualty with me and head off to bed with only minimal persuasion and bribing. I have literally never felt such professional pride as when his parents returned and I was able to report that the young master was alive and well and I hadn't burned down the house or killed the cats.

Over the next few years I had a fairly regular spot baby-sitting young Ian, and occasionally his sister, Eleanor, who made my job very easy by ordering her brother to bed herself. Over the years there were one or two memorable highlights, such as the time the cats escaped into the garden and we stood outside for about twenty minutes trying to coax them back in (possibly a bed-avoidance tactic, on reflection) or the time we played pool in the garage and Ian beat me in spite of the fact he was eight and I was cheating.

I also branched out occasionally and offered my services to the Rodgetts at Stanley House. This was a slightly longer commute but worth it for the convivial company of the two girls, the excellent biscuit cupboard provisions and the lift up the road in Dr Rodgett's Porsche."

WAR MEMORIAL

Villagers have commemorated Remembrance Sunday every year at the war memorial since it was built in 1920. In the days when there was a school at Blaisdon Hall, staff and boys joined in the remembrance. Today, the Catholic community that worship in the village hall join villagers in a joint service of remembrance on the nearest Sunday to 11th November. A few minutes is taken to remember those who died in conflict, both from our own community and elsewhere.

Above: Blaisdon War Memorial.
Below from left:
Remembrance order of service 2006.
An unusual peace-time visitor to Blaisdon.
Boys from Blaisdon Hall school. J Dunbar on cornet c1950s (J. Dunbar)

Above & right:
Remembrance service 2011.
Jack Alcock lays the wreath.
Below:
Order of service 1993.

Remembrance Day

HYMN

The Lord's my shepherd, I'll not want.
He makes me down to lie
in pastures green. He leadeth me
the quiet waters by.

Yea, though I walk in death's dark vale,
yet will I fear none ill.
For thou art with me, and thy rod
and staff me comfort still.

Goodness and mercy all my life
shall surely follow me.
And in God's house for evermore
my dwelling-place shall be.

SCRIPTURE READING

In the days to come
the mountain of the Temple of Yahweh
shall tower above the mountains
and be lifted higher than the hills.
All the nations will stream to it,
peoples without number will come to it; and they will say:
'Come, let us go up to the mountain of Yahweh,
to the Temple of the God of Jacob
that he may teach us his ways
so that we may walk in his paths;
since the Law will go out from Zion,
and the oracle of Yahweh from Jerusalem'.

He will wield authority over the nations
and adjudicate between many peoples;
these will hammer their swords into ploughshares,
their spears into sickles.
Nation will not lift sword against nation,
there will be no more training for war.

O House of Jacob, come,
let us walk in the light of Yahweh.

Prayer of St Francis

Lord, make me an instrument of your peace.
Where there is hatred, let me sow love;
where there is injury, pardon;
where there is doubt, faith;
where there is despair, hope;
where there is darkness, light;
and where there is sadness, joy.

Divine Master,
grant that I may not so much seek
to be consoled as to console,
to be understood as to understand,
to be loved as to love.

For it is in giving that we receive,
in pardoning that we are pardoned,
and in dying that we are born to eternal life.

LAYING OF WREATHS

Remembrance

Let us remember before God the men and women of all nations who have died as a result of war – those whom we have known and whose memory we treasure; those we never knew, and those who died unknown. We will remember all who have lived in hope, but died in vain – the tortured, the innocent, the starving and the exiled, the imprisoned, the oppressed and the disappeared...

'They shall not grow old as we that are left grow old: age shall not weary them nor the years condemn. At the going down of the sun and in the morning we will remember them.'
All then say, ... 'We will remember them.'
Silence follows

PRAYERS OF INTERCESSION

Let us now pray to God our Father:

1. Today we remember and we pray for those who died in the two great World Wars.
    We pray for the people of Blaisdon whose names are carved on this memorial. May the sacrifice of their lives bring lasting peace to the world.
    LORD HEAR US - LORD GRACIOUSLY HEAR US

2. We pray for the Old Boys of the School who died in the armed forces:
    for EDWARD DOWDALL, JAMES LANGRELL, JAMES JOHNSON, CYRIL McDERMOTT.
    May remembering them inspire us to work for peace.
    LORD HEAR US

3. We pray for those who are in the armed forces today, especially our past pupils and our relatives and friends. May God keep them safe.
    LORD HEAR US

4. We pray for peace in the world. Let there be peace in Northern Ireland. Let there be peace in the Middle East. Let there be peace in Yugoslavia. Let there be peace in South Africa.
    Lord, let there be peace.
    LORD HEAR US

Lead me from death to life, from falsehood to truth,
Lead me from despair to hope, from fear to trust,
Lead me from hate to love, from war to peace,

Let peace fill our hearts, our world, our universe. Amen

THE ODGE

The Lodge has remained in the ownership of Blaisdon Hall, so, as the Hall was sold its ownership moved from the Salesian Order to Hartpury College, Mr Tony Haynes and now to Mr Andey Zhelamskiy. During that time, various people employees have lived here. Mr and Mrs Austin (Volume 2) continued to live at The Lodge until leaving the village in the 1980s. On 8th December 1995, ownership of The Lodge passed to Hartpury College.

Above: The Lodge on a snowy morning.

Nicky Charlesworth and future husband, Ed, came to Blaisdon to work for Hartpury College:

"Ed and I arrived in Blaisdon in 1997, myself coordinating the conferences and weddings at Blaisdon Hall and Ed as a lecturer on the Rural Foundation Course for Hartpury College.

I moved into Blaisdon Hall Lodge from my previous home in Warwickshire in 1997. The Lodge hadn't been lived in for a number of years and I set about making it my own with redecoration and kitchen remodelling and slow reclamation of the garden. One of the nicest aspects of living at The Lodge was the walled courtyard adjacent to the house, which provided a wonderful, sheltered space for outdoor entertainment and evenings of frivolity with newly acquainted friends from the Village and the Red Hart pub. Ed acted as a warden for Blaisdon Hall and subsequently had a room on site (1997-99). It was a room with a fabulous view over the Severn Vale.

Unfortunately for Ed and I, Hartpury College decided to sell Blaisdon Hall in the autumn of 1999 so we were both out on our ear! Luckily we'd bought a house in Lower Lydbrook and had been restoring it in readiness for our homelessness. Regardless of relocation, our love affair with Blaisdon continued and we were married at Blaisdon church on a very snowy December 18th 1999. Then a few years later, the opportunity to buy St Michael's Cottage arose and we were able to move back to Blaisdon."

The Lodge Garden. (1982)
As the gardener for Blaisdon Hall from 1950s to 1980s, it is not surprising that George Austin kept the garden at The Lodge in immaculate condition, providing a lovely splash of colour behind the high wall.

BLAISDON HALL

The Roman Catholic Religious Order of the Salesians of Don Bosco had run a School of Agriculture and Trades at Blaisdon Hall since 1935 (Volume 2). In 1962, the Order sold the Stud Farm and changed the emphasis of the School. The training in Agricultural trades ceased and in its place was a broad and practical education given to disadvantaged boys.

Blaisdon Hall. (2012)

Father Sean Murray's time at Blaisdon Hall encompasses the final twenty eight years of the school at Blaisdon Hall. Since the Salesians had arrived in Blaisdon with their first boys in 1935 they had nurtured their boys with a firm but fair hand. The large number of ex-pupils who still return to Blaisdon for reunions demonstrates the success of this. Although the school was to change direction, the philosophy of the Salesians was to remain true to their original ideals.

Father Sean Murray continues:

"I first came to Blaisdon Hall on Friday 10th September 1965. Yes, I admit that I did go rather unwillingly and indeed in those unenlightened days I had no say in the matter. Inevitably though, like most boys and staff, I became immersed in the enormous challenge and was inspired by the loyalty and dedication of the staff and the mostly willing cooperation of the boys.

The Salesian School at Blaisdon Hall had opened in February 1935 as a joint venture of the Salesians of Don Bosco and the Westminster Catholic Crusade of Rescue. The Salesians of Don Bosco are an international Roman Catholic order of laymen and priests dedicated to show the love of God to young people, especially those who are disadvantaged. They now number 16,000 brothers and priests present in 128 different countries. Understandably, the Crusade of Rescue placed many of the early boys at Blaisdon and this continued until the farm closed in 1962.

The sale of Stud Farm on Monday 27th August 1962 was a defining event in the history of the Salesian School. In the foreword to the farm sale brochure was written, 'Changing conditions and new Government policy demanded new developments, so that the school has become a residential school for boys suffering from some degree of maladjustment, and farming is no longer taught.' Maladjustment is not a term used today. In reality the boys at the school at that time were the victims of some

Father Gilheney.
Headmaster.

difficulties in their home lives. Placement at Blaisdon, in a small school, took them away from areas of failure and gave them the opportunity to gradually resolve their problems, gain confidence and success in a secure, well-organised lifestyle.

Father John Gilheney was the head teacher in the 1960s and most of the 1970s and he led the gradual but remarkable changes in the 1970s. Father Dan Lucey who had been manager at Stud Farm for many years, left the day the farm was sold. His right-hand man Brother Joe Carter (Volume 2) stayed on and continued to farm on the Blaisdon Hall Estate. We took Joe out of the farm but we couldn't take the farm out of Joe!

At that time all the pupils were accommodated in the main house and teaching took place in the 'old school' behind it. This building had been constructed by the brothers and the boys in the early 1940s. This new building, situated beyond the main house, comprised classrooms, offices and sleeping accommodation and was opened in January 1966. In addition a new gymnasium/concert hall was built on the side of the playground. The new school building was demolished when new owners moved in but the gymnasium was kept. Two ornamental pools now feature on the school site.

School staff 1960-61.
Back row from left:
Br Tom Caulfield, Tony Quinn, Dennis O'Leary, Br Eddie Barron, Tom Palmer, Br John Finnegan.
Front row from left:
Br Dan Donohue, Fr Peter Wareing, Fr John Gilheney, Fr Joe Fairclough, Fr Henry Mulhaney, Fr Jim McGuire, Fr Dan Lucey, Fr Bill Boyd, Br Alan Garman.

Above:
Blaisdon Hall Staff 1963-64.
Back row from left:
Br Tom Caulfield, Dennis O'Leary, Fr Philip Spratt,
Br Alan Garman, Br Edward Barron, Br Joe Carter,
Fr Hugh O'Sullivan, Anthony Quin, Paul Jackson, Br Pat Coye,
Tom Palmer.
Front row from left:
Fr Bill Boyd, Fr Jim McGuire, Fr Joe Fairclough, Fr Bernard Higgins,
Fr John Gilheney, Fr George Hilton, Fr Frances Sutherland.

Left:
Old boy, Pat Murphy & his family visit the community c1985:
From the left, back row:
Pat Murphy, Fr George Robson, Fr Jim McGuire, Br Alan Garman,
Br Tom Caulfield, Jergan Murphy, Fr Sean Murray,
Br Neil McElwee.
Front row: Rita & Heidi Murphy, Fr George Hilton.

The staff in the 1960s were totally male until the arrival of a wonderful matron, Pauline Allen. There was always a long queue outside the school infirmary each morning. Pauline used to live in Dairy Cottage opposite the Red Hart and even after leaving, kept in touch over the years. The boys of those years were fortunate to have such a caring matron.

Over the years we always had a devoted hard working domestic staff. They all lived locally and were collected each day by Brother Joe Carter in the minibus whose driving would often give them the fright of their lives. Nobody from Blaisdon Hall will forget Joe Hurley who was cook for over thirty years. He was well known in the area, as were his assistants, Mrs Dowding who lived on Nottswood Hall and Mrs Hart from Huntley.

Br Neil with Hall staff, from the left:
Shirley Yemm, Susan Green & Jean Adams.

The Salesians, both priests and brothers, looked after the boys morning, noon and night. This was quite demanding and indeed more help was needed. That came, with the appointments of three lay-teachers in September 1972. The first lady teacher, Barbara Jackson came at Easter 1973. Barbara brought more than a touch of gentility and glamour to what could be at times a rather harsh male dominance. Barbara stayed for four years and later emigrated from Dairy Cottage to Canada. Unfortunately she died of cancer in March 2000.

At the time of the arrival of the new lay-staff, preliminary preparations were being made to establish separate teaching and care staff. Gradually under the leadership of Father John Kavanagh, Head of Care, five house units were established and new staff were appointed. Each house of about twelve boys had a housefather, housemother, one or two deputies, a teacher on extraneous duties and a community service volunteer. The care staff looked after the boys from end of school until the start of class in the morning and also at weekends. This was a much-needed arrangement and everyone, boys and staff, benefitted greatly.

There then began a golden era of life at the school. The staff were well qualified, dedicated and loyal. Another first was the arrival of Ron Smy as the first lay bursar and his wife Margaret was housemother in Brother Alan's house. Daphne Duberley and Eileen Beard who were already working at the hall, took over as housemothers and Alan Ferry, a past pupil who had been gardener, became one of the new housefathers. Brother Joe Adams was one of the early housefathers and became Head of Care eventually. Peter Knott was one of the housefathers, staying until

1. Fr Hilton on the occasion of his Golden jubilee with Winnie &
Eric Parsons.
2. Br Jan Orysiuk meets Pope John Paul II.
3. Fr John Kavanagh.
4. Br Charles O'Donnel.
5. Fr Bill Boyd.

Housefather Peter Knott, left, with pupils.

Back left: Fr Pat Kenna.
Front row, centre: Mrs Sandra Meadows &Mrs Linda McDonald.

the end of the school and is still living locally in Huntley. We had some great volunteers, young men like Sean Tarpey, who went to get suitably qualified, came back and eventually became Head of Care and led the never to be forgotten 'farewell trip' to Paris Disney in early December 1993.

The staff used their talent and experience to open up the world to the boys. Sandra Meadows who came in 1977 and stayed until the closure, ending up as a successful deputy head, together with Linda McDonald took the boys well beyond the local environment. They went to Cats and other shows in London, to Stratford and Shakespeare, to the Three Counties in Malvern, to the Last Night of the Proms and skiing in Italy and Bulgaria. They went all over the place. Sadly Linda who was one of the most inspiring teachers ever at Blaisdon, died in September 1985. It was a huge loss and we remember her with gratitude and love to this day.

Mention too must be made of Father Pat Kenna. Pat came as a young Salesian Brother in 1980 staying for two years, completed his studies and was ordained in 1985. In 1987 he returned as Head of Care, took over as head teacher in 1991 and led the final difficult years of the school with care and efficiency to a successful conclusion. Pat had a great affinity with young people who were always at ease in his company. Sadly Pat died in 2005 after a heart attack on the playground of the Salesian College, Chertsey.

The successes in art and pottery deserve mention. We, a small school of under sixty, stood up against the big schools of five hundred plus and took the top prize, the Frank Tuckett Trophy, in the annual national exhibition of children's art on more than one occasion. One of our boys in 1988 won Britain's Young Sculptor of the Year winning a ten-day tour of art galleries in Italy. The inspiration behind all this tremendous success was Mr Arthur Hickman, the Art and Pottery teacher. One year we had the audacity not

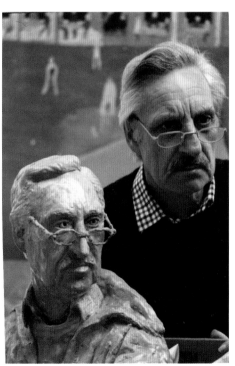

1. Pupils demonstrate their pottery to Prince Edward at Cowley Manor.
2. "Rat Race' by Kevin Barlow.
3. A group of Blaisdon entries for the National Exhibition of Children's Art.
4. 'A motor Accident' by Chris Barber.
5. Mr Hickman (Art Teacher) with his likeness sculpted by a Blaisdon pupil.

only to enter the Forest Schools sports but also to take the top prize, a school of 60 standing up to schools of hundreds!

Towards the end of the 1980s our numbers were falling. Government policy was to phase out schools like the Salesian one at Blaisdon Hall. Sadly in September 1993 the trustees and governors decided to close the school at Christmas. It was understandable that some staff would leave but most stayed to bravely and calmly lead us through to a successful closure. The governors provided all the expertise to ensure that the remaining boys got placements in other schools and that the staff had new posts with comparable or better salaries. It was a sad but glorious ending. The remaining 19 boys and many of the staff set off on a trip to Paris Disney, stayed in a lovely hotel with plastic cards, not keys for the doors and had a

Above: Sue Booth, school secretary.
Below: School trip to Euro Disneyland.

wonderful day at the theme park. The boys left on 19th December 1993.

The Salesian community stayed on until the summer of 1994 and then dispersed to other Salesian centres. Father Jim McGuire stayed on as parish priest, Father Aidan Murray as caretaker, Ron Smy as bursar, David Bastable as security and Sue Booth as secretary. They secured the whole place and disposed of most of the contents of the school and hall.

Father Jim McGuire who had been parish priest almost all the time since the early 1960s moved in to St Peters in Gloucester. Jim is now 96 yrs old and going strong. Father Aidan Murray became parish priest and settled in Dairy Cottage but is now resident in the parish house in

School trip to Euro Disneyland.

Newent. Brother Joe Carter who was at Blaisdon since 1945 stayed on to the end and then retired to the new Salesian home for the elderly in Farnborough.

It was a big wrench for all of us but especially for Brother Alan Garman who had been at the Hall since 1936, working on the farm, teaching metal work, instructing in archery and being coach driver. Brother Tom Caulfield was a skilled woodworker and passed on his skills to so many of the boys. Brother Charles O'Donnell took over the canoeing and was engaged in so many outdoor activities such as caving and rock climbing.

Over the sixty years the school maintained close friendly links with the village and surrounding area. Brother Joe was always around in his tractor, Roger Keyse grazed his sheep on the estate, Brother Neil was a frequent visitor to the Red Hart managed for many years by Johnny Dunbar, an old boy of the school. In the middle 1960s Mario Marco and Martin Jay could be seen walking to Mrs P. Manners for piano lessons. People in the village came to sing carols in the front hall at Christmas and our boys

Top: Br. Joe Carter. celebrating 50 years as a Salesian.

Above: Br. Joe with Fr Jim McGuire, left, & Jim Chayter.

Right. Sign reads:
Thank you for being
Wood carrier, port in a storm, clothes drier, tent mender, child minder, battery charger, cake taster, cake taster, plum provider, tea drinker and most of all, our BEST FRIEND.

The Salesian & Old Boys burial plot in Blaisdon churchyard.

returned the compliment. Father George Hilton was on the parish council for some years and always took pride in the fact that he was a guest at the wedding of Janet Royall in the village church.

Then there are five Salesians buried in the churchyard together with the ashes of a number of the old boys.

Fr Sean Murray
commemorates his years in Blaisdon on the Gloucester Rugby Club 'Walk of Legends'.

The connection continues to this day with the old boys' reunions at Easter and at the end of August. Father Aidan Murray is still around saying Mass in the village every Sunday, and Father Sean Murray is never too far away and is still a season ticket holder at Gloucester Rugby! Also there is George Austin an old boy who lived with his wife and family in The Lodge. He looked after the grounds magnificently and gave such good example and friendship to the many boys who helped him over the years. He was the best worker I have ever seen.

Another connection was the Angelus Bell. Every day for many years Brother Eddie Barron rang the bell high up in the tower at 12 noon and at 6pm. It was a call to prayer but people in the village could set their clocks by it and it was also a reminder to get dinner ready and put the kettle on! The Salesians and the past pupils are deeply indebted to the people of Blaisdon."

Blaisdon Old Boys have given permission for reprinting excerpts from their book, 'Recollections of Past Pupils of Blaisdon Hall, 1935-95' published in 2007. One contribution is from Terry Elcock on the 1970s and is followed by Madge O'Rourke on the 1980s.

Terry Elcock shares his memories of being a pupil at Blaisdon Hall between 1971 and 1975:

"I must let you know how I came to Blaisdon. My family are of mixed race; wherein my father was one of the fortunate/unfortunate people that was encouraged to leave their homeland in the 1950s to seek a better life in the then fading British Empire. My mother went through hell being one of the first people to start to integrate with inhabitants from the West Indies.

My mother and father separated (1966), and being a single mother with 5 growing children, she was finding it difficult to cope with 4 boys and one girl to care for. Fortunately St. Peters Catholic Church in Gloucester had a good safety net for its congregation and the eldest in our family, Robert, was allowed to attend Blaisdon Hall to help lessen the turmoil my mother was having in coping with being a single parent. Some of you may know my big brother Robert (Bob or Woolly) Elcock (1965 -1970) who was described as the model pupil when I arrived at Blaisdon Hall.

I don't really remember Robert leaving home or what was really going on, as I was only six at the time, though I recall the first time I went to see him at his school, Blaisdon Hall. It made such an impression on me. I thought he was a person to aspire to as he was articulate and he would keep many children from our area mystified with the ghost stories he would tell whilst at home.

I attended various schools through my junior years, then along came the shock of having to leave this safe period and think about going to a senior school. I asked my mother if I could go to Blaisdon Hall. She tried her best but to no avail. After being turned down to go to Blaisdon Hall, I decided that if I couldn't go there for my senior years tuition, I wouldn't go to school at all. This caused no end of problems. The School Board man tried his best to get me to go to most local schools but he felt the wrath of my determination to get what I wanted most. Eventually the authorities agreed that I should go to Blaisdon. Result! Soon, I was being driven to Blaisdon Hall. It was a lovely

summer day and the start of my first real adventure. Who knows what I was about to experience!

Greeted by Fr Pilling and Fr Kavenah in the main hall, we conversed about how the school was there to help me; also how the school was about to make my life a totally enjoyable experience in education. Then into the main hall came a person who I thought looked similar to images of Adolph Hitler I had seen. When he spoke, his deep growling voice made me think, 'Don't mess with this guy, he's trouble!'

Br Allen was the first year intake dormitory master. Actually when you got to know him he was a really nice guy, kind of like a gentle giant, but I've seen him explode at times in his metalwork classes. When he did, you just kept your head down and made sure you didn't have eye contact with him unless he spoke to you. When Br Allen was angry the thing to do was to work hard and try to do your best in the lessons he taught.

Life at Blaisdon Hall was a great experience. I still look back on my stay there and think to myself, from time to time, how lucky I was to have attended. How many schools at that time could you have participated in such great sporting activities: canoeing, archery, javelin, rock climbing, potholing, swimming, football and cricket. Need I say more; the list was endless. Oh yes, the academic lessons weren't too bad either.

Blaisdon Hall had such an impact on my life. I was taught guitar by Father Skivington and enjoyed playing in the church band most Sundays. Christmas carol singing in the village was really good too; I still use the guitar skills he taught me. Father Skivington's guitar tuition enabled me to join a group when I was eighteen. I released four singles in the early eighties and have released 3 albums. This all sounds impressive! However, it didn't make me rich, it was Punk Rock! And I still have a day job!!!

I join in appreciation and gratitude for my time spent at Blaisdon Hall. It was a shame that the school was sold and past pupils are not able to attend at the school for their reunions. Even worse is that young people today will not be able to experience and gain the skills that most of us took away from the Blaisdon school."

Madge O'Rourke taught at Blaisdon Hall in the 1980s:

"Each morning, I would get to the Lodge and have a quick word with the famous figure on the cross, and ask him to help me to cope with this 'typical' Blaisdon day.

The magic of Blaisdon will always be tied up in the different boys who have left their mark, one way or another! Any pupil at a new school would know how it felt to settle in, and get to know everyone, and it's just the same for a member of staff. I remember, as a new teacher, trying very hard to do a good job and at the same time, not seem over-anxious to the boys that I put on my 'super cool mask' and acted accordingly. So when a very vociferous Michael Hyne said, 'Hey Miss, I'm gonna do a bunk tonight, do you think I should wear my boots or my trainers?' I calmly replied, 'Well Michael, it looks as though we might have frost, I should wear your boots' and thought at the time that this was a big joke.

Imagine my horror next morning when I arrived at school

to hear that Michael had 'done a bunk' and even worse, when I opened his desk, there were his trainers. He had taken my advice but fortunately, as with all Blaisdon 'bunkers', all Michael got was a long cold walk and he was soon back with us.

It wasn't always out of school activities that provided a school day with its share of memories. A certain work-shy Paddy Mac will recall the lunchtime he spent holding the floodwaters of Blaisdon at bay. He had spent the morning idly tapping his foot against the pipe to the radiator in the terrapin, as he moaned about the quantity of Maths and English he was required to do. Finally, just before lunch, the poor old pipe had had enough and began to trickle water. Then a crack appeared and water issued over Paddy's Doc Martin boots. Well, there was nothing for it; only a finger over the hole would do until the plumber could be found. Of course, it had to be Paddy's finger and you know how hard it is to find a plumber when you need one. Imagine the whole dinner time passed before Fr Skiv. tracked down someone to mend it. Paddy didn't tap too many pipes after that!

As you probably know, many of my days were spent in the cookery room, where the boys and I used to shuffle from organised chaos to complete devastation. In the early days, when cookery started, the facilities were, to say the least, poor! We had three tables (the best bit), two very old cookers with ovens with doubtful temperatures, one sink and a floor, which looked like a cross between a football pitch and a skating rink. Simon Smith will remember trying to mop the floor after a 'session' and the flour forming into a sticky paste beneath our feet. However in spite of such odds, quite a few successful dishes were produced and as time went on, there were fewer horrific stories of mouldy mince pies, or crumbling cakes in lockers, as the young cooks learned that their efforts were for sharing with the rest of the unit and not to be hoarded for a rainy day.

Finally, even though many people have come and gone from Blaisdon and the school closed, it will always be 'home' to so many, and a place of treasured, loving thoughts for most."

Father Aidan Murray is the parish priest to the Parish of Our Lady of Lourdes, Newent and St. Michael's Blaisdon. He came to Blaisdon in 1970 and tells his memories of Blaisdon Hall 1970-95:

"When I arrived in Blaisdon Hall in 1970 I discovered a school of some seventy boys and a staff of Priests and Brothers who seemed to be able to do anything and everything; you have only to remember Br Joe Carter and his snow clearing, Br Alan Garman for metalwork, Br Tom Caulfield, woodwork and, of course, Br Jan Orysiuk, electrician, plumber, jack of all trades with his, 'I fix, I fix.'

Under Fr John Gilheney as Headmaster there was a new determination to give our boys a sense of their own dignity and worth. To that end we gave them many opportunities to improve their skills, to take part in events

Fr Sean Murray, left,
Fr Aidan Murray, right.
(J.Stokes)

and competitions outside the school and to learn social skills both with adults and with other young people.

Success in competition was easy to measure and they had lots. During the 1970s and 1980s they won many table tennis League Titles in Gloucester. They took part in pretty well everything that was organised by the Gloucestershire Boys' Clubs, the Gloucestershire Youth Clubs and among the Forest of Dean youth clubs: football, rounders, indoor games, cross-country, orienteering, 'Super Stars' etc. Often for Youth Club events we had to have girls in our teams and thanks to families in the village we were able to include Thursa Lilley, the Austin's daughter and a couple of girls from Gloucester.

Success in any event was a great boost to their self-confidence but they also had to learn how to lose and lose gracefully. This was quite evident in the many table tennis events we took part in and where there were mature adults who could step in and help them and let them know that losing well builds character. Besides that they had opportunities to take part in archery, judo, weight lifting (we had a National Champion), life saving, the Duke of Edinburgh's Award, pot holing, abseiling and canoeing.

For all of them, including those who had little or no sporting ambitions, we had an excellent Arts & Crafts section. Arthur Hickman from Huntley seemed to be able to get the very best out of even the most difficult boys. He was a painter and taught painting but it was in ceramics that he achieved the most outstanding success.

Year after year we entered items, once a coach load of over forty large and small items, in the National Exhibition of Children's Art. On two or three occasions we won the title of Best School Team and many times one of our boys won the top prize for Ceramics. We have a photo of Arthur Hickman beside a Ceramic model of himself and the likeness is incredible."

In 2012, Frs Aidan Murray and Sean Murray celebrated 50 years as ordained priests. ***Norman Taylor*** writes:

"On Sunday 15th April 2012, Father Sean Murray and Father Aidan Murray, two Salesian priests of the Order founded by St. John Bosco, celebrated fifty years since their ordination. With the inclusion of guests from Blaisdon, Gloucester and Newent parishes, together with Blaisdon Hall Old Boys, the numbers of guests exceeded two hundred. The Celebration Mass commenced at 12.15pm and every pew in the beautiful church of St. Peters, Gloucester was full. The hymn singing during the Mass was led by a small group of musicians, whose lead singer, filling the church with the glorious sound of her voice, inspired the congregation to respond in like manner.

After Mass, the congregation joined the Celebrants in the nearby church hall for lunch. The celebration closed with the cutting of a cake and a short address from Father

Sean and Father Aidan, with Father Sean commenting that the day of his ordination was a wonderful day in his life, but the greatest day in his life was the day he decided to join the Salesian Order. Today was a truly memorable day for everyone who had the privilege of being present to celebrate with Father Sean Murray and Father Aidan Murray the Golden Jubilee of their ordination in 1962."

Frs Sean, left, & Aiden.
(left & below: J. Stokes)

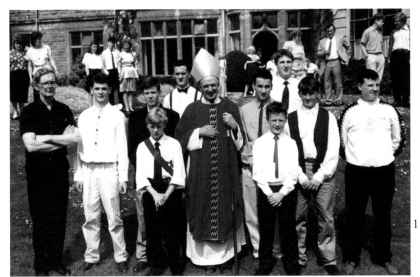

1

2

3

4

6

Blaisdon Hall folk:
1. Bishop of Clifton with Fr Sean Murray after service of confirmation.
2. Housemother, Eileen Beard, from Longhope with Carl.
3. From the left: Shirley Brickel, Sandra Meadows (Deputy Head), Wayne Howe (pupil), Sean Tarpey
4. Cedric Etherington, centre, with old boys Peter Lansborough, left, Freddie Evans & Charlie Springett.
5. Terry Elcock.
6. Old boys, Stuart Allport, left, & Joe Shott with Madge O'Rourke (staff).

5

Blaisdon School Photographs.
Above: 1985. Below: 1991.

Above: Blaisdon school photograph 1982
Below: leavers 1984.

Below: football team c1973 with Sean Murray back left are:
Ian Mole, Derreck Peters, Vlad Malinowski, Terry Elcock,
Mark Davis, Chris Buckles.
Front row: Neville Button, Andy Cahill, Tony Saunders, Phil Craig,
Melvyn Little, Rod Martin.

1.& 2. Fete days.
(c1980s)
3.& 4. Blaisdon Hall School Golden Jubilee celebrations.
(1985)
5. John Gilbert (youngest pupil) plants the Golden Jubilee commemorative tree, watched by Br Chris Gorton (oldest Salesian) and John & Ruth Magee with Ben Carter.
(1985)
6. Fr Robson makes a presentation to John & Ruth Magee
(1985)

Blaisdon Old Boys reunions.

Aerial view of Blaisdon Hall.
The school block built in the 1960s & now demolished is seen to the left of the Hall.

Having closed the school and secured places elsewhere for pupils and staff, the Salesians left Blaisdon Hall in 1994 but it was not until the following year that Blaisdon Hall was sold. It was bought by another educational establishment, Hartpury College, with the aid of a Government grant of £220,000 from the Competitiveness Fund. Their stated aim was to use it as an educational centre as well as a management and training centre. In the few years they owned the Hall, it never became an established centre and the Hall was put back on the market and sold in 1999 to Tony Haynes.

Tony Haynes' son, **Tony Haynes Jnr**, has written about his father on his website www.haynesfineart.com. Born to extremely humble beginnings, Tony Haynes Snr had little choice but to become the provider and carer for his then family of six brothers, two sisters and mother.

"There was very little time for the privilege of attending school; as a result he was mostly self-educated: Tenacious was his middle name! So, in hope of earning much-needed funds, the young boy started his working life by performing a wide array of imaginative duties - for example, looking after the prams of strangers whilst parents shopped at Woolworths.

For Tony Snr, art opened a window into another world; he would sit for hours at Birmingham Museum & Art Gallery in awe of the craftsmanship displayed. February Fill Dyke

Tony Haynes Snr, right with his son, Tony Haynes Jnr.

by Benjamin Williams Leader (British 1831-1923) was the very first painting to grab, excite and captivate him; amazed by Leader's depiction of figures in a landscape going about their business after much rainfall, struck by the realism of water as it pooled into passing cartwheel tracks and uplifted by the suggestion of sunlight breaking through the clouds all denoted to him that life goes on, to weather storms and wait, for the sun will come out again. Art, the educator, had taught him its first important lesson.

Fortunate to meet his equally determined future wife and life partner, Vivien, when he was just seventeen, Tony Snr, with Vivien's hard work and unflinching support, journeyed his way through a diverse succession of employment (including selling hot dogs and window cleaning) from a lowly position through to that of a firmly established and widely respected international art expert and dealer, as well as both founding and heading the successful company known today as Haynes Fine Art. A self-made man in all aspects - and yes, we are all very proud of him and miss him very dearly, God bless.

Tony Snr and Vivien's ultimate pride and joy were their children. Sadly only two of four survive. The youngest, Alison, followed her path into performing Arts (Guildhall

School of Music and Drama) singing at The Royal Albert Hall and on national radio before her passion for world music took her to South Africa as music director for a touring theatre company; consequent ill health has, for the time being, paused what promises to be a notable career.

Nurtured amongst a wealth of beautiful and important art works, it came as no surprise when eldest son, Tony Jnr, decided to follow in his father's footsteps. From an early age the Haynes children were encouraged to interact with art, including regular trips to public art galleries and museums, alongside frequent invitations to share in their father's often exhaustive research procedure - the promise of a reward was always lucrative! Over the years Tony Snr patiently shared his encyclopaedic knowledge of art and well thumbed comprehensive collection of art books and catalogues. Indeed with his guidance and motivation, the next Haynes generation had an exceptional start into the art world."

Tony Haynes and his wife Vivian lived at Blaisdon Hall untill selling it in 2009. During that time he undertook extensive restorative work on the main building. Although the exterior of the Hall remained unaltered, the interior underwent many changes, removing many later additions and restoring it to its original state whenever possible. The 1960s school block was demolished and ornamental ponds laid out instead.

In 2009, Blaisdon Hall was again sold, the new owner being Andrey Zhelamskiy. He is continuing the refurbishment of the main house and outbuildings as well as developing it as a centre for weddings and other functions.

Blaisdon Hall,
main entrance and tower.

Top: Blaisdon Hall from Velthouse Lane.
Above: Blaisdon Hall in the snow. (1982)
Right: A balloon landing in front of Blaisdon Hall.

THE  ATHOLIC CHURCH IN BLAISDON

Father Aidan Murray SDB, Parish Priest to the Catholic Parish of Blaisdon & Newent, writes about his parish and parishioners

"From 1935, the priests in the Blaisdon Salesian Community, took it in turns to say Mass for the scattered Catholics of the Forest. They celebrated Mass in Blaisdon Hall and also ventured out to Cinderford and Newent. The OMI priests came in the late 1930s to cover Cinderford, Coleford and the rest of the southern area between the Wye and the Severn. Blaisdon/Newent was set up as the Salesian Parish. Probably the first full-time Parish Priest was Fr Bill Boyd who took over in 1952 and stayed till 1970, becoming Military Chaplain in Rheindahlen. One of his biggest tasks was to build a permanent Church in Newent, which he did with a lot of help from Bro. Joe Carter, Bro. Alan Garman and the Blaisdon boys. The Church was officially opened in December 1960.During this time the number of Catholics grew so much that it became necessary for Br Joe or Br Alan to take the school coach round the lanes to pick up parishioners around Flaxley, Westbury, Rodley etc.

Fr John Chadwick took over as Parish Priest from 1970 to 1972, but died rather suddenly. Fr Jim McGuire then took over and developed a thriving parish during his twenty

two and a half years in charge. He took several coach-loads to attend Mass on Coventry airfield when Pope John Paul II came in 1982 and again to Ninian Park, Cardiff. Fr Jim was particularly noted for his pastoral concern for the elderly and the housebound, visiting them regularly at home or in hospital, never thinking of the fact that he might be missing his meals or extending his day beyond the call of duty. When the school closed down and the Community dispersed to other Salesian Houses, Fr Jim was most disappointed to be asked to retire, after all he was only seventy nine. Although he did retire from the parish, he continued to work in St Peter's, Gloucester. Some years later he had to undergo a couple of operations and was forced to retire to Farnborough. However, when he felt fully recovered he asked for another job and became Chaplain at Nazareth House Nursing Home in London. He was about ninety four when he eventually retired but he's still hale and hearty now.

When Blaisdon Hall was sold the local Catholics needed a place for Sunday Mass. Blaisdon C. of E. parishoners were more than happy to allow them to use the Church of St Michael and All Angels, which they did for a couple of years. Nothing seemed too much trouble for the Anglican community and they did everything to make us feel welcome and help us fit in. Together we arranged for a new car park behind the church. We did a feasibility study to see if the church could be adapted to suit the requirements of our young people and quite significant changes were proposed! However, the Catholic families eventually decided they would rather leave the church as it was and migrate down to the village hall, where we have happily thrived ever since."

The Catholic Community
outside Blaisdon Hall
with Father Aidan Murray,
centre in blue shirt.
(2012)

BLAISDON COURT

Above & below:
Blaisdon Court. (2012)

Frank and Doris Brown (Volume 2) lived in Vectis, Blaisdon Court's former name, till moving to Cinderford. David, one of their sons lives in the village at Stanley Lodge. Another son, **Peter Brown** reflects on his time in Blaisdon and his early married life:

"We moved to Vectis in Blaisdon from Tuffley when I was about two in 1954. I went to school in Blaisdon, and then went on to Mitcheldean School. I feel very fortunate to have been brought up in such a beautiful village as Blaisdon.

My marriage to Christine took place in 1971, when I was nineteen, at Blaisdon church conducted by the Rev. D.J.Bick. It was a very cold November day, but the ladies of the village still turned out to see the bride arrive.

We love to tell a funny story with affection about Bertie Buckett playing the organ on our wedding day. As my wife entered the church, instead of walking into 'Here Comes the Bride' Bertie played 'Onward Christian Soldiers' this made my future wife and her brother-in-law Jim, who gave her away, feel like marching down the aisle to the beat! Then after the ceremony, Bertie decided to play 'Here Comes the Bride' as we walked out! We often wondered as we still do, if this was a genuine mistake or just maybe it was down to Bertie's sense of humour. We like to think it was the latter.

We started our married life living in a caravan in Mrs Renee Bowkett's orchard along Velthouse Lane. She was a

The Brown Family celebrating the golden wedding anniversary of
Frank & Dorris.

lovely lady who was happy to help two young newly weds on their way in married life. We have now been married for over 40 years.

Our reception was held in the former village school, now the village hall. Blaisdon village hall seemed fitting for our wedding reception, as I was one of the last to attend the school when it closed. My Mother and sister Janet did a lovely spread of food for our guests. My Grandparents, Mr & Mrs Matthews, were there, making three generations of our family at the wedding.

We spent many happy hours in the Red Hart. Frank and Elsie always gave us a friendly welcome and with characters like Albert Pithouse around we were never short of a good laugh!

In the hot summer of 1976 we were invited to use the swimming pool at the Salesian school in Blaisdon. We had a son Eddie who was three and our daughter Leah was about two months old. We would put our sleeping Leah in a Moses basket, that we placed by the side of the swimming pool, while we all played in the water watched by one of the Brothers, it was plain to see he loved children and one day he asked if he could take Leah out of her basket to look after her by the pool. He nicknamed her Moses because of the basket I'm sure. He would sit down on the grass bank in the warm sunshine and rock her in his habit like a cradle.

Top:
Eric, David & Peter Brown.
Centre:
Eric, David, Sally & Gill Brown.
Bottom:
Peter Brown.

We moved from Velt House lane to Flaxley and from there to Sussex in 1977 where I live with my family today, but we often visit my brother's and sister's that still live in the Forest of Dean. It was a time I will never forget and my memories are full with great fondness of those days."

David and Joan Risborough moved to Vectis from Tewkesbury in 1978, buying the house from the Harris family. They have three children, Martin, Andrew and Deborah who were in their twenties at that time:

"Having moved into Vectis, we were surprised given the house's position to be flooded in the first year. Water came off the hill behind and through the back door. Joan and Miss Smith swept water out of the front door for 2 hours while David and the boys dug a trench to divert the water round the house. We later installed a land drain as a permanent solution and never had a reoccurrence.

In 1983-4 we built a stable block that is still there. Joan had bought a new horse that went straight through the thin concrete floor of the original wooden stable and created a hole that needed barrow loads of rubble every other night.

We enjoyed living in the village and watching the changes that occurred during the twenty five years we lived there. Keeping horses was

Above: David & Joan Risborough,
Below: Vectis in 2002.

a dream came true. Having an orchard behind the house was lovely and our goats enjoyed it to, especially when the plums were ripe. The Blaisdon plums used to be sold to Ron Walton but sadly those trees, like so many others, disappeared over time."

The house was the bought and developed by Ed and Nicky Charlesworth befor being sold to Brian and Alison Evans.

"My first memories of Blaisdon," says **Brian Evans**, "are when Blaisdon Hall was just about to be bought by Hartpury College in 1995. At that time, my wife Alison and I were running our own language school in Cheltenham and we were in discussions with Hartpury College about using their facilities in Hartpury as a venue for a summer school. On the verge of taking over the Hall, they invited us to look around it with a view to us using the facilities there as a residential Summer School for overseas students the following year. After a good look around the impressive, although, at that time, rather tired looking hall, we retired to the Red Hart for dinner. It was at that moment that I thought to myself, wouldn't it be great to get out of town and come and live somewhere like this?

Although we never did go ahead and use the Hall as a Summer School, the idea of moving to the area did not go away. It was about four years later that we upped sticks from Cheltenham with our then two boys and moved to a wonderful newly converted barn in Westbury-on-Severn. This was to be the house where we would stay and bring up our family, until a year or so later when Jamie came on the scene and we suddenly realised that eventually we would outgrow it. The final straw came in 2004 when the latest addition to our family came in the form of Poppie, the Springer Spaniel. She is possibly the most expensive accessory we ever bought!

The arrival of Poppie coincided with our selling our business in Cheltenham and so realising that the world was now our oyster, we set about investigating all those different places where we could go and live. However, the decision was staring us in the face. Why move away from an area where you are perfectly happy and which has everything you could want anyway?

So in January 2005 we set about looking for a new five bed roomed house in the area and almost immediately came across Blaisdon Court, its name recently changed from Vectis and renovated and extended to a high standard by Ed and Nicky Charlsworth. The house was everything we could have wanted. It was perfect for a family of five with a dog, close to our friends in Westbury, the children could continue at the same school in Westbury and of course we already knew several families living in Blaisdon through the school. Ben was in the same class as Sam Batham (Western View) and Sam with Liam Selwyn (Claremont) and Callum Batham.

We immediately put our own house on the market and waited. Not long after, however, and before we even had a buyer for our own house, the bad news came. Blaisdon Court had been sold! That was it then, we were scuppered!

We accepted an offer on our own house in April and then the pressure was on to find something else. We eventually found a house that we liked in Hartpury, which we decided would have to do. Then, one evening an e-mail arrived from Steve Gooch Estate Agents announcing that Blaisdon Court was back on the market! I immediately picked up the phone to Ed Charlesworth; we agreed a price there and then and the next morning called Steve Gooch with the formal offer. We moved in around 23rd August 2005 - it was clearly meant to be!

Within a couple of weeks of arriving we were visited by a brother and sister of the Brown family who told us they had lived in the house from the 1950s to the 1970s and asked if they might have a look around. They told us how they had lived in the house: there had been no running water so each of the ten children would take a bucket down to school each day and return with water from the well. Apparently the garden was divided up into sections and each child would grow fruit and vegetables in their own plot. The house at that stage was just the front half of what existed when we moved in, with two downstairs rooms, two on the first floor and a converted attic making two more rooms. There was, I believe, a small lean-to kitchen to the rear. Access to the house was from the small gate to the left when looking from the lane and the front door was on the south west side, since made into a window.

Since moving to Blaisdon, our life has remained focussed primarily around Westbury-on-Severn largely because of the school connections, but also because of various family involvements in Westbury Players and Westbury Youth Project and other Parish Hall based activities.

Blaisdon, itself, has been a great place to see the children grow up. It is great that we can all walk straight out of the house into beautiful countryside without the need of getting into the car and much use is made of the walks on the hills and in the woods behind the house.

There is a lovely community spirit manifesting itself several times in the year with the various celebrations that go on. We have particularly good memories of the year Blaisdon fete took on a Dr. Who theme and every year we

played on the Tenor Horn and Euphonium respectively. I think I managed to play at one house and then politely asked Nigel Hogg (Syston Cottage) if he would mind awfully if I could leave it with him and pick my instrument up the next day. I'm not sure if it was the weight or the dreadful sound I was producing that prompted this!

Since coming to the village, we have developed a particular

Bonfire night. The Young Farmers' bonfire at the Red Hart is burning well.
(William Faucett)

live in trepidation of the bombardment of rockets during the spectacular Young Farmers' bonfire at the Red Hart, of which we have a privileged view. Roger Keyse's carol singing at Christmas is always something of a delight! I remember one year when Ben, probably about eleven at the time, and I decided to help out with some accompanying music

interest in fruit and making it into alcohol! Every year now, with the help of our Little Garth neighbours Steve, Nicola and Emily Atkinson, we press the apples from the five or so trees in the garden at Blaisdon Court and make cider. 2011 saw the best year yet with the production of some twenty eight gallons! Blaisdon plums make an excellent

The Evans family in front of Blaisdon Court.
From the left:
Ben, Alison, Jamie, Brian & Sam.
(2012)

plum gin, although we unfortunately lost two trees in 2011, and we planted a particularly vigorous quince tree - great for quince cheese, particularly well crafted by Parkside neighbour Glenys Barnard and, of course, quince vodka!

Although Blaisdon Court had recently been renamed and renovated before we moved in, over the years we have continued to make our own mark on the property. In 2006, with three boys to keep occupied and with myself being semi-retired, we thought it would be a good idea to

install an outdoor pool in the garden.

With Phil Woodman and James Boyer's help we set about digging a rather large hole behind the house. This was our first taste of the delights of Blaisdon clay. Six swelteringly hot and sunny weeks later the hole was finally dug and we could get on with building the pool, which took another seven weeks or so. When it was finished the sun went in and has hardly been out again since, but we live in hope!! In spite of the inclement summers we have had since moving to Blaisdon, the pool has had great use and has been the scene for many a party or get together involving not only family and friends but also the local community. Undeterred by the prolonged efforts of our first attempts to develop the property, in 2010 we decided that the two front rooms in the house were not really the best use of floor space. The decision was therefore made to take down the stud partition that separated the two rooms and make one large room across the entire front of the house. Of course none of these projects go quite according to plan as on taking down the wall we realised that two previously hidden rather flimsy-looking upright pieces of wood were holding up the original beam above which in turn was holding up the entire house. Several discussions with the structural engineer later, it was decided that the only way to achieve what we wanted was with an RSJ. A couple of weeks later the joist was not only in place but also clad in distressed oak and looked like it had been there forever.

Our second major experience of Blaisdon clay came during the week of the Jubilee celebrations in June 2012 when work commenced on our new hardwood conservatory. The day the digger came, it started raining and didn't seem to stop. The Somme had arrived in Blaisdon! The trench for the footings filled up, was pumped out and filled up again ... and again ... and again! But in the end we got there and by August it was all finished bar the painting.

Once again wanting to ensure that anything we did to the house looked like it had always been part of the house, we were keen to build something very much in keeping and hope we have achieved that.

So what's next? No immediate plans to develop the house more. I can't really imagine us moving away from Blaisdon

in the near future. We are all very settled and happy here and to be quite honest we don't really feel we would want to live anywhere else. I think Alison and I at least would quite happily grow old here. Let's see if we make the next volume of this book!"

At the time of writing in late 2012, Brian continues his work as a house husband and is involved in tutoring and in graphic design. He also does some consultancy work in the language school industry, while Alison continues to work at Frontier Medex in Mitcheldean, having recently changed her role from HR Manager to Operations Manager (Support). The boys (now aged 11, 13 and 15, are currently studying at three different schools - one in Westbury, one in Mitcheldean and the third in Gloucester."

The Evans family. From the left:
Alison, Ben, Sam, Jamie & Brian.
(2005)

PARKSIDE

Parkside in 2012.

Harriet Selwyn (nee McCreery) now lives at Claremont but she spent the early years of her life at Parkside:

"My family lived in the village from 1968 -1974. There were my parents, John and Jean McCreery, my four brothers, Richard, Stephen, Mark and Kevin, plus me when I was born in 1972. My father was stationed in RAF Hullavington when he moved here but wanted to settle down and make roots, so he left after twenty seven years in the service to work for Rank Xerox in Mitcheldean.

The garden was very overrun when my parents moved in and so they set the 4 sons to work with scythes in the garden to cut the brambles down. Dad added a single storey side extension, which has now been replaced by a two-storey extension. He also built the front porch and black shutters which are still on the house today. My first pet was a donkey, 'Jeb', which dad bought when I was around 12 months old and he brought home from work in a van he borrowed from work. He got into trouble for the smell left behind.

They often had visitors from the Blaisdon Hall and became friendly with a few of the 'Brothers'. My first word was

'plum' as I was shown the plum trees in our back garden. One of my first memories was sitting on the bar in the Red Hart, when Johnny Dunbar ran it, and being allowed to drink my Granny's Guinness!

Miss Smith who lived opposite was a lovely lady who was very kind to all the children in our family, often giving us sweets, she also gave me a beautiful old rag doll whose hair was made with fur. She commissioned a painting from Mrs Davies from Claremont when I was born. It was a picture of some bluetits painted onto yellow silk. I still have the painting to this day; little did I know I would one day live in the house where the painting came from."

1

2

3

4

5

1. Parkside and, nearer, Vectis. (1971)

2. Mark McCreery. (1971)

3. Jean & Harriet McCreery (1975)

4. Harriet McCreery. (1974)

5. Mark, Jean, John & Harriet McCreery. (1973)

6. Jean & Harriet McCreery. (1975)

6

The McCreerys sold Parkside to Angela and Keith Foster. **Angela Foster** tells of her family's time in Blaisdon:

"Keith and I arrived in Blaisdon in March 1976 after Keith began working in Mitcheldean at Rank Xerox. At that time there were 3600 people working there and our intention was to stay in Blaisdon and bring up our family in the village. We subsequently had 3 children: James born August 1976; Emily born February 1978; and Alice born January 1980.

Having three babies to spoil was an absolute delight to Auntie Lilla (Lilla Smith), who lived in the cottage opposite to Parkside. She became part of the family and attended every birthday party. She would often take all the children from the party for a walk, each one holding on to the rope that she brought. It was quite a sight seeing them walking down Velthouse lane. She often took James on 'environmental walks' and today James is still very interested in the environment and we suspect Auntie Lilla had a lot to do with that .

It was interesting that Auntie Lilla was a dairymaid and whenever we had a dinner party she would create a basket made of butter and filled with butterballs. They were always a great hit. I remember that she made butter with the children. They all sat there with jam jars with fresh cream and they sat and shook them until they had butter. Very exciting!

While life in a village should have been idyllic it was probably the busiest time of our lives. We grew our own vegetables, harvested the fruit, made jams and wine and also added a large extension to the rear of Parkside. While

we were in Blaisdon my Father, Billie Piper, and Auntie Mildred Woodall, came to live with us.

In the end we left the village purely because of job reasons. Xerox was down to 1100 people with more reductions likely. So, in 1984, we went to live in Scotland and, later on, we moved to Canada.

We still maintain contact with our friends in Blaisdon, some of whom have visited us here in Canada, as well as

Above:
The Fosters' Fancy Dress
party with:
A pirate (James),
Andy Pandy (Alice)
Worzel Gummidge
(Emily).

Left:
Angela & Emily Foster

200

1

2

3

4

5

1. From left: Keith Foster, Jean Waters, Nigel Hogg, Angela Foster & Brandy. (1983) (N. Hogg)

2. The Foster family.

3. Keith Foster a & 2 helpers clearing snow in front of Parkside. (1982-3)

4. Dick Hawker with Alice, James & Emily Foster at Niagara Falls.

5. From the left: Hilary Hawker, Keith & Angela Foster, Lilla Smith, Dick Hawker.
In Front: Alice, Emily & James Foster.

seeing many of them on our two return visits to Blaisdon. It was really very special to see them all back in Blaisdon. It felt like we had never left."

When the Fosters left Parkside for Edinburgh, the house passed into the hands of Ken and Glenys Barnard. *Glenys Barnard* continues:

"In 1985 we were living in the Forest of Dean. Our family were grown up. Rebecca was at university in London and Julian was undergoing training as an RAF pilot at Cranwell. Only Alice was still at home, doing A levels at Haberdashers Monmouth School for Girls. Our jobs involved a fair amount of travelling and so we started looking for a village house in the area. After viewing several other houses, we came to see Parkside Cottage.

The house had been empty for six months since the previous owners, the Fosters, had moved out. Lilla Smith was the house's 'custodian' and held the keys. She treated potential buyers with suspicion. Would they be suitable for Blaisdon?! Although the house had not been occupied over the winter, it still felt welcoming and we moved in April 1985.

Aunty Lilla, who became a very good friend, provided a very long and comprehensive list of information essential for life in Blaisdon such as milkmen, paper boys, the once a week bus service! She also told tales of an American couple who had recently rented the property. They had put in a pale stair carpet, which was totally unsuited for dealing with the Blaisdon mud! This narrow staircase was the first problem we encountered. It had to be removed in order to get beds, wardrobes and other items of our furniture upstairs.

The house has grown over the years, with the addition of bedrooms and bathrooms. A garage and stables have been built and in recent years the stables have been converted to a snooker room complete with woodburner and bar! It is the scene of a long running duel between Ken and Dick Hawker with no outright winner as yet.

The house, which overlooks the village, has a large garden enjoyed over the years by numerous horses and ponies, dogs, cats and the rabbit, Thugs, who lived in the greenhouse. In the spring it is covered by snowdrops, all originating from a single clump planted soon after our arrival. There are also two huge chestnut trees which grew from conkers planted by the children of the previous owners.

One of the most memorable events during the early years in Blaisdon was the Plum Festival, which involved a competition to create the essence of the Blaisdon plum. To this end Alice and Rebecca locked themselves in the garage for several weeks, to secretly create 'SUPERPLUM'! This was a plum so large he is on an aerial photograph taken at the time.

Historically the cottage was added to Blaisdon Estate in 1911. It was possibly known as Hyetts Cottage after a previous owner. When a new name plaque was recently being fitted, a stone with the initials 'T + H' and the date 1849 was revealed beneath the rendering. It has yet to be discovered who put it there, and whose initials they are."

1

3

2

4

1. Alice Barnard with Fritz & Superplum for the Plum Festival.
2. Ken & Glenys Barnard. (2012)
3. The bank in front of Parkside in full bloom.
4. Parkside in 1985.

CHERRY RISE

Cherry Rise in 2012.

Elaine Lanciano (nee Smith) moved to Cherry Rise with her family around 1957-8 with her parents, Ronald and Cynthia, brothers, Peter and Martyn, and sister, Sharon:

"My dad was a Fire Officer with Gloucester Fire and Rescue Service. He built a bungalow just below Blaisdon Hall on Velthouse Lane, which was called Cherry Rise and we lived there for about 10 years.

I can remember my first day at Blaisdon Village School. It was a lovely sunny, spring day. I walked the short distance to the school with my mum and sister. Sharon was crying, as she didn't want me to leave her. The playground seemed very big and there was a strong smell of carbolic soap in the lobby entrance where I hung my little brown, tweed coat.

Brother Joe Carter (Volume 2), from Blaisdon Hall, used to cut the grass, which grew behind our bungalow and bale it for hay. My mum would make a pot of tea with some baked cakes and we would chat over the fence while Brother Joe had a rest from working in the fields. This was to lead to a lifelong friendship between Brother Joe and myself, even though I was only 6 when I first met him. I still think of him most days and it was a great privilege to

have known him. In the school holidays, I would rush to join him working in the fields. When he was constructing the top playground at Blaisdon Hall, I would sit alongside him in his Massey Ferguson tractor as he flattened and levelled the ground. We would sing songs such as, 'We're coming round the mountain.' We had great fun.

My birthday is 24th May and I was told that the Union Flag was flying above Blaisdon Hall in honour of this. When I got older, I discovered that it was, in fact, Empire Day.

The family were involved in Blaisdon Church. Peter and Martyn rang the bells, while Sharon and I sang in the choir. On Sunday mornings, my sister and I would go to

Father McQuire greets Elaine Smith & brother, Martyn, who gave her away. (1976)

A young Elaine Smith

Elaine & Antonio Lanciano walk down the aisle in the chapel, Blaisdon Hall. (1976)

Sunday school, held by Miss Rees in The School House. There only ever seemed to be four or five of us at most. We used to have a book and when we attended, we would be given a sticker to put in it. The stickers looked like miniature stained glass windows. On Mothering Sunday, we would make posies of wild primroses and violets to take to Church where they were blessed and given to our mums.

My two brothers used to go fishing in the old reservoir in Blaisdon Woods, hoping to catch tench or roach. Martyn held the record for catching seventy six fish. At one time,

the boys from the Hall used to swim in the reservoir. Some of them built a raft using oil drums and branches to push it around. I think the clay lining got punctured and as a result, it no longer held water as well and often dried out in the summer months.

I married Antonio in Blaisdon Hall in 1976. The weather had been awful for the week before with torrential rain, but on the day, the sun came out and it was lovely. Brother Joe had been unable to attend the wedding, as he was unwell. However, when we heard his tractor we knew he wasn't far away and his arrival minutes later made the day special for us.

I continued to visit Brother Joe about once a month. When our daughter, Sophia was born in 1988, she would come with us. By then Brother Joe was almost bedridden, so Sophia and I would go up to his tiny room in the top floor of the building. Sophia would sit on his bed and play quietly whilst we would talk about everything and anything. It meant a lot to us and Sophia would often say he was her very best friend. Indeed, he was mine too and always would be."

Shirley Brickel moved from Huntley to Blaisdon in 1984 when she lived at Iona. Her parents, Tom and Gladys Collins had moved to Cherry Rise in 1978, having bought the house from Peter Ellis.

After Tom died in 1981, Gladys continued to live at Cherry Rise until she too passed away in 2000. Shirley then moved from Iona to Cherry Rise in 2001.

"I arrived in Blaisdon with my four children, Scott, twins Tom and Chris, plus daughter, Amy. I think they loved growing up in Blaisdon. They had a great time plum picking and also sold produce from Gary Yemm's smallholding at Blaisdon Lane Nurseries, now Bramble Orchard. Sometimes they would make £20 a day but Gary always made sure they paid him for the produce they sold. They also had a great time in the summer playing on the tennis court that Vic and Enid Woodman built at Parkwood. They loved the fetes, especially the skittles and 'fruit machine', where three children would appear in holes holding up a fruit at random. 3 in a row would win a prize.

Top:
Tom Collins in the garden at Cherry Rise.
Above:
Gladys Collins.

206

1. Chris, Tom & Scott Brickel with dog, Sam.
2. Tom, Amy, Chris & Scott.
3. From top: Scott, Chris, Tom, Amy.
4. Angela Foster with twins, Chris and Tom.
5. Shirley & Scott.

Now, they have moved away from the village. Sadly Chris has passed away, but the others are all well. Scott is a market gardener in London; Tom is an artist and a car bodywork sprayer; while Amy is a potter. I now have 4 grandchildren, all being Amy's children. Much of the time now, I find I am on my own, but I enjoy the peace and quiet here in Blaisdon.

I worked as a House Mum at Blaisdon Hall for 13 years, till it closed. It was a lovely job and I enjoyed thoroughly looking after the boys. When on duty, I would sleep up at the Hall. My children used to enjoy coming up to the Hall, mixing with the other boys there and using the pool and other facilities, as well as joining in the camp-fires in summer."

Above:
Shirley Brickel with Sons
from left,
Tom, Chris & Scott.

Left:
Shirley Brickel, right,
with from left,
Marilyn Morgan, Bernie O'Carroll
& Angela Philips.

LITTLE GARTH

Little Garth. (2012)

Sheila Evans remembers Lilla Smith who lived at Little Garth, formerly Buena Vista, from the 1970s:

"Lillian Smith, known as Lilla or Auntie Lilla, lived at Little Garth with her cat and surrounded by her much loved garden, full of plants and flowers named after those who had given them to her.

Lilla was the fourth of five children brought up at Chosen Hill where she lived until her retirement when she moved to Blaisdon, a village she would have known from her working days.

Following her time as a Dairy Student in her working life, Lilla became a Dairy Inspector for the Ministry of Agriculture, Fisheries and Food and was highly respected for her forthright manner and expectation of high standards. She loved demonstrating butter making at the major agricultural shows and reunions at the Three Counties Show were highlights of her years well into her late eighties.

She was of the generation who just got on with things even though her life was greatly affected by the war, when she had to drive her handle-cranked car around the county with shaded headlights to prevent detection by enemy aircraft!

Lilla was a dedicated church-warden from 1979 - 94 and she donated the ornate churchyard gates, made to match those in the porch. She spent hours singing hymns while cleaning and polishing her beloved church which earned her the nickname 'The Holy Duster' and her displays for Harvest Festivals were thought provoking and beautiful, with her trade mark baskets and roses which she made from butter.

Her notes regarding when to do things in the church and which altar-cloths etc to use are still very much in evidence today, relied on by the new generation of church-wardens and sidesmen. A plaque was placed by her seat and the window nearby restored in memory and recognition of her devotion to the church.

Auntie Lilla was the name by which she was affectionately known, as she was so kind, thoughtful and caring. Anyone who was going through a difficult patch would find a tiny posy on the doorstep. It may have only been of daisies and buttercups but it said so much and she always kept her overnight bag packed just in case someone should need her at short notice.

When her greenhouse blew down Lilla set about chopping up the wood as kindling for the 'old dears' in the village, who were all younger than her. When she was nearing her ninetieth birthday she got on her knees to scrub the aisle of the church for a forthcoming wedding as she didn't want the bride's dress to get dirty!

Nothing was ever too much trouble and she made no concession to her age. 'It's better to wear out than rust out' she would say and she continued as church-warden until her ninetieth birthday in April 1994, with a birthday party at Blaisdon House, and she died the following September when she returned to the top of Chosen Hill near Churchdown.

Auntie Lilla Smith
at her 90th birthday party in 1994.

The Blaisdon church bells rang out a full peal in her memory on 22nd October 1994 and this is commemorated in the belfry."

Angela Foster lived opposite Aunt Lilla and she tells more of the relationship Aunt Lilla had with the Foster family in the section on Parkside. Here she recounts a particular tale that happened to them one Wednesday:

"On this particular Wednesday morning in the spring of 1979 it was raining and Auntie Lilla came round to give us the sad news that Pollyanna, her long time cat and friend had been run over. Someone had come to tell her that this had happened outside Mrs. Griffith's house (Hillcrest or the Old Post office). Pollyanna had broken her back and needed to be put down. I called my vets in Lydney and I was told if we went straight away the vet was in the office and he could help us put Pollyanna out of her misery. Auntie Mildred came to the rescue and said she would look after James and Emily and then I could drive Auntie Lilla to Lydney. She was too upset to drive herself.

On the way back to Little Garth Auntie Lilla noticed that people were waiting at the entrance to Blaisdon Hall, for the weekly bus to Gloucester. She went down the road to tell them her sad news.

We set off with the cat in a cardboard box. I had a quick look and thought Pollyanna had lost a bit of weight but decided that was just due to the accident. Auntie Lilla talked to the cat all the way and tried to comfort Pollyanna on her last journey. We arrived at the vets to find another patient in the waiting room, a young rambunctious puppy. Auntie Lilla did not like how this upset Pollyanna and persuaded the owner (as only Auntie Lilla could) to take the dog outside, as it was causing the cat even more distress. Auntie Lilla was called in and soon Pollyanna was out of her misery.

Pollyanna was now placed in the boot of the car for the journey back to Blaisdon. We quietly talked about Pollyanna's life with Auntie Lilla and how she came to Blaisdon. She was a pregnant stray cat that Auntie Lilla had found and took into her life. She decided that if she was going to be welcomed into life at Little Garth then there should be no more kittens. So Pollyanna was taken to the vets with a note (Something Auntie Lilla was famous for). The note read something like this:

'Dear Dr. Vet, I have been a naughty girl in the past and if I am going to live with my new owner I cannot have any more kittens. Can you please help me in this situation as I really want to stay with this kind lady?' The vet laughed so much that he did not charge her for the surgery.

We also talked about would she have another cat, but she thought that Pollyanna would be the last of her furry friends. On our arrival back in Blaisdon I asked Auntie Lilla to come and have a coffee with us. I thought about

offering a brandy but it was early in the day. She had the coffee and then said she would go and bury Pollyanna in the garden that she loved. James, as always, was very willing and wanted to go help Auntie Lilla to do this. I thought that this was probably not a good idea and suggested that changing the beds would be a much better idea; perhaps I would let him bounce on them. So off Auntie Lilla went and we went upstairs.

Shortly, there was a shout from downstairs. I went to look and saw Auntie Lilla stood at the bottom of the stairs with her raincoat covering her head. She said Oh you will never guess what has happened. I thought that perhaps the vet had not given the cat enough medication and that Pollyanna had come round. Then I was told Pollyanna was at home eating her breakfast. Auntie Lilla was deadly serious but I was laughing. I kept apologising for the laughter but I just couldn't help it.

Now Auntie Lilla had two problems. First, she had to wait for the bus to return from Gloucester, so she could tell everyone that Pollyanna was still with us. I can just imagine everyone walking back to their homes. I'm sure there were smiles on their faces. Secondly, the other and a more pressing problem, was to find the owner of the poor cat that Auntie Lilla had put down. Well, after some detective work, she found out who it was. It was an Etherington cat, so Auntie Lilla set off on her final errand of the day to relay the sad news to the owners of the poor cat.

Auntie Lilla was well known for her involvement in the village and this was just another story in support of that."

2

3

1. Lilla outside Little Garth.
2. Lilla with Catherine Higgins. (1984)
3. Lilla with Ian Waters at his christening at Blaisdon Church.
4. A typical note from Auntie Lilla.
5. Text from above note.

4

5

Home of Ceri & Sheila Evans.
April 10th at Blaisdon House
Tea Party for my 90th Birthday April 5th
Now retired ChurchWarden. My fellow
Church Warden Dick Hawker "saying a few words."
As ?? the Beautiful cake made
by Sheila and iced by Icing expert Artist
kind Lynne hogg
thank you
Auntie Lilla.

Little Garth was then the home of Megan and Gerlad Kear who moved from Woodgreen Cottage and later moved out of the area.

In 1998 Little Garth was sold to **Stephen and Nicola Atkinson**. Their daughter, Emily was born in 2000:

"We found Little Garth in March 1998 and moved in by May. We had previously lived in Quedgeley having sold our semi in search of somewhere that needed a bit of renovation.

On our first viewing the particulars mentioned a sun lounge and second toilet and all seemed just what we were looking for but there was no description of the view. As we looked around, the sun lounge was in fact a breeze block lean-to with a plastic corrugated roof in poor repair. The toilet was in a green shed to the rear of the house and outside there was a patchwork of concrete slabs where an Anderson air raid shelter had recently been removed. As for so many before us, this did not matter for once we saw the amazing view everything else could be sorted in time.

The garden so lovingly tended by many previous owners, including Lilla Smith who we are told planted the more exotic trees still there namely a Gingko Bibalo and Tulip tree, was now overgrown with vegetables and flowers mixed together throughout the garden and weeds all standing two feet tall.

The alterations we have made are many but to list a few:

The garage previously mirrored the original boundary of the house and was about six feet narrower at the back than

Two views of the front garden of Little Garth in 2012 and a view of work in progress trying to tame the garden,

213

at the front. The previous owners between 1996-8 had also purchased a further strip of land so were able to re-build the garage, this time in the more common rectangular shape.

As much as we enjoyed our very airy sun lounge, we had this extended in 2003 and this time with a slate roof!

In the previous edition of the Blaisdon book mention was made of the countless flies that infested the dormer bungalow attic bedrooms and sixty years later the flies were still prevailing. They would multiply under the roof tiles and on warm days manage to find their way in. Nothing we did seemed to stop this flow, so in 1999 the re-plastering and lining of the roof began, with momentos along the way from the original builders who had left their cigarette packets in the rafters. Bats are plentiful in Blaisdon and have also been known to whistle through the house.

In the garden a lot has changed since we have bought the property. We have done various improvements including adding paths, veranda, patio and in 2009 planted a yew hedge at the front. One thing that hasn't changed is the heavy clay soil, which is still hard work but does provide most of our vegetables throughout the summer.

A normal week in Blaisdon would start with the arrival of the primary school bus at the memorial cross at 8:10am which collects the village children and takes them to Westbury–on–Severn primary school. This is closely followed by the secondary school bus for Dene Magna stopping at the Red Hart pub at 8.15am.

Our first few days in our new home were marked by a kind note from one of our neighbours, Sheila Evans, who left a card welcoming us to the village. This was the start of joining in with the village activities and in 2003 Nicola joined the Parish Council and helped collate the villagers' views and published a Parish Plan. Also we took our place in the annual village fete on the face painting stall.

One of the things that we liked was the lack of street lighting and on clear nights Stephen can be seen setting up his telescope for an evening of astronomy. During the spring of 2010 we started bee keeping in a plot of land on Guy's field behind the pub with payment via jars of honey. We needed strong stock fencing around the plot to keep Guy's pigs at bay. Stopping his pigs and in particularl the piglets has been a feature over the past few years and we have been seen more than once chasing piglets around the lane to return them to their field.

Stephen was born in Little London and remembers spending his summer holidays picking the famous Blaisdon plum and many hours playing on Nottwood Hill. His mother, ***Amelia Meek*** (nee Hall), wrote a poem in 1977 about these plum picking days. Also her father Ray Hall remembered Little Garth being built when he was in his early teens and was on his way to visit the Red Hart, the only place that would serve him real ale!

 We had been to the Red Hart before as Stephen's dad, Harvey Atkinson, was a Forest of Dean Morris Man and they danced in the road outside in the summer and also mumming at Christmas, where he would play either ragged Jack or the Turkish knight."

1. Emily Atkinson in an apple tree with Gizzy.
2. Nicola & Emily Atkinson build a snowman.
3. Easter egg hunt with cousins at Little Garth.
4. Nicola, left, & Emily check their bees.
5. Stephen Atkinson admiring his new vegetable patch.

Plum Picking (1977)

I've been plum picking today
Oh what a tiring job. Up high
ladders. Down steep banks
Just to earn a few bob

Lorries are loaded as
soon as their full
Baskets are emptied
Away they pull

Some go for canning
Some go for jams
Some even get sold
Down at old Sam's

At twelve we stop for a well
deserved break, Blaisdon Plum
Jam sandwiches and a
piece of fruitcake.

Plum picking's over now
That's it till next year. No
More getting stung from
Wasps, nesting near.

Legs can be rested
Aching backs eased
Plum pickings over
Oh I'm so pleased.

Amelia Meek
(1997)

Above:
The view from Little Garth's
bedroom. (1998)
Left:
Stephen laying the
greenhouse foundations
beneath a heavily laden
Blaisdon plum tree.

ST. MICHAEL'S CLOSE

St. Michael's Close comprises of three bungalows, built in the 1970s by the Salesian Order when they ran the school at Blaisdon Hall. Their purpose was to house staff of the school, especially married staff who required family housing.

Under subsequent owners, they have been occupied but are at present unoccupied. The close is for sale at present (2012) with planning permission granted to demolish them and build three detached properties.

Right:
Two views of No. 3 St. Michael's Close.
(2012)

WEIR COTTAGE

Above: Weir Cottage in 2012.

Joyce and Doug Inger moved into Weir Cottage in 1979. Joyce continues:

"We bought Weir Cottage from Mrs Moss and moved in on April 4th 1979. Before that a Reg and Peter Fisher were living there. We had been living and working in Zambia for fourteen years and were planning to settle down and establish a trout farm. Tate and Lyle had sent Doug there, originally for three years, first working at the Refinery in Ndola on the Copper Belt and then on the Nakambala Sugar Estate in Mazabuka. This is where he became interested in fish farming as they were stocking the dams used for irrigation with indigenous fish.

We bought Weir Cottage mainly because the Longhope Brook bordered the land, with the weir and mill leat, which ran just in front of the cottage, were ideal for directing the water into what would eventually be a large building with the tanks inside for growing fish.

Left:
Weir Cottage c1979.
A traditional tapering
fruit picking ladder can
be seen on the right.

Right:
Weir Cottage,
winter 1981-2.

The cottage was then still a two up, two down building, but a kitchen and bathroom had been built on the side. There was about one and a half acres of land with around a hundred plum trees. These were all the local Blaisdon plum, very popular with all our visitors who usually went home with a boot full during the fruit season. A number of these trees had to be cleared before we could start any building.

We started the actual excavation of the land at the end of the year. Building of the shed, to house the tanks and equipment, putting in the pipe work, plus double garage and packing area took most of the spring and summer. The tanks were eventually delivered and in place and we had our first tiny trout, fingerlings, delivered in September 1980.

We did a lot of work on the cottage during October and November 1981, mainly so that it could be easily extended in the future. We eventually built on a kitchen extension in 1982, making the original kitchen into a small dining room.

December 1981 was a really dreadful winter; we were snowed in for about ten days. Our neighbours in Wood Green Cottage, Gerald and Megan Kear, and ourselves, took it in turns to walk up to Longhope where the helicopter dropped fresh bread and milk at the local

Doug & Joyce Inger.
(1981)

shop. The phones were also off, but we did manage to walk into the village to the Red Hart to meet the rest of the village residents to discuss the situation, exchange stories and have the odd drink!!

Blaisdon has always been an extremely friendly and sociable village. Very hard working and enthusiastic when it came to fund raising events, with lots of people willing to organize fete days, harvest suppers, plum festivals, usually in aid of the church and village hall, two buildings always in need of repair or maintenance. The Plum Festivals covered four days with numerous events going on, lunches and afternoon teas were served in Blaisdon House, plus a concert in the Church on the Saturday evening. Blaisdon also had a very active branch of the WI.

Things were always happening, like the time we spent the evening pulling one of the sheep from Gaulett Farm out of the brook. It had such a thick coat which, when wet, weighed a ton. We were both in the brook in our wellies, when Doug lost his glasses!! We deposited the sheep on dry land in the end but had to wait until morning and the water settled to retrieve Doug's glasses.

Or the time Doug parked the car outside the egg farm in Velthouse Lane only to find it missing when he

1. Doug Inger in Trout Farm.
2. Joyce, a talented Soprano singer, with Dorothy Davies and their trophies
from the Bayley Lane End Music Festival.
3. Neighbours, Dick & Hilary Hawker help out during floods. (1982)
4. John Dunbar & Foster Yemm lend a helping hand to Doug Inger. (1982)
5. & 6. Doug & Joyce beside the Trout Farm sign, winter 1981-2.

Doug & Joyce Inger
with their last trout, dressed for the table. (1986)

Doug & Joyce Inger
Celebrate the Queen's Golden Jubilee. (2002)

returned. It had gone down a bank backwards, crossed a road, and negotiated a number of trees in a field before crashing through a wall into a pigsty. Fortunately no pigs were hurt, although the farmer was a bit surprised. It is always better to put the brakes on when parking a car!!

In January 1982 we had a flash flood; our brook suddenly became a rushing torrent. The cottage was on high ground but the barn, where we had a couple of fridges for keeping gutted trout packed and ready for delivery the following day, was soon under gushing water. We had to try and lift everything onto whatever was available to keep them out of the water. Everybody helped in situations like this and Hilary and Dick Hawker from the Stud Farm were soon

there giving us a hand.

Unfortunately disease came into the stock twice and once we had very bad pollution down the brook. We then faced the fact that we really weren't big enough to cope with these things and sadly decided to close the business and sell the property.

We eventually left Blaisdon and the lovely area of Weir Cottage in 1986 but as we live in Huntley, we are not far away from our friends or the lovely village of Blaisdon."

Weir Cottage was then owned by the Wiggins family for some years and is now owned by Jeremy and Sarah Aston.

Jeremy and Sarah Aston continue:

"We moved to Blaisdon in December 2006 from a village called Chilbolton in Hampshire with our children, Penny, aged 12, and Charlie, 9. We also have two lovely dogs, a flat coated Retriever mix called Chester (4) and a Beagle/Spaniel mix called Jemima (2).

Penny attends Dene Magna secondary school in Mitcheldcan and Charlie attends Hope Brook C. of E. primary school in Longhope. One of the reasons we moved to this area is because the schools had an excellent reputation and we have not been disappointed.

Apart from redecorating we have not made any changes to our house. We chose this house because it has a fantastic garden of approximately two acres for our children to enjoy as they grow up. The Longhope Brook runs through the garden so the children and the dogs have endless fun with that.

There are long rope swings hanging from the tall trees, a cabin to sleep in during the summer, various campfire sites, the children made a bridge of wood and rope to get across the brook and there is also a 'proper' bridge further up. The children drive tractors, motorbikes, lawnmowers and cars around the garden as well as riding their bikes. They play various games like hide and seek, football, rounders, ball and hoop games with the dogs, they do archery and have air rifles. We hope to have a zip wire soon. Our garden borders Mugglewort Wood, which provides many lovely walks.

Buzzards fly overhead all the time and by the weir it is possible to see kingfishers and a heron.

We love living in Blaisdon because it is a quiet, peaceful and friendly country village, with The Red Hart Pub at its centre hosting many events. Children can take their time growing up here."

Above:
Jeremy & Sarah Aston.

Opposite:
Penny & Charlie Aston
1. Swinging high.
2. On a bridge over Longhope Brook.
3. Alongside the weir.
4. Outside their cabin with canine friends.
5. The weir on Longhope Brook.

1

2

3

4

5

STREAMWAYS

Ivor and Enid Jones (Volume 2) lived at Streamways from 1938. Enid moved to The Cottage in Blaisdon in 1969, her husband having died in 1960.

In 1962, Robert (Bob) and Mary Bird had taken over the prep. school, Brightlands, in Newnham on Severn. Being Headmaster at a boarding school meant living on the premises for much of the time. They bought Streamways as a base for when they were not at school. Later, Bob relocated to Devon and the property passed into the hands of Sheila Sparks and her family.

They still own Streamways but have lived abroad for some years. Streamways has thus been a rental property for that time. One of the families who rented it were John and Danielle Price together with their young children, Robert and Grace. More is said about Danielle by the Waters family in the Spring Cottage section, as she was nanny to Eleanor and Ian for nine years.

Streamways.
(2012)

WOODGREEN COTTAGE

Woodgreen Cottage in 2012.

Few houses in the parish of Blaisdon have undergone as much change as Woodgreen Cottage. Derelict when Gerald and Megan Kear bought it in 1971, it has grown substantially since then; additions being made first by the Kears and more recently by Mike and Tracy Bayliss.

Gerald and Megan Kear together with daughters, Nicky and Debbie, describe the major project they took on when they bought a derelict Woodgreen Cottage:

"We bought Woodgreen Cottage at Auction in 1971 for the princely sum of £1200. It came under West Dean District Council at that time and I must say we had a tussle to get planning permission to renovate it. John Holman, an Architect from Longhope, did the drawings and applied for planning permission. Because of the problems we were having I remember him saying if we can't get planning permission I won't charge you.

Planning permission was given for a small extension of 1750 cubic feet. If this fitted in they would then consider further enlargement. The original cottage was very small with wattle and daub walls and the timber supports to the ceiling were logs that must have been taken from the surrounding woods.

There was no mains water available so we had to go for a borehole; we were told that there was an underground lake at Woodgreen. Anyway the hole was sixty odd feet down and the pump was down forty feet.

Nicky and Debbie were both at Denmark Road High School at the time and when we moved in, in 1973, they had to catch a bus from Gloucester and walk down the lane which was not very nice in winter time. However, Bernie Knight the postman from Longhope would be on his round collecting the post, which coincided nicely with the time the bus was due in Longhope. He took pity on them and asked if they would like a lift, which they refused at first but on a wet evening they accepted and they have been good friends ever since , it was also a great relief for us as we both worked in Gloucester.

Woodgreen Cottage:

1. Before any work 1971.

2. End result of Kear's years.

3. Before any work 1971.

4. After initial work.

5. Before any work 1971.

6. Drilling the borehole.

7. Woodgreen Cottage after the Kear's alterations.

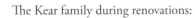

The Kear family during renovations:
1. Megan, Nicky & Debbie.
2. Debbie, Megan, Nicky.
3. Nicky, Debbie, Megan.
4. Debbie & Nicky cross Longhope Brook.
5. Nicky loved mixing cement.
6. The finished garden.
7. Megan, Debbie, Gerald, Stephen.

Our shed was well known in the village and beyond. We had our own Pub sign, the 'Woodgreen Arms' and most of our visitors would have spent time in the shed. We had all the creature comforts there, a chaise longue, cheese biscuits and flapjacks. Most left feeling very happy. We proved that wine could be made from almost anything, our favourites being blackcurrant and raspberry.

I did my stint as Secretary and handyman at the village hall and the Parish Council, becoming Chairman after Bob Pickering stepped down. The highlight I suppose was when we won the Bledisloe Cup for the best kept small village. That was in 1993. It was never a difficult job. We always had so much support from the Village and everyone joined in .

We feel very privileged to have spent almost thirty years in Blaisdon and I can't think of a better place to bring up children, our girls think the same too!!"

2

1

3

4

1. In the famous garden shed.
Gerald & Megan Kear's 40th wedding anniversary:
2. Megan with her backing band.
3. Gerald & Megan arrive for their surprise party.
4. The anniversary waltz.

Debbie Rowe (nee Kear) describes her 'enchanted childhood':

"I was lucky enough to experience a wonderful childhood in Blaisdon with the support of a loving family. What a 'playground' my parents had bought in Woodgreen Cottage. At the fun loving age of nine, I was introduced to a house that hadn't been lived in for thirty years, a neglected garden full of trees and a trout stream, where do you start!!

A united family effort lead to a lovely home being built, we had never been closer. From my brother Steve digging out the foundations with dad, to my sister Nicky working the cement mixer and me, the youngest, collecting water for the cement from the well. Mum and dad led the way working from dusk until dawn.

Our neighbour, for a short time, was Mary Griffiths, who lived at Gaulett Farm. She was such a gentle lady, who had a soft spot

Christenings:
Top: Debbie Rowe, Rev. John Magee holding Amy, & Olly Rowe.
Above: Debbie Rowe, Rev. John Magee holding Chris, & Olly Rowe.

for Nicky and me and we would often be invited in for tea and toast. Mary moved from the farm into the village and most Sunday mornings we walked along Velthouse Lane to visit her and pick her a bunch of wild flowers from the hedgerows. Rob and Marg. Allen came to live at the farm afterwards and introduced us to the fascinating world of farming.

Nicky and I went to school at the High School for Girls in Gloucester. Every morning I remember dad 'honking' the horn and mum running up the drive, we never arrived at school early!! Coming home was via Cottrells bus service, which dropped us off in Longhope.

One wet afternoon, we started our walk home along Velthouse Lane and the local postman Bernie Knight offered us a lift. Dutifully, like good girls, we said no and continued our journey drenched to the skin. Several days later, Bernie offered us another lift and after a quick look into my sister's eyes, we agreed yes and there was the beginning of a beautiful friendship. Bernie continued to pick us up and drop us off near home for the next 5 years, a friendlier local postman you couldn't meet and with him we were 'safe'. I am pleased to say we still see Bernie and his family and correspond every Christmas.

Saturday 25th August 1984 was the year Olly and I were married at Blaisdon Church, by Reverend John Magee; it was also the month of the Blaisdon Plum Festival. Again we realised how lucky we were to live in a close village community. Sheila Evans, who lived at Blaisdon House, adorned the church in beautiful flowers to match my bouquet and Dave Lilley from The School House, who always had a glint in his eye, prevented us from leaving the village by 'roping out' the main road, until we had handed him some cash!!

All the villagers made our day very special and we have very fond memories of a Blaisdon wedding.

Following our marriage, Olly and I moved to Newent and later to Cheshire. Having made a special relationship with Reverend John Magee during our wedding, we were so honoured that he could christen both of our children, Chris and Amy over the following years. Whenever we met John Magee, he would hold our hands, give us tremendous encouragement and they were the moments when I felt closest to God, he was a very special man.

At moments of quiet contemplation, Woodgreen and Blaisdon is where I take my minds eye. An enchanted childhood, safe with a loving family and safe in a close and caring community, I was so very lucky!!"

Mike Bayliss continues the story of Woodgreen Cottage:

"Tracy and I bought Woodgreen Cottage in 1997 and over the forthcoming years we have extended and modernized it to today's property in the picture at the start of this section. We also own the small woods at the front of the property that used to be an orchard. We have three children, Callum, 16, Alfie, 12, and Evie, 8.

We have recently found coins dating back to 1615 showing good proof there was activity on the land in those times"

Mike has opened a micro brewery, situated in Mitcheldean in the Forest of Dean on the site of the old Wintles brewery. The Bespoke Brewery is a has a 5.5 barrel brewing capacity and uses traditional high quality ingredients with their own bespoke twists, producing such beers as 'Running the Gauntlet' and 'Saved by the Bell'. There is a range of quality ales available in casks or bottles. They have won Camra beer of the year award at the Postlip Festival 2012 with their stout, 'Money for Old Rope'. The brewery also has its own bar and counter sales area where a drink can be enjoyed every Friday evening and their beer can be bought from their trade counter.

Another innovative twist is the bespoke labelling facility that enables personally designed labels for personal and special events. Mike produced a special commemorative label for Spot of the Red Hart and this is reproduced in the section on the pub.

The Bayliss family:

1. Mike in his Bespoke Brewery, Mitcheldeaan.
2. Callum.
3. Tracy.
4. Evie.
5. Alfie.

RCHARD HOUSE

Bert and Sheila Daniell (Volume 2) built Orchard House when they retired and sold Velt House Farm next door. When they moved to Mitcheldean, **Peter and Katherine Davis** bought the house:

"We are the Davis family, consisting of Peter, Katherine, Ewan (15) and Lewis (13) and we live in Orchard Cottage, Velthouse Lane, Blaisdon. Pete and I have lived within four miles of Blaisdon pretty much all our lives so know the area very well, having grown up in Huntley and Birdwood. We moved here in March 2000 from a terraced house on the main road in Huntley, which was quite a contrast. Initially, when we first moved here it was

Above;
Orchard House in 2012.

Below:
Orchard House prior to the extension.

hard to sleep at night because it was so quiet and if a car went by it woke us up!!

The property is a converted granary, which attaches to the main farmhouse, Velthouse Farm. It was converted around 1990 by Bert and Sheila Daniell who used to live in the farmhouse from a young age and had worked the farm all their lives. They converted the granary for their 'retirement' then decided that they wished to move to Mitcheldean to be nearer the shops and doctors. Bert and Sheila have remained our good friends and 'advisors' and have given us a rich insight into the history of the area. For example, when trains used pass in front of the

Bert & Sheila Daniell, front with Ken & Glenys Barnard.

Katherine & Peter Davis.

house. Also they have many an anecdotal story to tell. The property suited two people adequately but was not really big enough for a growing family and we applied to extend it to create a three-bedroom dwelling. The extension took us some time to complete (about five years!) Pete carrying out all the building works himself in his spare time, with me as his labourer.

Moving to Blaisdon was only a few miles down the road from where we lived but it was a massive change to our lives. Pete had the land that he dreamed of (just under 10 acres) and the children had oodles of space to run free. I had my eyes opened to a whole new ball game. My first Christmas present from Pete was 'the present that keeps on giving', when he bought me six ewes in lamb. That was the start of several ventures involving animals that we have encountered, having now dabbled with pig farming, chickens, ducks, ponies and their respective offspring.

When we moved here the children were two and a half years and one year old. Keeping tabs on Lewis who was just finding his feet was difficult and sorting out sheep and lambs with him in tow was not easy, he subsequently spent a good deal of time on my back in a baby carrier! One day I was trying to stop our dog, Ben, from chasing a lamb when Lewis was unceremoniously catapulted out of the backpack over my head and landed face down on the floor some distance away. A good job he still had all his chubby baby fat to cushion the landing and no damage was done. Ewan was that bit older and his love of nature and collecting things soon took full hold. We would often go fungi foraging in the wood behind the house for hours and trawling through books to identify what was what. His collection of stones and fossils rapidly grew, especially when we discovered the fossils in the rock at the quarry at the end of our land. He was like a kid in a sweetshop! He often went to school with a plastic container housing some

Ewan & Lewis Davis:
1. In Blaisdon Wood.
2. 'Let them eat mud!'
3. Hose down.
4. New piglets.
5. Pony care.
6. Ewan foraging.
7. Lewis at Golden Jubilee.

Peter Davis with Ewan & Lewis

Katherine labouring!

piece of 'treasure' that he'd found – sometimes not so nice, for instance a dead hornet he'd found in his bedroom!

When the property was converted, the land adjoining the Farmhouse was basically split and everything on the side of the Granary formed part of the new development. Unfortunately there were no farm buildings on this side and we applied for planning permission to build some outbuildings in 2006, which was granted and now we have somewhere to bring the sheep in for lambing and the pig for farrowing and we can even watch from the bedroom window to see if anything is happening!

Pete has worked for Glevum Conservatories at Elton since we moved here and I have fortunately been able to work from home as a legal costs draftsperson, fitting this in around looking after the children and animals.

The boys attended Huntley Primary School, which was in fact the same school that both Pete and I attended, although he was in an older year than me! They are both now at Dene Magna Academy School in Mitcheldean. There are lots of children in the area around their age group and they have a lovely bunch of friends, a lot of whom they have known since Playgroup.

I often think about how 'unfazed' the children seem about the things they see and experience living here, for instance: the first time we watched chicks hatching from eggs under our hen; the time we found a live mole wandering along the roadside; watching Pete get his friendly pheasant to eat out of his hand; seeing new born lambs stand up and feed from their mother within minutes of being born and cleaning off piglets' noses and latching them on for their first feed; investigating bright green lights glowing in the grass which were glow worms; coming across a hornets nest in the wood (mind you Lewis was a bit freaked out by that!); rolling bales of hay down from the top of the bank; swimming in the stream in the summer; watching the buzzards soaring and mewing above our heads and the bats flying low at dusk. To name but a few, of which there are many!

There are of course some memories that won't be so fondly remembered, our aptly nicknamed 'killer cockerel' for one. Lewis will remember how his childhood consisted of constantly watching his back whilst in its vicinity for fear of being attacked! Pete, in his wisdom, tried to deal with the problem by getting Lewis to 'man up and face up to it' with a newly bought 'super soaker water pistol', however the logistics of filling up the water pistol and it being to hand just when you needed it proved pretty impossible and the only thing to do was run back into the house for safety! Lewis did finally outgrow the cockerel and then it seemed justice was done when the cockerel met an untimely death by the jaws of the fox. Lewis felt he'd lost a close friend and even posted on Facebook 'killer cockerel RIP', to which most of his friends came back with comments to the effect that they would miss him too, because they'd all had to watch their backs as well!

Another instance of a memory that won't be forgotten in a hurry is when Pete had left his horse tied up on the gate at the top of the drive and I looked out of the window to see it charging down the drive with the gate dragging behind it. Pete's never moved so fast but only managed to catch up with it after it had travelled quite a distance down the lane. Luckily the horse wasn't hurt and thank goodness no cars came along. It wouldn't be the sort of thing you'd want to be confronted with on your leisurely Sunday morning drive in the country.

There was of course also the dreaded day the rain came in 2007 and believe it or not despite living on the side of a valley in an elevated position we were flooded. At the back of the house there are steps down to the back door and I was at home that day and had to watch it fill up like a swimming pool and eventually come into the house, despite Pete's idea to use his mastic gun to seal the bottom of the door. By the time he returned home from work that night, the water had gone and he couldn't understand what all the fuss was about! Luckily I'd taken pictures of the stream, which was unrecognisable as a raging torrent of brown water covering half the field.

We do occasionally frequent the local pub, the Red Hart,. Pete a little more than me! In fact, Ewan is frequenting it more than either of us at present because he has a job helping in the kitchen, which he seems to enjoy, but not enough to do the washing up at home too.

Moving to Orchard Cottage was a bit like a dream turning to reality for us, we own our little piece of England and we couldn't have asked for a more beautiful spot, with a lovely community spirit."

When ***Ewan Davis*** was asked if he would contribute to the book, he decided to write a poem:

Upon these fields of summer's gold
And in these brooks of waters cold
Were memories made to grow old?
          In this place of Blaisdon

All these creatures that pass us by
And tree houses built up so high
And winter's frosts slowly die
In this place of Blaisdon

We're the lucky, who have seen
What lives of us could have been
Saddled upon those horses keen
          In this place of Blaisdon

But now the woods are all explored
And the childhood dreams are all but moored
Yet still these fields are not ignored
          In this place of Blaisdon

And now the dawn of tiring day
Sat down upon these bales of hay
We let our memories unfurl and fray
          In this place of Blaisdon

Summer & winter views of the land next to Orchard House.

VELT HOUSE FARM

When Bert and Sheila Daniells (Volume 2) decided to retire, they sold Velt House Farm and part of the land whilst continuing to live for some time in the other part of the building, Orchard House. Roger and Christine Leyfield bought the farm and **Christine Leyfield** reflects on living there:

"We moved into Velt House Farm in July 1993. We had been living in Pembrokeshire and moving day was memorable because the lorry in which the cows were being transported couldn't get down the narrow lane. We therefore had to borrow a cattle trailer from Bob Allen of nearby Gaulett Farm and transport the cows down the lane in small numbers; stressful for all!

Roger worked the farm, where we had a suckling herd of Dexter and Hereford cows, together with some sheep. I worked at Littledean Primary School and James, who was seven at the time, attended Hopes Hill Primary School.

We found everyone to be very friendly and helpful and enjoyed the various village activities, particularly the annual fete. I enjoyed attending the talks, events and outings with Blaisdon WI and Roger and I used to regularly walk the footpaths in and around Blaisdon. It was a real pleasure. We have very fond memories of our time in Blaisdon."

Above: Velt House Farm in 2012.

Below: James, Roger & Christine Leyfield.
(2011)

The farm then passed into the hands of David and Catherine Goldthorpe before being bought by Sean Taylor. **Helen Taylor** continues:

"My husband Sean and Mother-in-law (Angela) moved into Velt House Farm on 20th May 2005 from Marlow in Buckinghamshire. Sean and I met in 2006. Up to this point changes had been made but the most significant changes in Velt House Farm happened after we met. I moved to Blaisdon in 2007 to be with Sean. I moved from Evesham in Worcestershire where I grew up. We married in 2007 at Blaisdon Church with a reception at Velt House Farm in a marquee in one of the fields.

In 2007 a new barn was erected in place of an old hay barn and a new drive was added to get better access to the fields from Velthouse Lane. A log cabin near the house was also finished that year. In the latter part of 2007 work began on Churn Cottage, turning an old animal shelter into a one-bedroom cottage for Angela. Builders came in to do the roof, work on the stonework and some of the internal walls. This work was completed in early/mid 2008. From this point, Sean and myself completed most of the work with help from my mother, Hilary Packham. Angela moved into Churn Cottage at the end of February 2011. Work still continues on Velt House Farm with the next project, the redevelopment of the big barn already started.

In 2010 Sean and I were blessed with the arrival of Laura

Mr & Mrs Taylor, just married in Blaisdon Church.

Winnie our daughter. She was born at Gloucester hospital on 2nd July. Sarah Hobbs visited us at home to bless her birth. Laura was christened at Blaisdon church on October 3rd 2010. Laura's first birthday party was held in one of the fields at Velt House Farm.

While we do not have any animals, we have had cows in the field from one of the local farmers for the last three years, although not this year. The first lot of cows we had were probably the most spoilt cows ever to have lived. Sean used to go and feed them a variety of things. Biscuits and chocolates we didn't want and on one occasion a new packet of cheddars, much to my disgust, as they were my cheddars! They were so spoilt and tame they would come running when people came into sight, particularly Sean. On one occasion one of the cows was in such a hurry to reach Sean that it fell over. Luckily she was fine. We spent many an hour chasing cows round the field when they got out. Sean's nemesis was cow number 895 who was auditioning for a remake of the great escape.

We are very lucky to live where we do. We look out on fields and woodland. It is unbelievably quiet. Laura is getting to learn about nature first-hand. We have a lovely place to have celebrations; a marquee in a field with only the sounds of nature is just great. My parents moved from Evesham to this area to be near us. They now live in Grange Court just a few miles away. They love living down here, they have views both to the front and back of their house.

It is always difficult when you move to a new area to make new friends and find a place to fit in. Sean persuaded me to join the WI as a way of getting to know his mother better. So I joined Blaisdon WI. I met a number of ladies from the village and surrounding area. They made me welcome and when Angela stopped going I continued to attend. Unfortunately in 2009 Blaisdon WI had to close due to insufficient numbers and most of the members moved to Longhope WI, as did I.

I started attending church and was confirmed in 2009 through the parish. I have continued to attend church with my daughter Laura, who enjoys the family communion services, particularly when there is cake afterwards. We enjoy going to the village fete and in 2009 my nieces Morgan and Annie also had great fun at the fete.

Sean and I have enjoyed going to the Red Hart pub both for dinner and drinks, from our first meal together to a barbecue the night before our wedding and meals both with and without our daughter Laura today. It has always been a good place to find out what is happening in the village. Sean and I used to go to the pub every Sunday and Tuesday night for a drink and to catch up on the local news. We used to cycle until I became pregnant with Laura. After Laura's birth we continued to go to the pub in the evenings until she was six months old. She would happily sleep, smile at people, or sometimes I would feed her in a quiet corner. The change in the smoking laws made this possible.

It wasn't until I had Laura and started to attend some of the baby and toddler groups around the area that I really met many people of a similar age. Until then younger people were limited to those that we met in the pub. Since starting to attend the baby and toddler groups I have met many more people in Blaisdon, Longhope and Northwood Green.

From Blaisdon Laura and I, joined by various family members, have visited and experienced many things. Laura is well on her way to filling her National Trust passport and particularly enjoyed the egg hunt at Westbury Court gardens this year. We went to Ross on 25th May to catch a glimpse of the Olympic torch on its journey round the country.

Living in a rural community such as Blaisdon can be what you want it to be. For me it is a community of which I am part with friends and community spirit. There are some great events to attend such as the fete, bonfire night, and Sheila and Ceri Evans' cheese and wine evening, accompanied by the rather unusual auction with £20 chocolate cakes. There is a supportive church community headed by Ian Gobey and Sarah Hobbs, to both of which I can only say a really heart-felt thank you for the support they have offered me whilst I have lived here. All of which makes Blaisdon a happy and lovely place to live.

Milestones that have come and gone since I first came to Blaisdon include getting engaged, getting married in Blaisdon, getting my PhD, being confirmed, birth of my daughter Laura, getting my PgC (Laura was just 11 days old at the ceremony), Laura's christening, Laura's first birthday. I hope there will be many more."

1. Laura &Helen Taylor.
2. Helen at herPgC graduation, with a young Laura. (2010)
3. Laura watching the Olympic torch in Gloucester. (2012)
4. Sheila Evans with Laura.
5. Laura in the garden with her favourite beer, Fynnie. (2012)
6. Laura & friends party in the Garden.
7. Laura's christening, dressed in Helen's christening gown.

241

1

2

3

4

5

1. Helen & Sean's wedding party at Velthouse Farm.
2. & 4. Before (2007) and after (2011) photos of the barn that became Churn Cottage.
3. Sean Taylor mowing the field.
4. Velt House Farm in the snow. (2010)

SHERTALLY

Shertally sits on the site of an earlier bungalow, built in the 1920s and occupied for some time by Mrs Alice Hyett, prior to its sale to Venk and Anna Shenoi. **Venk Shenoi** describes his and his wife, Anna's time in Blaisdon:

"Shertally is the last house on Velthouse Lane in the Parish of Blaisdon and the views of Whitehouse's farmland, and the sylvan hills across Longhope Brook constantly remind me of the Dooars landscape in North-East India where I worked as a Tea Planter in the early sixties.

Above: Shertally.
Below: The preceding bungalow, replaced by Shertally.

There is a bit of railway history too, the Gloucester and Hereford railway line through the parish opened in 1885 and ran through the land. An old shed, adjacent to Shertally, was reportedly used to store Blaisdon plums waiting to be loaded on the railway.

The line was closed in 1965 and Severn Trent then installed a buried thirty inch diameter water supply main along the railway alignment in the Seventies. Bits of sleepers, rusty carriage bolts and other hardware kept turning up during excavation for the foundations for Shertally.

Shertally would not have been built but for Anna's pushing me to the auction held at the Yew Tree Inn Longhope on 24th June 1997, only a few days after an eye operation. I could only see the old bungalow and adjoining land

243

through a painfully hazy eye and dark glasses and it was raining but it reminded me of my days in Tea. It rained there too.

There may be prettier parts of England or grander but we both fell in love with this corner of Blaisdon on day one, and that was to motivate us to travel almost every day for over two years from Quedgeley, where we lived then, to manage the building and landscaping work.

The deciding factor was the view and one is never disappointed, whatever the season or time of day, the view is ever changing. Being in a valley, we also have our own micro-climate. The stretch of Longhope Brook was the icing on the cake. We even constructed our own bridge across the brook

The bungalow that stood on the site was built in the 1920s and as we developed our ideas for its replacement, we found the district planners to be very helpful as we were on a fast learning curve. We made sure the floors, walls and roof were well insulated and constructed to meet the best that was available in the trade at the time. The SAP rating, or how much energy was lost from the house, was near perfect.

Top:
The old railway alignment.
Above:
Old storage facility, possibly used for plums

After early disappointments, we were lucky to find Steve Jayne who lives in Broadoak near Newnham on Severn to take on the building work. Evans the roofing contractor did a splendid job with the clay tiles and lead-work, replacing the hand moulded Rosemary tiles that were installed over eighty years back on the bungalow that stood in its place. Reclaimed Rosemary tiles from the old bungalow went on the garage roof. The timber roof had to be specially designed and cut on site because of the span and supported on steel purlins fabricated by Longhope Welding. We were also lucky to have Haskets from Littledean do the plumbing which after twelve years (2012) has proven to be leak-free.

We moved into Shertally in October 2000. Planting the trees and shrubs took a little longer, a never-ending but wholly satisfying occupation if at times tiring.

Apart from resident bees, robins, bull-finches, sparrows, tits, pigeons, pheasants and blackbirds, there are occasional sightings of foxes, badgers, weasels, snakes, buzzards, hawks and storks. The valley provides a defined route for migratory birds. A family of ducks regularly nest on the banks of the brook and a large black cat was seen strolling quietly by the brook one evening during late 1999, long before I came to hear about black beasts roaming in the Forest of Dean and other parts of the county. A Muntjac deer comes occasionally to graze, an inquisitive little visitor who inspects every nook and cranny around the garden before disappearing into the bushes along the stream.

Forest of Dean folk are naturally reticent and our nearest neighbour is hundreds of yards away. Anna and I are not great socialisers and we like our space. Our nearest neighbours, Roger and Christine Leafield at Velthouse Farm, made us welcome on day one. So did Bob, and his sister Marge from the Gaulett, ever helpful with local advice and more importantly with contacts which we needed with the self-build project.

We also got acquainted with Philip Snow who lives in Little London and is a man of many talents. Philip is ever ready to help out with all those awkward tasks from tree-felling to excavating trenches, road levelling, stock fencing and erecting heavy gates. What is most striking is Philip's local knowledge, and the sympathetic manner in which he works with the land and the environment. We would not have achieved so much without his continued help over the years.

Twelve years is quite a bit of one's life, Blaisdon is a great place to be and every day reminds us how fortunate we are to have one of the loveliest views in the Forest of Dean and Shertally is our corner of this green and pleasant land."

From the top:
Bridge over Longhope Brook.
The apiary at Shertally.
(2012)

ST. MICHAEL'S COTTAGE

Above:
St. Michael's Cottage after recent alterations..
Below:
An earlier view of a snow covered St. Michael's Cottage.

Dorothy Baylis recounts the lives in Blaisdon of her father-in-law, Francis Joseph Baylis the Second (Senior), her husband, Francis Joseph Baylis the Third (Junior), and herself:

"It was in 1973, I believe, when Francis Joseph Baylis senior came to St Michael's Cottage, Blaisdon. He wished to continue researching his family tree as the family originally came from Westerley, near Yate, Bristol.

The house was partly one-storey with the large kitchen area originally reaching up to a high sloping roof with no ceiling. His sons thought that he had come to live in a barn and not a recycled one. A few years later, when in his 80s, Frank had builders in to install a ceiling with a further bedroom, bathroom and storeroom, also further stairs at the back of the building, quite an undertaking for a man of his age, but that was Frank Senior.

While he was in Blaisdon he became a churchwarden at St Michael's Church and also climbed the church tower to wind up the church clock until the year before he died at eighty seven years old.

1

1. Frank Jnr, Dorothy, Frank Snr, Mr & Mrs Charlie Baylis
2. Frank Snr carrying out alterations. (1981)
3. Frank Snr with sister, Beattie on left & Dorothy Baylis.
4. Frank Snr with Andrew & Nigel Hogg, plus Brandy.
5. Frank Snr with sons, George & Charlie.

2

3

4

5

Francis Joseph Junior and I came to St Michael's Cottage in August 1987 after his father had died suddenly in Gloucester of a heart attack. We were with him at the time and it was a great shock coming back to St Michael's Cottage without him.

Later in the year, after consultation with George and Charlie, Dad's other sons, we decided to sell our house in Blackpool and come to Blaisdon. It was quite a big adventure, to come from a busy seaside town to a quiet country village,. but we soon settled, especially with 'Auntie Lilla' leaving us a welcome flag on the back door.

After our furniture arrived, added to Dad's, we had to spend some time sorting out where we could find room for everything and some of the boxes hadn't been opened several years later. However, we soon found time to join in with various village activities. I joined the WI and Frank became Chairman of the village hall and was also a bit of an odd-job man around the village. Round our village, Frank had soon become known affectionately as 'Young Frank,' a nod to his father, despite the fact that he was not exactly young at the time!

We also attended evensong once a fortnight at St Michael's Church, as we were members of Littledean United Reformed Church, which we attend on Sunday mornings. I also joined the church cleaning rota and later the Gardening Club although I am not a gardener; Frank loved his garden and spent many happy hours there tending the dozens of plum and other fruit trees and growing tomatoes, peas, strawberries (which the squirrels loved) etc, and cutting the lawn. That was quite a mammoth task. I gathered the lavender for the craftwork I did, some of which ended up on a stall at the village fetes.

While we were at St Michael's Frank made some alterations, mainly putting in a partition in the kitchen to cut off the draughts from the back stairs. I also assisted by making curtains for the windows.

We enjoyed meeting friends in the village and looked forward to the various village occasions such as the harvest supper and the fete. We also thoroughly enjoyed the cheese and wine parties at Sheila and Ceri's, when we managed to acquire various items in the charity auctions and also had a lovely happy evening with lots of laughs.

We became quite friendly with some of the 'Old Boys' from Blaisdon Hall. Once Frank met Kevin Cummins when he was going down for his paper, which was put in a pipe in the hedge. Kevin was so surprised when Frank got back so soon, as he thought he had been to the newsagent. After that he became Frank's firm friend and, of course, everything was 'brilliant.'

My husband Frank died in a road accident near home in January 2005, eleven days after driving to Amsterdam to collect our nephew who had gone there for Christmas. On his first day there, he had fallen and broken six ribs and was obviously not able to fly home. Frank took him back to Blackpool on New Year's Eve and returned to Blaisdon on the morning of New Year's Day, a journey that several of his younger friends said they could not possibly have undertaken- a chip off the old block obviously.

Frank's death was a great shock to everybody and I stayed in Blaisdon for the next twelve months, coming to terms with being without him but eventually I had to decide what to do. I loved living in Blaisdon and everyone was so kind, but living in a rambling old house, quite isolated and on my own, I realised that I needed to be nearer people and to have more local amenities. So I sold the house to Ed and Nicky Charlesworth and returned to my home town of Blackpool where I now live. I could say a lot more about our friendships with various people but I think it is best now to say I do miss all my friends in Blaisdon who were all very kind to me. I also miss the beautiful area and the views of the Cotswolds from the hill above the house but I have many happy memories of our time in Blaisdon and wish everyone well in the future."

1

2

3

4

5

6

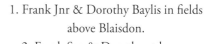

7

1. Frank Jnr & Dorothy Baylis in fields above Blaisdon.
2. Frank Snr & Dorothy at home.
3. Frank Snr in his garden. (winter 1999)
4. Frank Jnr on the Kevin Cummings memorial seat.
5. Dorothy Baylis with Paul Baylis, George's son, on the Frank Baylis jnr memorial seat.
6. St Michael's Cottage garden looking down past the house to the church.
7. Frank Jnr , left, when a navigator in 2nd World war, with pilot, Danny.

Nicky and Ed Charlesworth had lived at The Lodge before leaving Blaisdon when Hartpury College sold Blaisdon Hall. They had hoped to move back to the village and when Dorothy Baylis decided to move to Blackpool, the opportunity to purchase St. Michael's Cottage arose.

Nicky Charlesworth continues:

"Needless to say we always hankered to get back to Blaisdon and several years later (2006) we were delighted to be given the opportunity to buy St Michael's Cottage from Mrs Dorothy Baylis. This was a dream come true. With a bit of remodelling, it was to be our ideal Blaisdon home. It still has many intact features from its origins as the laundry to Blaisdon Hall.

We began work with enthusiasm in the summer of 2006 with an ambitious programme of works. Over the next three years we stripped the building back to its bones and rebuilt it with the addition of a garden room and a full height atrium on the west elevation. Where possible Ed and I did all the work ourselves.

In the garden we decided that the original outhouses were obscuring the best view, so we took them down brick by brick and rebuilt them at the top of the garden along with a double garage utilising further reclaimed bricks from the site.

Along with landscaping and planting, one of the last labour intensive jobs was the complete restoration of the original brick built reservoir at the rear of the house. This would presumably have supplied the laundry but had sadly fallen into total disrepair and had been filled with the detritus of generations. Slowly and painstakingly Ed rebuilt it and having installed a water collection system (from the roofs of the garage) and pump, we were able to enjoy a few months of our living plunge pool!

Sadly, as a consequence of the recession, we made the difficult decision to sell our 'home for life' and in the summer of 2009 we handed over the keys to Mr & Mrs Timberlake.

We thoroughly enjoyed our years in Blaisdon. What a magical village it is; from the daffodil lined verges in springtime to the orchid filled walks through the woods and the marvellous hospitality of Ceri and Sheila Evans in festively decorated Blaisdon House.

On a cheerier note we have now emigrated to north Pembrokeshire and are thoroughly enjoying being by the seaside! With very best wishes to all still fortunate enough to live in this special village."

Mr and Mrs Timberlake only lived In Blaisdon for a matter of months before work necessitated another move. The house was then sold to ***Liz Tandy***:

"We have been living at St. Michael's Cottage for nearly 2 years and love it! After an unsettling time and moving house twice in 9 months, it has been a total joy to move to Blaisdon and to find such a wonderful home.

We moved into St. Michael's Cottage in September 2010, my daughter Georgina and I initially, then later my partner Jerry.

We fell in love with the house and garden on first sight; there are not many who wouldn't! I knew the area a little as my family had previously lived in Awre, near Newnham-on-Severn.

The cottage had been 'yenovated' in 2007/2008 and looked wonderful. A glass atrium in the kitchen gave the whole area wonderful openness and light, which I have never known in my previous houses. But more than that, the cottage felt like 'home' immediately!

It took a short time to realise the many quirky aspects to the cottage. One of the strangest being that many of the doors had no door catches and could not be closed! One of the biggest problems we found was that the garage roofing timbers were not supporting the weight of the roof tiles. We have been gradually improving things, including a new kitchen, decorating and new guttering and drainpipes at the back of the house! In January the rebuilding of the garage was finished and looks fabulous.

The garden is a wonderful part of the property and it has been my aim not to kill anything over the last 2 years! We have a huge mix of plants and many are still a mystery! The views from the garden over the village towards the river are always stunning. It is just a short stroll up to the woods and that view must be one of the best in the county!

The garden remains a challenge, including the 'pond', which was used to launder sheets etc. from Blaisdon Hall. We are in the process of building retaining walls to, hopefully, simplify the work in the garden. The position of the cottage and the views make everything worthwhile and everyday I love the house more. Our dog, Jess, a 13-year-old border collie, has been a happy and relaxed dog since living here; she hated living in town. Jess can often be seen taking herself for walks in the field, or joining other dogs and their owners! Luckily there have not been many fights!

My daughter, Georgina started University in September 2012 but returns home every few months. My son, James, is at University and lives in Cheltenham.

Blaisdon is a wonderful village to be a part of and everyone has been very friendly and welcoming since our arrival. We are often getting nuggets of information about the cottage as it used to be, the previous owners and about the things that were done there. I think we will have had to be here a good few years to really be part of the village but we are always willing to help out with events and did enjoy last year's summer fete!"

Below: St. Michael's Cottage with magnolia.
Right: Jess.
(2012)

T. MICHAEL & ALL ANGELS, BLAISDON

The Church of St. Michael & All Angels, Blaisdon has continued to be a focus for the local community through the second half of the 20th century. Present churchwarden, **Mandy Howell**, reflects on the church and its role in the lives of those who live in the village of Blaisdon:

"Standing proud upon the hill above the village sits the Church of St Michael and All Angels, Blaisdon, one of the most beautiful churches anyone would ever wish to visit. Its origins date back to Norman times and the first rector, the Rev. Capella was recorded in 1294. Although not the original, the oldest part of the church now is the tower, which was built in medieval times. The rest of the church fell into disrepair and was rebuilt and enlarged in 1869. It is amazing to think that people have been meeting to worship on this very same spot for over 700 years and probably even longer.

Blaisdon Church has an idyllic setting with awe inspiring views over the Severn Vale; a sight that makes you catch your breath and makes you feel glad to be alive. To the weary traveller or investigative relative a church is an oasis of peace and tranquillity and a treasure trove of stories. Blaisdon Church is the keeper of many stories about people, those who have lived

Blaisdon Church.

Blaisdon church.
(Lower right: E. Perry)

253

in or are connected with the Parish, stories of birth and baptism, marriage and worship, death and burial. There are stories about life changing events like the fire that destroyed most of the village in 1699 and about acts of great heroism like the memorial plaque to the brave young men who gave their lives in two World Wars. Also there is the story of our faith told through the cross, the altar and the stained glass; a story that is telling us what happened in the past gives us hope for the future.

This is our church to which people from far and wide are drawn by family ties or by the sheer love of churches, leaving touching messages of thanks and remembrance in our visitors book.

Above: Blaisdon church interior. (N. Hogg)
Below: Mandy Howell.

On a summer's evening in the still before the congregation arrives for an evening service, all you will hear is God's wonderful nature at work; against the steady beat of the ticking clock there is the sound of the odd barking dog or crowing cockerel, bird song and the quiet humming of bees in the tower. In autumn opening the newly restored tower door in the west allows the mellow

setting sun to flood into the church. As it sweeps up the aisle and comes to rest on the altar it warms the backs of congregations and dazzles the vicar and readers.

On a clear crisp early winter's morning the sun shines through stained glass windows behind the altar in the East bringing their stories of faith to life in shades of blues and reds. Then, as if to spite the difficulties of heating such a spacious building, it travels southwards during a morning service filtering through glass of yellows and greens and warming and glittering like a ray of light and hope, reminding us of the spring to come.

I came to the Parish in 2003 and have been churchwarden since 2008. For a momentary blink in its 700-year history I have the very great honour of acting as custodian of this beautiful church to ensure that it endures for generations to come. This not only means maintaining the fabric and contents of the building, for which there is a long list of jobs but also ensuring there is a welcome for all who enter and that their stories are preserved.

The task of churchwarden would, however, be impossible to carry out without the help of a silent army of people who give their time voluntarily and willingly to undertake a multitude of tasks like flower arranging, cleaning, cutting and keeping the grass neat in the graveyard, restoring the furniture and fittings, oiling the bells, ringing the bells, sides duties at services, and playing the organ to name but a few.

The clock in the tower is one example of a task that needs particular dedication as it has needed winding once a week, since it was presented to the Church in 1912. Over the years one person has usually taken on responsibility for this task, finding somebody to cover for them when they are away.

A plaque in the Tower tells the story of Frank Baylis, churchwarden 1975 – 1985 and clock winder 1975 – 1986, who, it says, was 'a good time keeper and for whom time now stands still'. Frank made a great commitment not only as churchwarden but also as clock winder for 11 years. It was clear that he loved the clock and the files even note thanks being given to him for painting the clock face in 1975, which must have been a pretty precarious feat. Clock winding, it seems to me, is a classic example of the generosity and commitment of the silent army of helpers, especially when you consider the fact that two of Frank's successors, having completed their

watch, each clocked up nine and seventeen years respectively.

Whenever I hear people talk about Frank it is always with great affection and when looking through Church files from years ago I found several poems dedicated to him, this one I think aptly reflects his dedication to our church and to the hands of time:

For many years Frank had a pact
Fridays at 10am was this act
To climb steep stone steps to wind his friend
This Friendship will never end
His ashes will rest within sight and sound
In years to come as the hours go round
Rest in Peace
A life well run.

Ensuring the congregation is comfortable and well looked after during the services is an important part of a churchwarden's job. This could mean anything from welcoming people when they arrive to making sure the church is warm enough for people to sit still for a good while. Whatever the task required I have always been able to consult the copious notes, instructions and diagrams left by another predecessor of mine, Lilla Smith, churchwarden 1979–1994. They remain an excellent aide memoire. There is a plaque on 'Aunty' Lilla's favourite pew and the ledge of one of the south windows, which was restored in her memory. It is clear from the affectionate stories you hear about her in the village that Lilla was a valued and greatly loved member of the community. Her memory lingers on, even in those like me who were sadly unacquainted with her, as I always think of Lilla as an example to follow and often find myself thinking 'I wonder what Lilla would have thought about this?'

My mentor and predecessor Dick Hawker, churchwarden for a second term 1986–2008, said that Lilla would regularly give him a dig in the back to remind of something he should be doing. Dick brought in the excellent tradition of the occasional 'accidental on purpose' mistakes made by a churchwarden that serve to amuse the congregation and at the same time ensure they are paying attention. These mistakes could be anything from forgetting to light the candles on the altar to putting up the wrong hymn numbers, all adding a little challenge to the smooth running of a service.

This is a tradition, I'm pleased to say, that has continued to this day. Dick always made people feel at home and part of the running of the church. One of his favourite sayings was 'Have I got a job for you', as he handed you a reading when you walked into church at Evensong, or as he unexpectedly placed the collection bag beside you at the start of a service.

I expect I should have smelt a rat, however, when the 'jobs' he blessed me with began to get more and more involved as he gradually got me used to the idea that even I could take on the task of churchwarden. I shall always be thankful to Dick for encouraging me and for teaching me the tricks of the trade. He instilled in me the ethos that Church is for everyone no matter who they

Stained glass windows in Blaisdon church (E. Perry):
Above: Depicting the nativity scene. Placed in memory of
Colin & Mary MacIver.
Opposite: window above the altar, dedicated to Peter & Isabella Stubs.

1

4

2

3

5

7

8

6

1. Rev. Clive Edmonds.	5. Rev. Sarah Hobbs.
2. Rev. John Magee.	6. Rev. Paul Green.
3. Rev. Ian Gobey	7. Rev. David Colby.
4. Rev. David Bick	8. Rev. John Thorpe.

Above: Dedication of new churchyard gates, donated by Lilla Smith. (8th April 1979)
Rev. John Thorpe, left and John Magee, right.
Below: Cross donated to celebrate the centenary of the rebuilding of Blaisdon Church (14th June 1967).

are, everyone is welcome and that although there are times when reverence and decorum is demanded you also need to keep your sense of humour as there are also times when a little smile goes a long way. At the end of a service Dick would turn round to the congregation and say, 'Good job done!' I would say this sums up his watch as churchwarden very nicely.

When Lilla retired in 1994, Ceri Evans, churchwarden 1994–2012, took on the role. For the last four years of this time I was privileged to have worked with him, following his lead and regularly referring to him for much needed advice and guidance until his retirement in March 2012. I would describe Ceri as a pillar of our community, his service to our church being only one of a number of public duties that he has undertaken during his lifetime. To our Church he has been a stalwart supporter, generous and respected. For many years he and his wife Sheila have opened up their home, organising and running fund raising events, like the famous and much loved cheese, wine and auction evenings, that became one of the principal annual fund raising events for the church. Ceri presided with his usual wit and banter as Sheila totted accounts due in

Easter gardens
and, right,
Christmas crib.

between making sure the guests were amply sustained with wine and as many different types of cheeses as you could ever imagine possible. All who attended had a thoroughly jolly and enjoyable evening. Although a number of his roles might demand a degree of solemnity Ceri maintains a cracking sense of humour throughout. My favourite of his jokes used to happen when the national team of his beloved homeland, Wales, triumphed at rugby. To celebrate this event, especially if their opponents had been England, he would change the candles on the altar from white to red. This caused great amusement and generated much animated discussion after the service and sometimes before, about the highs and lows of play, the ins and outs of rugby law and very often about the ability of the Ref.

successful each year and everyone enters into the spirit of things, donning fancy dress or themed tee shirts or aprons. There is always plenty of food, ploughman's lunches, burgers, hot dogs, ice creams, tea and cake and there are all the usual stalls and games like the tombola, the coconut shy, darts and the bookstall among others.

Bell ringers: in Blaisdon Church.
From the left:
Frank Baylis, David Brook, A visitor, Dick Hawker, John Gibson, Lynne Hogg.

Churchwardens and Vicars do their bit as well. I am usually on tea and cakes or the raffle. Traditionally there are the local Blaisdon plums for sale either as fresh fruit or made into jam along with a wide range of other seasonal produce. Sometimes there is a special feature like the year we had a gallery where local photographers displayed their work and the year Blaisdon Hall grounds were opened up for guided tours. It is a great day out. The whole village comes together and you can really feel the pride and community spirit in the air and everyone, whether from near or far, thoroughly enjoys and appreciates the day.

Another great annual fund raising event, which is led by the Village Hall Committee, is the annual Blaisdon fete the proceeds of which are shared between the church and the village hall. This is always well attended and enjoyed by everyone. The village works hard to make this event

A church of course also makes an excellent safe haven for wildlife and Blaisdon Church has its fair share of cohabitants to remind us how close nature is to us and how endearing and precious it can be. At one morning service a very surprised member of the congregation, Hilary Hawker, found what she thought was a sleeping bat hanging underneath the pew where she was sitting. Sadly we found the bat was not sleeping at all but that it had died which is probably the reason why it stayed put.

During one evening service a mouse dared to impose upon the sanctuary of a visiting Reader's trouser leg. A fascinated few in the front pews watched as the mouse ran out of its hole, across the floor and up the trouser leg. A very surprised Reader merely shook his leg sharply; the mouse was spat out on the floor where, recovering its dignity, it scuttled under the nearest pew for cover. The intrepid Reader, much to the amazement and delight of the congregation, carried on as if nothing had happened.

St. Anthony's Well, near Gunn's Mill, Flaxley.
Traditional source for christenings at Blaisdon Church.

Then there are the swallows that return each year to build their nest in the South porch. Unfortunately baby swallows being the fastidious creatures they are, turn around to do their business outside of the nest. This means that you can clean the porch floor of their droppings just before a service but you can bank on it being just as bad when the congregation depart.

Along with the normal weekly services the church year wouldn't be the same without some special services where we try to encourage everyone in the village to join in. There have been Songs of Praise services, Harvest festival services, Mothering Sunday services where people are encouraged to join in by choosing a favourite hymn to sing or by reading a favourite poem or bible reading. Refreshments are always an important part of these special services, as indeed they are to our regular twice-monthly morning services. A cup of something and a morsel to eat not only warms and fortifies but it also gives people a chance to stay and have a bit of a chat, to catch up with friends and neighbours and to hear what is going on in the village. Harvest festival is always fun with the church dressed up to the nines in the colours and fruits of autumn. After one Harvest service one young lad was heard to say, 'please could you do another of these around January time as its my birthday?' When Lilla was churchwarden, she would make a harvest table, which would hold a little of anything and everything to do with what we harvest from the earth, from bread and fruits even down to a piece coal.

At Christmas the church looks splendid, there is an abundance of candles placed between the pillars, above the altar and on the windowsills. There is the Christmas tree with its fairy lights, which makes a very welcome sight. There is the crib telling the story of the nativity and to which characters are gradually added as the story unfolds. The Christmas Christingle service tells the story of the world (an orange) and Jesus who is the light of the world (a candle inserted in the top of the orange) the fruits of the world (sweets) surround it and tied round the middle is a red ribbon reminding us that Jesus died so that we might be saved. Lights are dimmed and we sing a carol in the light of our Christingles, which is a very special sight.

For as long as I can remember and as I've been told, for many years before that, the Christmas tree and copious well prepared Christingle oranges miraculously appear on cue, given each year by the same members of that silent army. This is another very good example of how important the silent army troupers are and how they give generously without prompting or seeking thanks.

For a while the church was regularly home to both Catholic and Church of England congregations. It is now only used occasionally by Catholic folk as their regular Sunday services are now held in the Village Hall. We do, however come together for shared Christmas Carol service, each of us taking turns to be host. This is usually a great event at which it is very nice to see some people who would perhaps not regularly attend church. I recall one year when we hosted at the church and Guy and Louise Wilkins, the landlord and landlady of the Red Hart pub, brought along all those in the pub who had been attending a lunch they had arranged. It was a wonderful sight to see the church so full and even Spot the dog attended and was very well behaved to boot. We also join our Catholic colleagues each year at the War Memorial in the village for a service of remembrance on Remembrance Sunday.

Christmas at St. Michael & All Angels, Blaisdon.
Top: Rev. Sarah Hobbs lights the Advent candle.
Centre: The congregation.
Bottom: After the service, from the left,
Francesca & Jill Rodgett, Eleanor & Ian Waters.

Music is an important part of church life. The church bells are rung before church on every first Sunday of the month, at weddings and other important events. Our Bell ringers are a merry band and the melodious sound of the bells, the ringers delight on achieving a successful session and the happy banter that ensues, is a familiar and homely sound as we wait for the service to begin. On the walls of thetTower you will find plaques telling stories of peels rung in years gone by, names of who rang which bells, how long it lasted and what the peel was for. You can even find a list of rules dating from 1913, which remind everyone that 'a fine of one half penny shall be levied on all late attendees'.

As well as our bells we are also very proud of our Walker organ, which is over one hundred years old. It has recently received much needed restoration thanks to the sterling fund raising efforts of that silent army of helpers; a fund to which the proceeds of Volume 2 in this series was a major contributor. With its new lease of life our organ is resplendent in body and sound and will now boost our singing and accompany many more brides down the aisle for many years and generations to come. I always feel that the organist adds a great deal to a service and always try to remember, at the end of each service, to say a special thank you to them."

Rev. Clive Edmonds became vicar in 2000:

"Prior to coming to Blaisdon, I was rector at Haslemere in Surrey. I'm originally from Petersham, Surrey and Linda is a Londoner from Bow. When I came to Blaisdon House for my interview I had been asked to make a short presentation. Suitably prepared, I arrived with a bundle of prompt cards. As I stood to start my presentation, I took the cards from my pocket, only to drop them. They scattered all over the floor, so my presentation was embarrassingly delayed whilst I collected and sorted them back into order. Surprising to me at least, I got the job. Six years later at my retirement dinner, Ceri Evans did the same. On purpose I think, much to the amusement of everybody there.

I was vicar of Blaisdon from 2000-2006 when I retired to Longhope. My years spent in the parish were very happy indeed. I found people very friendly and supportive and it was a particular joy to see how the whole village came together for the annual Plum Fair, raising funds for both the village hall and the church.

The church was the scene for a fair number of weddings, baptisms and sadly funerals during my six and a half years as vicar. The monthly Family Communion was for me one of the highlights and it was always so good to see some young families attending. The sermon was, for that service rather more of a talk with plenty of 'audience participation!' During my time we had two excellent and dedicated churchwardens, Dick Hawker and Ceri Evans to whom 1 shall always be grateful for their personal support.

In a real sense, St. Michael and All Angels became our family church with the wedding of our son, Matthew and his wife, Katherine in 2003, followed by the baptisms of our grandchildren, Henry and his sister, Mathilda (from Canada) and Joseph and William who live in Nantwich.

I remember particularly a very full church for the Christingle and Carol Services, for Easter and other festivals. Lovely bells and music, lovely people and lovely memories."

1

2

3

4

5

The Edmonds family:
1. Henry, son of Tara & Richard, at his christening.
2. Matthew & Katherine at their wedding.
3. William, son of Matthew & Katherine.
4. Mathilda, daughter of Tara & Richard.
5. Joseph, son of Matthew & Katherine, at his christening.
Clive & Linda Edmonds to the left.

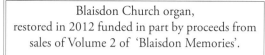

Blaisdon Church organ,
restored in 2012 funded in part by proceeds from
sales of Volume 2 of 'Blaisdon Memories'.

Above: Organist Guy Reeves.

Left: Organ removed revealing window, far left
that bears the marks of generations of Blaisdon
children.

Top left & centre: Some of the hundreds of
components that make up a church organ.

Rev. Ian Gobey arrived in Blaisdon in 2007:

"I realise that I do not live in Blaisdon, but I have been the vicar of the Blaisdon, along with Westbury-on-Severn, Flaxley and Minsterworth since 2007. I actually live in Westbury-on-Severn. During my time as vicar we have been successful in carrying out some minor re-ordering of the church and thanks to the work of a small dedicated team of people have given the interior of the building a really good refurbishment and arranged for the churchyard and its boundaries to be brought back into good order. The organ has also now been fully restored thanks largely to the monies raised by 'Blaisdon, Memories of a Country Parish 1935-64'.

Blaisdon holds a very special place in my heart. The setting of the church is wonderful and what better place can there be to sit than on the seat outside the church gate and admire that spectacular view over and across the River Severn to the distant hills beyond. That view, together with the one from the hill behind the church at the edge of the woods is, for me, a constant reminder of what a gracious God we have in giving us such a wonderful part of his creation in which to live and work. Blaisdon is a village with some real community spirit from time to time and the annual village fete demonstrates how everyone pulls together to enjoy themselves and raise money towards the village hall and the church, thanks to the dedication of the team of organisers."

Rev. Sarah Hobbs, associate priest has the final thought:

"As an ordinand in training, a curate and now as associate priest I have appreciated the congregation's patience and

encouragement as I learned my ecclesiastical trade at Blaisdon Church, as part of the Westbury Benefice.

The church and community will always hold so many good memories for me of baptisms, weddings and funerals as well as our weekly services."

Ian & Cheryl Gobey.

Vicars	
St. Michael and All Angels, Blaisdon.	
Rev. David Bick	1963-73
Rev. John Thorpe	1973-85
Rev. John Magee (NSP)	1978-94
Rev. Paul Green	1985-91
Rev. David Colby	1991-99
Rev. Clive Edmonds	2000-06
Rev. Sarah Hobbs	2004-
Rev. Ian Gobey	2006-

Queen Elizabeth II Diamond Jubilee.
Planting of a commemorative tree.

Right:
Rev. Sarah Hobbs, planting the tree.

Above:
The congregation of St. Michael & All Angels, Blaisdon.

NATIVITY PLAY

In 1985, Sheila Evans rediscovered the text of a Nativity play that the village of her childhood used to perform each Christmas. A wave of nostalgia resulted in an idea to perform the play in Blaisdon the coming Christmas. Not content with just performing the play, Sheila decided it should be a true village event with somebody from each house involved in the production, so she set out knocking on doors and slowly the cast was selected, some more willingly than others! Patricia Manners arranged the music and Joyce Lilley and Sue Booth made costumes.

There was a certain amount of typecasting. John Dunbar, landlord of the Red Hart was, not surprisingly, the Innkeeper. Steve Waters, who hoped his soon to be born child would be the representative of Spring Cottage as the baby Jesus, was thwarted by Eleanor not arriving till just before the production. He was suitably typecast as the Grumpy Shepherd as he came straight from the hospital to the stage for the performance, a little tired but very happy!

Sheila got her wish. Every house in the village was represented in this special Christmas production.

NATIVITY PLAY   Sunday 22nd December, 1985

The object of this play is to begin Christmas, 1985 with the story of the very first Christmas. Everyone, who has been involved with the production, wish you and your families a truly happy and peaceful Christmas.

Cast in order of appearance

Prologue . . .	John Magee
Gabriel . . .	Joyce Inger
Mary . . .	Jill Rodgett
Hostess . . .	Rosemary Wagstaff
Innkeeper . . .	John Dunbar
Orange Girl . .	Shelley Adams
1st Traveller .	Dick Roberts
2nd Traveller .	Dave Lilley
Servant . . .	Brian Jones
Joseph . . .	Dick Hawker
Angels . . .	Rachael Yemm
	Denise Yemm
Old Shepherd . .	Vic Woodman
Caleb . . .	Steve Waters
Shepherd Boy . .	Sam Evans
Angel . . .	Nicky Kear

Angels . . .	Alice Dazeley
	Sue Gent
King of Power	Martin Risborough
King of Wisdom	Cedric Etherington
King of Love .	Ben Evans
Pages . . .	Darren Hyett
	Andrew Hogg
	Scott Brickell
Child . . .	Marianne Daly
Woman . . .	Ada Keyse
Boy . . .	Francis Booth
Man . . .	Gerald Kear
Angels . . .	Nicola Brown
	Elizabeth Higgins

Costumes	Joyce Lilley and Sue Booth
Music	Patricia Manners
Producer	Sheila Evans

AT BLAISDON HALL

Above:
Cast List for Nativity Play. (1985)

Left:
Rosemary Wagstaff, right, as Innkeeper's wife with 2 travellers, Dick Roberts, centre, & David Lilley.

Blaisdon Nativity Play.
Christmas 1985.

AROL SINGERS

Carol Singing at Blaisdon Hall.

Carol singing has been part of the Blaisdon Christmas for at least fifty years. Started by the Rev. Lane in the early 1960s, it has continued ever since under the leadership of Roger Keyse. Indeed Roger has now clocked up fifty years of carol singing around the area.

At the time the singing started, the churches of Blaisdon and Flaxley were combined and so it was that the singing took in the two parishes. The carol singers spend every evening during the week before Christmas touring the two parishes singing at as many houses as possible. This is no mean feat as it takes in the two villages, Popes Hill, Nottwood Hill, Woodgreen, travelling in Land Rovers and tramping across fields in wellingtons, whatever the weather.

On Christmas Eve, the locals of the Greyhound, Red Lion and finally the Red Hart are treated to the singers' renditions. Finally, tlhere is a Boxing Day trip round a select few homes. Highlights over the years have included singing in the original part of Flaxley Abbey and, in the days when the Silesians owned Blaisdon Hall, singing inside the house. Every so often, the singers are treated to a very welcome mince pie and a glass of something to warm them up. Both are always welcome!

The singing has developed over the years, from a very conservative approach such as, 'There's a child here so lets sing Away In A Manger.' Jean Waters recalls the shock that greeted her suggestion that they could sing different hymns. Then she, Jill Rodgett and Joyce Inger took great delight in introducing descants. Now, the repertoire provides something for every taste, though it hasn't stopped the occasional request of paying us not to sing!

The collection from the carol singing goes to the Children's Society. Over the years, it is estimated that over £40,000 has been collected and donated.

1. Carol singers in Blaisdon House, from the top:
Peter Adams, Gail Jones, Roger Keyse, Louise Lisseman, Kevin &
Emily Baker, Nathalie Mignotte, Stephen Waters,
Paul & Philip Lisseaman, Dick Hawker.
(2012)
2. Roger Keyse, right, & Dick Hawker.
3. Carol singers at Woodgreen Cottage.
4. Carol singers at Stanley House.
5. Hospitality from Glenys & Ken Barnard, Parkside.

FAR VIEW

Stuart and Susan Gent purchased Far View in July 1978, moving from Ebley, Stroud:

"Far View is situated between St Michael's and All Angels Church and Blaisdon Lane. It has a long and mixed history. Formerly the property was a poorhouse after which it became the village school, then its use was changed to a reading room for the workers of the Blaisdon Estate, and then in the 1930's Miss Whittard purchased it. She, by all accounts, was a very handsome woman who gave dancing lessons in the former schoolroom. The property, when it was sold to Mrs Anne Pitt, became a domestic residence with no other ancillary uses.

Our connection with Blaisdon had started many years before. A Blaisdon 'old boy', Lawrence Stanton known as Curly, had lodged with Sue's grandmother in the 1950s-60s and by coincidence was living in Huntley when Sue's parents went to live in Byfords Road. This long-standing family relationship still exists today.

Stuart had previously visited Blaisdon Hall when he was a pupil at Central Technical School for Boys. The two schools occasionally competed against each other. Stuart was a member of the cross-country running team. He ran against Blaisdon Hall in races that took the teams through Blaisdon Wood and beyond. Visiting teams would often

Farvuew. (2012)

get lost in the woods as the marshals were all Blaisdon boys who, it was suspected, had a vested interest in the outcome!

In the mid 1970's Curly Stanton was maintaining the garden for Mrs Anne Pitt; he had known Mrs Pitt and her son Mark for many years. In conversation Mrs Pitt indicated she wished to sell the property and move into Newent where she had a business. Through Curly, Sue got to know about the pending sale and as she had always wanted to live in the country an offer was made to buy the house. The offer was accepted and that's how a long relationship with the village started.

In 1978 the layout of Farview did not make a comfortable

Above: Stuart Gent outside Farview c1970s.
Top Right:
Sue Gent on the steps to Farview c1970s.
Right: Fireworks & food at Farview i support of wildlife charity,
Tusk c1985.
From the left:
Dorothy Baylis, ?, Jean Waters, Andrew Rodgett, Hilary Hawker,
Jean Guy, ?.

home. The former schoolroom had high ceilings and having inadequate headroom compromised the two bedrooms above. The building backed on to the churchyard and different ground levels meant soil was banked up against the back walls. To overcome the problems a faculty was obtained from the Gloucester Diocese to reduce the ground levels and so remove a source of damp ingress. The ceiling height in the former schoolroom was reduced and smaller windows fitted. This enabled two full sized bedrooms to be created above.

As part of the improvement works a new staircase was fitted, a damp proof course installed and a new kitchen replaced the old fittings. The bathroom was relocated at the top of the new staircase and the old bathroom became a third bedroom.

In 1978 the house had no central heating but there was an old Aga in the kitchen, which provided hot water. It was inefficient because it was difficult to keep alight and while it kept the kitchen warm it did little else to make the house comfortable. When the kitchen was refitted a

Stuart & Sue Gent outside Farview. (2012)

Over many years several improvements were carried out. At ground level new concrete floors were installed, a walk-in larder was built off the kitchen and one open fire had its chimney lined. A new lining was also installed to serve the new central heating boiler. A new fire surround was fitted in the large room but the brick faced fireplace in the old sitting room (now the dining room) was left in-situ.

gravity fed solid fuel boiler was installed. That has been replaced with an oil fired range boiler/cooker; that has proved to be a big improvement.

Throughout their tenure of Farview Sue and Stuart have continued with their careers – Sue in pharmaceutical manufacture and Stuart in Local Government. In the early years they did spend most evenings and weekends repairing and decorating the house but always found time to travel. Trips to Asia, the Far East and to the southern parts of Africa, the USA and Canada were regular destinations. Many of the journeys were taken to observe wildlife; sometimes it was in the deserts of Namibia or on occasions to the edge of the Arctic Circle to watch polar bears or harp seals.

In 1990 the opportunity to purchase about five acres of plum orchard arose. The land had a common boundary with Farview therefore was a useful addition to the house. The vendors were the executors of the estate of the late Herbert Knight, a well-known fruit farmer who had lived in Huntley. The majority of the orchard is still planted with Blaisdon plum trees but a small area of land has been cleared to extend the garden of the house. One of the benefits of owning the extra land is that Sue has somewhere to position her beehives. The bees in turn benefit from the blossom and the trees benefit from the bees, a good outcome.

Since 1978 the house has accommodated more than just people! A total of three cats have lived with Sue and Stuart along with a stock dove. The stock dove was rescued from the church tower after being close to death; magpies had killed its siblings. Its parents had abandoned the surviving chick as it had been pecked to within an inch of its life and was covered in maggots; but it was still alive! It was taken from the nest one Sunday afternoon in late autumn, a vet was contacted and the bird was taken to Newent for treatment. It was not certain if the bird would live but it did survive and so presented Sue and Stuart with a problem. It had injuries that took time to heal so, by the time he could

have been released, it was winter and survival was going to be a huge challenge. It was decided to keep him through the winter, teach him to fly and then offer him the chance to go free in the spring. Spring came and the windows in the bedroom next to where he had spent the winter were opened. The bird, which by now had been named Booster, chose not to leave. What was to be done? The answer was to build an aviary in the garden. The aviary was built and when finished Booster was rehoused, for all of one night! He simply did not like the outdoors; he did not like the cold and was unaccustomed to the noises of nature. Next morning he looked a very sorry bird, so the aviary was abandoned and he was brought back into a dry warm house. He had a small room to himself and for the next twelve years or so, flourished as a pet. He became old and in 2010 died, a very sad day. Stuart and Sue miss his welcoming face at the window when they come home.

Like many properties in Blaisdon, Farview has been continuously improved. In the early 1990s the outbuildings on the north gable were taken down and rebuilt. The layout of the new extension roughly matched the footprint of the old utility building and former school lavatories. Two new external stores, a new utility room and a ground floor toilet and shower room were built. This alteration proved to be a better use of the space but as time goes on needs constantly change. In 2012 the north end of the house is again being redesigned to provide a new sunroom, a new utility room and cloakroom complete with shower and WC.

For the moment the house meets the needs of its occupiers but there is only one thing for certain, it will change again when Farview has new owners."

SHARON

Sharon in 2012.

John and Ruth Magee (Volume 2) lived in Sharon after Ruth inherited the house from her father, Bill Brewer, in 1963. John was admitted to Holy Orders at Gloucester Cathedral on 2nd July 1978. Although he became a non-stipendiary priest attached to the parish of Westbury-on-Severn with Flaxley and Blaisdon, he was considered by the people of Blaisdon as their vicar and remained so for the rest of his life. The whole community mourned him when he died in 1994. Ruth continued to live in Sharon almost to the end of her life in 2004.

Ownership of Sharon then passed to Kevin and Angela Baker, who moved there with daughters, Katie and Emily.

Angela Baker continues:

"We moved to Blaisdon from Highnam, Gloucester in 2005. Our first experience of Blaisdon had been around 1985 when a work colleague Kevin Cookson, whose wife Margaret Ashcoft was born in the village, invited us to a fete held in the grounds of Blaisdon Hall. We came to view Sharon sometime in June 2005. We parked in the field gateway opposite the house waiting for the estate agent to arrive with the key, just as the Library Bus was

pulling off from Stud Farm Driveway. The gentleman that had been on the bus strolled over to ask what we were doing and introduced himself as Dick Hawker, we were asked many questions. We now often talk about that time we were interviewed by our now good neighbour, Dick Hawker, to 'join the village.'

The house was hidden behind an 8ft tall hedge and thirty feet tall fir trees. The garden had been untouched for many months, the grass was waist high and the path way around the house over grown. There was a Marley type garage that was full of old tools with initials WB, being William Brewer who had first bought the house when it was sold by the MacIver's. There is a well to the side of the house that for four years we thought was an old septic tank that had been filled in. There was still a lot of furniture and

1. Notice of the ordination of John Magee.
2. John Magee.
3. Ruth Magee.
4. & 5. Presentation by Father Robson to John & Ruth Magee
at Blaisdon Hall 1985.

belongings in the house. It would need a lot of work but we could move in with our two daughters Katie and Emily and get the work done over time. There were two aerial photos in the lounge, one taken around 1995 we think, as the extension was build about then and was complete in the picture. The other is earlier, before the gas tank was fitted which was pre-1991. There is a man stood on the porch roof and the old vegetable plots can be seen. These were left for us when we moved in and we have now mounted them on the wall in the dining room.

On 26 September 2005 we completed on the purchase of Sharon. The first thing we had to do was make the drive entrance wider to get in three cars. Luckily a man with a digger had a cancellation and was able to come the very next day. We then emptied the house of its contents. We moved in three days later, three of us having been living with Angela's dad in a two bedroom bungalow in Highnam with four dogs living in the conservatory for that last 2 months as our sale had gone through and the purchase of Sharon was delayed for a short time, as there was some question over the legal ownership of the property dating back to the 1990s. This was sorted out and the executors of Mrs Magee's estate were able to proceed with the sale.

During the first day a 'posh' gentleman, Mr Ceri Evans, stopped outside to welcome us to the village and introduced himself and said that he lived in the 'large pink house' in the village. Nigel Hogg called in to see if we would like a parish magazine delivered each month.

Mr Hawker came by on his way to ring the church bells, he said that he knew Ruth Magee very well and after the extension was finished, he brought over his tractor and buried the tin sheds and all their contents in the back garden. Looking at the aerial photos, that must have been a big hole. We still find rusty metal and rubbish rising to the surface even now.

During the first spring the cows had been put out to grass and were very excitable. Kevin went down to Stud Farm to see Donald Rich for something and he always remembers, Ann Rich coming to the door with a worried look on her face; 'You haven't come to complain about the cows making all that noise have you?' He replied; 'It's taken us the best part of twenty years to get to live where I can see and hear cows next to our back garden.'

We promised Emily that she could have chickens when we had moved to the country and in April 2006 they arrived. We started with six; she now has fourteen, with three geese. Emily went to Newent School and was able to get a free bus that came through Blaisdon at 8.05am and returned at 4pm. After the first year we had to pay for this service. She is currently at the University of the West of England studying Bio-Medical Science, with her final year starting in September.

Katie was in her second year at Hartpury collage studying Equine Science and not having passed her driving test Angela drove her to Hartpury for the first six months in Blaisdon. She is currently working in Newent, whilst studying for an Open University Business Degree. Katie remembers getting the large bedroom because a fox or something had dug up what we thought might have been the remains of Ruth Magee's cat under the fir trees which could be seen from the window and Emily didn't want to look at it. There was a stone figure of a cat in the same area as the bones that had been dug up.

Every year we have been in Blaisdon so far there has been major road works on the A40 into Gloucester. The traffic has got increasingly more each year and Kevin now has to leave for Gloucester to work before 7.15 or sit in traffic for 45minutes for a 15 minutes journey. Kevin was asked to join the Parish Council in 2008. Kevin along with Pete Adams has helped with the tidying of the trees around the churchyard. Kevin designed and made the railings and gate on the house.

In 2007, with no one else stepping forward, Angela was asked to join the Village Hall committee and be treasurer. Then later in 2007 Nathalie Mignotte took over cooking the Harvest Supper and Angela along with Jean Adams became part of the team. One thing that surprises us every year about the village fete is that we struggle to get people to the meetings but on the day the village comes alive, with people all over the place to help and support this very important fund raising event. In 2010 and 2011 Pete, Jean and Shelley Adams, Nathalie Mignotte, Stuart and Sue Gent, Kevin, Angela, Katie and Emily Baker organised a Christmas market in the village hall along with the help of some other villagers. All dressed up in Victorian clothing.

Over the past seven years we have now got a productive vegetable plot and some flower borders. Having removed the Marley garage, we built a stone and timber garage and carriage house with a tarmac drive. The house was rewired and a new plumbing and heating system installed, we also have two wood burners. Interestingly, we have found invoices for a Solid Fuel Parkray with seven radiators at a cost of £1489.25 installed 1985 then, from 1991, a Baxi Bermuda Propane heating system at a cost of £1385.33. We have had to replace some of the windows on the side of the house but would like to keep the original window on the front.

For the first six years of living in Blaisdon, if anyone asks where we live, we would explain and they always said, 'ah!! Mrs Magee's House.' One day it may be the Baker family's house."

Above:
Emily Baker looks over the snowy landscape with St. Michael & All Angels Church visible.

1. The Baker family, from the left: Katie, Angela, Kevin, & Emily.

2. Emily Baker with young geese & surrogate mother.

3. Kevin Baket and canine friends.

 EW HOUSE

Dick and Hilary Hawker bought the Stud Farm in 1965 from H. Knight (Huntley) Ltd of Yew Tree Farm, Huntley. The company had owned the farm for three years, since they bought it from the Salesian Order in 1962 for £30,000 plus £600 stamp duty. The farm had been used as part of the Agricultural School run by the Salesians (Volume 2) since the Blaisdon Estate was sold in 1935. The farm had then been purchased for £9,200 plus stamp duty of £92.

Above: New House in 2012.
Below: New House In 1965.

Hilary Hawker continues:

"We moved to Blaisdon in 1965. We had been dairy farming in South Gloucestershire but the M4 was built on

part of it and we wanted a more rural position. The first Severn crossing had not been completed, so none of our friends knew anything about The Forest of Dean and it was thought to be quite a wild place!

The Stud Farm had two houses on it. The old house had been split into two flats, which were not completed. So we moved into the new house, which had been built by the previous owner of the farm two years earlier but had never been lived in. This was good for us as our first farmhouse was large and cold with a leaking roof, so a modern weatherproof house felt like luxury. Although we owned the farm for many years, we never actually spent a night sleeping in the original farmhouse. Our son, Michael, was born in 1967 and daughter, Louise, in 1969.

1.View over New House & Stud Farm to the River Severn.(2012)

2. Dick Hawker, Snow Warden! (1988)

3. 4. 5. 6. Silage making around Stud Farm. (1988)

7. Milking parlour Stud Farm.

In 1965 we milked about 50 cows and had 200 to 300 laying hens in deep litter and by 2000 we milked about 150 cows but no other livestock. In the early days we grew corn but in later years concentrated on growing grass, mainly for silage. David Brown was already working on the farm and he stayed with us for thirty five years, until we retired in 2000.

The old farmhouse on Stud Farm had two flats. Roger and Hilary Etherington lived in the bottom one for over eighteen years. The top one was let to various people. David and Pauline Brown moved in. After they moved to Stanley Lodge, Mike and Rosemary Wagstaff had it for several years and son Michael and family lived in the bottom flat. Lynne and Nigel Hogg and Roger and Gail Jones moved in while their houses were being refurbished. Steve and Jean Waters also had a caravan at the farm, for the same reason. As Michael's family grew, we made it back into one house. During this time we found a very large inglenook fireplace and two bread ovens.

Above:
The 'Oldest Residents' in Blaisdon 2012,
Rosemary Wagstaff & Dick Hawker.
Below;
Flash floods cover New House Garden but not, thankfully, the house. Dick Hawker & Harvey play in the water.

Ruth and John Magee were neighbours at 'Sharon' and were very helpful in giving us local information. After John died, Ruth came shopping with me. She was always waiting for me at the top of the farm drive. She was never late!!

In 1965 we had a mobile grocer, butcher, baker, greengrocer, fish man and chemist. The Post Office was still open at the Old Post Office but soon moved up to St. Michael's Cottage and was run by Mr and Mrs Keating for a short time before being closed completely. There was a very basic shop at Parkside but that soon closed.

We used to visit Bertie and Mrs. Buckett at Stanley Lodge. There was no road so we had to wear Wellingtons. We were given bread and cheese and told to help ourselves to sherry. They played the piano and sang old-fashioned songs to us. One of her last outings was to the village fete, which was in our garden and paddock.

On retirement we stayed in the same house but as it was no longer

1

2

3

4

5

The Hawker Family:
1. Louise, left & Mike.
2. Louise & chickens.
3. Mike taking a tea break on the farm.
4. Dick, Hilary & Louise celebrate Christmas.
5. Louise.

284

The Hawker family:
1. Dick & Hilary with grandchildren Charlie, left, & Poppy.
2. Dick with grandchildren Adam & Chantelle.
3. Great grandchild Skye.
3. Adam & Chantel with mum Mandy, at Louise's wedding.

connected to the farm, we changed the name from The Stud Farmhouse to New House. The original name of The Stud Farm, before 1900 was New House Farm, so we have gone back to the original name.

Dick was church warden for many years and mowed part of the churchyard until 2012. He was also snow warden. Many children in the village thought that he could order snow for them. The roads were usually kept clear by the council so that the milk lorry could get in.

Hilary belonged to Blaisdon WI until it closed and was President for two years. Dick is eighty and I am seventy and we are enjoying our retirement in Blaisdon"

Louise Stoddart (nee Hawker) arrived in Blaisdon in October 1969, growing up in the village and only moving for college and work in 2002. Now married to Nick and with twins Charlie and Poppy, she remains a frequent visitor saying:

Michael & Lin Hawker, just married in Blaisdon church.

"My heart is in Blaisdon and the village will always be home. I grew up in The New House, then part of Stud Farm. My earliest memories are playing outside beneath the carport, bathing my dolls in a toy bath. The area covered by the carport is now built on and is occupied by what is still called the playroom, though it is now used by my mum for her computer and photographic work. There used to be an old oak tree in the garden. Dad hung some old tyres from ropes, which we used as swings, which were

very popular with all. They seemed much more exciting than an ordinary swing! I was allowed to walk down the field to the farm as long as there were no cows in the field. Neil Dunbar, Chris Lilley, Mike and I turned my old pram into a go-cart. This we raced down the main farm driveway, getting up a decent turn of speed.

I started my education at Brightlands in Newnham from 1974-80. I then went onto Selwyn School in Gloucester before training in health care and child care and, later in social care. I also seemed to have worked almost everywhere in the village, first as a baby-sitter, then I helped out on the farm as needed; milking, cleaning the parlour, silage and hay-making and tractor driving. I've also been decorating for Lee Barrett, worked as a plumber's mate for Roger Allen and in the Red Hart as a waitress and barmaid.

Stud Farm Christmas parties at The Red Hart were a fixture for many years, my contribution being making the mince pies. Originally they were for those who worked on the farm. Then it was extended to those living on the farm and then to those who had lent a hand during the year, doing such things as moving cattle and sheep through the village. This was always fun as the animals always wanted to go where they shouldn't, namely people's gardens. Such was the popularity of our Christmas parties that people always seemed to be looking for ways to help out even if we weren't aware that we needed help in the first place!

Flood parties also featured. As the village is situated on a hillside, there can be a lot of water running through the village when it rains hard. Longhope Brook has also been known to break its banks. When houses are threatened, all available hands arrive to help, moving furniture where necessary and holding the water back where possible. Afterwards, a party would be held to thank the helpers.

The farm equipment came into its own during winters with heavy snowfall, especially in1981-2. With no way out of the village for ordinary cars, we used the tractor and trailer to reach homes, dug a path to their door and gave them some farm milk. At the time there were quite a few elderly folk in the village, so we were able to dig them paths around their houses to give them some access to the outside. Whenever the snow was deep enough, David and Pauline Brown would arrive with tin trays and heavy-duty plastic bags to use as sledges, sliding down the fields. When we got a proper sledge, Mike would pull it through the snow behind a quad-bike.

Although I was christened at Flaxley church and confirmed at Westbury, Blaisdon is my special church. Nick and I were married there and our first son, Edgar is buried near the west door. Our twins were christened there in August 2012. I also learnt to bell-ring when I was 17-18 with the other 'originals,' Lynne, Pat and Rita. John and Vick

Nick & Louise Stoddart walk down the aisle in Blaisdon Church.

Gibson came from Westbury-on-Severn to teach us. Dad originally came to watch but after six months, decided to join in and Frank Baylis also started then. I love bell-ringing and have rung bells all over the country.

During my teens and early twenties, there seemed to be a great atmosphere in the village, with lots going on and everybody joining in. There were village parties and cheese and wines, after which, I have had to walk people home and sometimes help them to bed! We had farm barbecues, summer or winter and whatever the weather. Blankets and sleeping bags were provided if it got chilly and a standard light was sometimes produced as the evening grew darker. Vic Woodman grew the best strawberries and raspberries, to which we all went to 'pick-your-own'.

When I was married, Ceri Evans was unable to come due to illness. Shortly afterwards, Rosemary Wagstaff arranged for a repeat wedding meal at her house so Ceri wouldn't feel left out. We were to come in whatever clothes we wore on the day, so I was in my wedding dress. Ceri arrived…In his pyjamas!! This was not a village first though. Some years earlier, Doug Inger worked through Christmas, so a group of us held an alternative Christmas lunch in midsummer just for Doug. This came complete with turkey, Christmas pud, a Christmas tree and a blazing fire despite bright sunshine outside."

Four generations of the Hawker family celebrate Dick's 80th birthday.
From the left:
Hilary, Michael, Louise holding Charlie, Dick, Chantel holding daughter Skye, Adam, Lin (Michael's wife),
Nick Stoddart (Louise's husband) holding Poppy. Also Harvey the dog.
(2012)

STUD FARM

Following the sale of Stud Farm in 1962 by the Salesian School at Blaisdon Hall (Volume 1) and the subsequent sale of its herd of cattle, the farm was owned briefly by H. Knight (Huntley) Ltd before passing to Dick and Hilary Hawker. It was run as a dairy farm till they sold it in 2000. At this time, the land sold with the farm amounted to 194.86 acres (78.751 Hectares). The herd of Holstein Friesian cattle was also sold at this time.

Above:
Stud Farm in 2012.
Below left:
A snowy Stud Farm prior to conversion of outbuildinngs.
Below right:
Sale particulars for the Friesian Herd owned by the Salesian School, Blaisdon in 1962.

SALESIAN CHOOL, BLAISDON, LONGHOPE
Adjoining the Hatley to Westbury-on-Severn Road. Within 2 miles of Loghope, Huntley and Westbury-on-Severn.

CATALOGUE OF

102
DAIRY AND STORE CATTLE
including the ENTIRE
BLAISDON HERD
OF
Dehorned BRITISH FRIESIANS

Comprising 24 Pedigree and S.R. Cows and Heifers in milk, 10 younger Heifers, 29 Non Pedigree Cows and 20 younger Heifers, also 12 Friesian Steers and 7 Aberdeen Angus Steers and Heifers

2 TRACTORS
Ferguson 35 and T.E.A.

IMPLEMENTS AND MACHINERY
including Ferguson Ploughs, Cultivator, Seed Drill, Zig-zag Harrows, Mower, Crop Sprayer, Vicon Lely Acrobat, Bamford Forage Harvester, 4 ton FYM Spreader, Cambridge Rolls, Trailers, Disc Harrows, Concrete Rollers, Cattle Yokes, etc.

which

BRUTON, KNOWLES & CO.

are instructed by the Rector of the Salesian School (Father Higgins)

TO SELL BY AUCTION ON

FRIDAY, 14th SEPTEMBER, 1962
at 12 Noon
The Pedigree and S.R. Cattle will be sold under the Auction Sale Rules of the B.F.C.S.
LICENSED CATERER WILL BE IN ATTENDANCE
Further details from the Auctioneers, Gloucester Market. Tel. 25717.

An Aerial view of Stud Farm in 1971.
(R.Etherington)
Right:
One of the Stud Farm's bulls looks over the fence.
(J. Higgins)

The Stud Farm chapel when the Salesian school owned the farm.
(1968)
(Father Sean Murray)

Dick and Hilary decided to make the recently built New House their home. The original farmhouse, complete with the small chapel used by the Salesians was converted into 2 flats, one on the ground floor, the other upstairs. Over the years there were many occupiers of the flats. Many village residents were grateful to stay at Stud Farm when building work on their houses deprived them of basic facilities at home.

Whilst most of those stayed for a few months at most, there were other residents who stayed longer. Rosemary and Mike Wagstaff (Nettlestones) used the upstairs flat for 10 years when they lived at Windsor. However, the record for longevity is held by Roger and Hilary Etherington who occupied the ground floor flat for over seventeen years.

Roger Etherington continues:

"Some twenty years before moving into the Stud Farm, I had arrived in Blaisdon seated upon the crossbar of my father's bike. Cedric had shallots to plant in the cottage garden prior to our moving into The Forge, the house he was about to rent from a local farmer.

We as a family were about to retreat into the countryside from wartime London, with the constant threat of enemy bombs. We would possibly never have chosen Blaisdon had we known that a few months earlier a German aircraft had delivered several bombs across the village, cratering the potato fields and demolishing the little humpback bridge over the village brook. So, not knowing, we came anyway and I'm glad we did. Blaisdon for so many others and us was always going to be special.

On this first day, it looked very pretty among its white blossoming fruit trees and up a lovely winding path through the woods spangled with primroses and starred with wood anemones.

Now, returning in the late spring of 1966 to stay on a farm, still called The Stud farm from the old estate days but now home to a herd of Friesian cows. With the permission of farmer Dick Hawker we were able to rent the lower floor of the old farmhouse for a few months at least. Eventually, we stayed for around seventeen years!

For Hilary and myself, bringing up children on a farm was an experience to savour. I'm sure they look back on that time with affection too.

The village school, which had been such a big part of my childhood, was closed, leaving a large space in the heart of the village. However, the Catholic teaching college at Blaisdon Hall continued, though in a different direction. This meant that there wasn't the same interaction between

1

3

2

4

1. Hilary & Jamie Etherington with Marian (Hilary's sister) holding Annabel.
2. Hilary Etherington.
3. Hilary & Jamie Etherington with Annabel in the pram.
4. Jamie & Annabel Etherington.

boys and village that there had been in my own childhood days. In the post war years, the Hall was a training college for young theologians as well as a boys' school, having its own cadet force with manoeuvres taking place in the grounds. A strange conflict of interest no doubt but of little concern to we village lads who collected the spent cartridge cases left lying around under trees that had hidden the camouflaged soldiers. When all had returned to barracks, we village boys moved in and collected our trophies, stuffing the still warm cases into our pockets. Although all make believe and firing only blanks, life in the village could never be as exciting for my own children.

They never to the best of my knowledge were able to swim across the old reservoir up in the woods, pushing out to the centre on a raft of old oil drums. They weren't able to jump across the twenty foot drop through which water from the millpond fell into the village brook. I hope too they never pushed large boulders onto migrating eels as they emerged from the tunnel under the railway embankment, upon which we trespassed carelessly, not heeding the warning signs that promised fines of forty shillings or six months in gaol. To the best of my knowledge our children experienced none of the thrills of village life in the 1960s when the village seemed a lot safer. The large slurry pit on the farm was always a concern but stern warnings prevailed.

Above: Inglenook fireplace in the Stud Farm.
Below: Interior view of the former chapel.

The farmhouse had altered little since it was used as part of the farming school run for the boys at Blaisdon Hall until the farms were sold in 1964. The house had its own chapel, which is now a living room with a fireplace where the altar once stood.

Now, along with the farm boys, the steam trains, the stand of elm trees in front of the church, the tall row of Lombardy poplars along the eastern boundary, as high as steeples, and much else besides, exist only in the memory and recollections of those of us lucky enough to live in this most special of villages."

Another family that lived on Stud farm were Roger and Gail Jones, plus sons, Simon and Christopher. They now live on The Slad, opposite Nottwood Hill but prior to this occupied the top flat on the farm.

Roger Jones continues:

"My paternal grandparents lived at Northwood Green and my grandfather was the head gamekeeper for Blaisdon Hall, but unfortunately died in his early forties, in 1916. This meant that granny had to move to Nottwood Hill with 6 children. My grandparents are buried in Blaisdon Church, amongst other Jones relatives. Also, there are two great uncles names on the Blaisdon war memorial, hence my close attachment to Blaisdon.

In 1940, after a bombing raid, I was evacuated to granny's cottage, which was at The Slad, Little London, Longhope. I was 18 months old and I continued to live with her until she died when I was fifteen years old.

Granny and I often visited Blaisdon to tend the graves and occasionally she would have a quick port and lemon at The Red Hart, sustenance for the walk back up to The Slad. In 1953 she died and I returned to my parents, to live the urban life in Bristol. On weekends, I regularly cycled the one hundred mile round trip from Bristol to Longhope to visit friends and relatives. In 1955 I moved back into lodgings at Hinders corner, but in 1957 was summoned to join the army.

In 1991, I again returned to Blaisdon with my wife Gail and sons, Simon (10) and Christopher (8). We were about to live the dream of building our 'house on the hill', but needed to live somewhere in the meantime. The top flat at Stud Farm became our temporary home. We ended up staying there for 22 months with Dick and Hilary Hawker being our landlords, with their son Michael and family living in the ground floor flat.

We had a collie pup, May, whilst at Top Flat and she used to make a nuisance of herself by regularly taking a drink of milk from the calves feeding buckets. The cowmen were not amused and she would be chased away with the yard broom. As a result, she developed a lifelong dislike of men in dark overalls and once we had moved to Rose Cottage no one wearing overalls would be allowed through the gate!

Simon and Christopher roamed wild on the farm, but the best story is the day the cows were let out of their winter quarters in the spring of 1992. We were all positioned in the field to help with this annual event. We had the dogs with us and realised that they needed to be on leads. As there was no sign of the cows, Christopher decided to run

across the field to get the leads from Top Flat.

At that moment the cows appeared and as anyone will know, cows are very energetic when let out. They literally run and jump for joy at the prospect of freedom and fresh grazing. Everyone screamed at Chris to get out of the way and poor Dick Hawker nearly had a heart attack. Christopher, not known for his speed, certainly ran for his life that day."

The new millennium marked the start of a new phase in the history of The Stud Farm when the Rich family moved there in 2000. Since then the farm has been run by brothers Ben, Nat and Laurence with support from their father, Don.

Don Rich continues:

"I come from a Somerset family of farmers. Before moving to Blaisdon I had been living and farming in nearby Churcham. I moved to Churcham at the age of 19, in 1959. I joined the local branch of the Young Farmers as a way of getting to know the local younger folk. It was not long before I met Ann, a local girl from High Leadon and it was not too long before she became my wife.

Above:
Gail & Roger Jones.
(Millenium eve 1999)
Left & Below:
Simon & Christopher
Jones on Stud Farm.

Our children are Ben (45), Nat (42), Laurence (40) and Vanessa (38). Ben is married to Anna and they have 3 children, Tom (9), Max (6), and Abbie (5). Laurence and partner Jo have a son, Stanley, who was born in March 2012. Vanessa is married to Gareth and their children are Rosie (5) and Austin (3)."

Front & back views of the Stud Farm house. The chapel protrudes from the back in the lower view.

Left:
Post-conversion of dairy
& milking parlour
showing the new house
& cottages in 2011.

Lower Left:
Dairy & milking parlour
prior to conversion.

Below:
The next generation of
the Rich family get to
work on the farm.

Ben and Anna Rich continue:

"Although Don had been involved in dairy farming for over 30 years, when we moved here. Ben, Nat and Laurence decided that they would take the farm in a different direction. The farm now supports a rotation of crops such as wheat, maize, grass, fodder beat, hay and haylage, together with raising young dairy heifers till they are ready to sell for milking.

We have made quite a few changes to the buildings as well. Don and Ann live in the original farmhouse, which has had quite a lot of work done inside, making the most of features such as the beautiful inglenook. In 2007, the old dairy was converted into a lovely house for us. Behind this the original buildings have been replaced by 3 holiday cottages, which are run by Anna. Ben's brothers don't live on the farm. Nat is currently in Tibberton and Laurence in Flaxley, though both are fully involved in running the farm. Laurence and Jo also have their own business, 'Helpful Careers Co.'

We were at school together and, afterwards, Anna went on to the Royal Agricultural College, Cirencester to study Land Management. Anna puts this to good use on the farm. Anna was brought up in Gloucester and moving to the quiet of Blaisdon was a bit of a shock for a town-girl. Now, however, she loves it, as long as she has her car to get around.

Ben has loved Blaisdon since the day he moved in. When he was doing some contract work on Stud Farm 20 years ago, he remembers thinking how lovely it was out on the fields in the peace and quiet of the early evening. He

thought how lovely it would be to live in such a wonderful place. Little did he know that that the opportunity to fulfil his dream would arise and he can't believe his luck."

Ben and Anna's 3 children also had thoughts about where they live.

First, **Tom Rich** says:

"I like being the oldest and being able to tell my brother and sister what to do. I like visiting the pub with my parents. My brother and I have motorbikes that we can ride on the farm. I am also allowed to move bales with the tractor. When I am older I would like to join the army."

Younger brother, **Max Rich** says:

"I want to stay on the farm when I get older and work with my dad. I love playing tennis and biking around the farm. Once, when I was playing tennis in the rain, I was told to come inside. I said that it was alright as I was playing and having a shower at the same time!"

Abbie Rich, who was born during the alterations on the farm, says:

" I would like a pony to ride on the farm with my mummy."

In 2011, as the Rich family moved into their second decade at Stud Farm, the whole family gathered together on the farm to celebrate Don's 70th birthday.

The Rich family celebrate Don's 70th birthday:
Top row from left: Vanessa, Gareth, Austin, Laurence, Jo.
Middle row from left: Anna. Ben, Max, Don, Ann, Nat, Tom.
Front row from left: Rosie, Abbie.
(2011)

Stud Farm families:
From the left,
Ann Rich, Hilary Hawker, Dick Hawker, Don Rich.

STANLEY LODGE

Bertie Buckett (Volume 2) continued to live at Stanley Lodge with his mother until her death in 1973 and then on his own till increasing frailty necessitated a move to Westbury Court Residential Home. Until then, he continued to play an active part in village events and playing the organ at church. He died at Gloucester Royal Hospital in 1987, aged seventy eight. Dick Hawker of Stud Farm rented Bertie's land and subsequently bought the land and Stanley Lodge. The house was then bought by David and Pauline Brown and they continue to live there.

Above:
Stanley Lodge in 2012.
Below:
Bertie Buckett with Myra Royall & Dick Hawker at a Blaisdon Plum Festival..

David Brown:

"I lived in Vectis as a child, going to the village school. I count 22nd February 1965 as one of the best days of my life. I left school and went to earn a living. For a few months I worked for Bert Knight at Stud Farm. When Dick Hawker bought the farm, I continued working for him until he retired from farming thirty five years later.

So much has changed in those thirty five years. We used to cut hedges, dig ditches and fruit picking, all done by hand. Perhaps the biggest change of all though is the hairstyles!

Far Left;
David Brown, left, &
David Lilley of School
House.

Left:
Pauline Brown.

Looking back, bell ringing and Flaxley Youth Club were the highlights of the week. In 1967, ballroom dancing started in the Village Hall, a hobby that was perhaps one of the most enjoyable experiences of my life.

I believe the best events the village held over the years were the Plum Festivals. The whole village pulled together, everyone was involved and we had a wonderful response from the visitors"

Pauline Brown:

"Coming to Blaisdon in 1975 was quite a cultural shock. Having come out from a town the slow pace of life contrasted with the bustle of the town. However, in no time at all I had been made to feel welcome by the locals and soon felt part of the village and its ways, gin parties, flood parties, snow parties, you name it and we had a party!

Pretty soon after arrival I was seconded into the local WI Something I wouldn't have dreamed of a little while

before. Wasn't that for older women? First task, bake some scones for a competition next week. Lo and behold one week later and I won the scone competition! Now I really was a WIer. Sorry to Miss Smith who I was told ALWAYS won the scone competition.

Plum festivals, fetes, plays at Blaisdon Hall, rounders teams that the whole village joined in, we had plenty of things to join in. With David working and us initially living at Stud Farm there was plenty to keep us busy with all the comings and goings. Half the village at some time or other took up residence outside at the farm!

Then, in 1981, we moved up to Stanley Lodge and began the renovations that have been going on ever since and we hope will finish by Christmas 2012."

Niki Janneh (nee Brown):

"Growing up in Blaisdon was a privilege for me and living at Stanley Lodge was a dream come true.

Robert Brown, Niki Janneh & Pauline Brown.

For me as a child, Blaisdon offered a community that has been like an extended family; they have grown with me as I have grown with them.

My favourite memory of being a young 'Blaisdoner' has to be carol singing at Christmas. Spending the build up to Christmas travelling around the surrounding villages in Uncle Dick's Land Rover, eating far too many sweets and cakes and having a sneaky alcoholic drink when the adults weren't watching or at least, they pretended they hadn't noticed. Competing with the other kids to make sure the money was dropped into my collection tub and ultimately staying up late, even on Christmas Eve. It to me was like you now only see in films.

I also have very fond memories of the village fetes, plum festivals and Christingles. Everybody from the village joined in and pulled together, making them enjoyable events for visitors that we could all be proud of.

I've watched families come and go from Blaisdon over the years. My generation of kids have grown up and moved on but we all still have a draw back to the village, I'm sure I'm not just speaking for myself, but it's where our hearts are and still many of our parents and Godparents, etc, live there.

The main focal point of the village has to be the Red Hart Pub; it's a place where we all frequent either often or occasionally. With memories ranging from the ladies darts team, which my mum played for, the peacocks in the garden and the ploughman's lunch (only for the hearty) to the now more elegant food and Saturday BBQs, it's had its array of characters behind the bar also.

My dad has put his heart and soul into developing and maintaining Stanley Lodge. It's not a house, it is a warm welcoming family home.

I have been a part of the development of Stanley Lodge from a three bedroom house with a small garden, to what it is now with various additional extensions and buildings sat in acres of farmland and surrounded by a lovely lawn.

Thank goodness for the land surrounding the house as being a country girl and an animal lover, I have buried in the fields everything from our family pets under the old apple tree to field mice in match boxes that our cats Beryl & George (named after our Godparents Beryl & George Austin from the Archway) brought home.

If you asked a child to draw a house, they would draw

1

2

4

3

1. From the left:
Niki, Ben, Robert & David Brown.

2. An impressive snowman with Ben
& Niki Brown, Plus Honey.

3. David Brown with Ben in the
tractor.

4. Bonfire night with, from the left:
Niki, David, Robert & Ben Brown,
Jill & Andrew Rodgett.

Max Janneh.

Above;
A penny for the Guy?
With Ben, left, Niki & Rob Brown.
Below:
The Brown family, from the left,
David, Rob, Ben, Niki with Pauline, sitting.

something very similar to Stanley Lodge and that to me says Stanley Lodge is what every child feels a house should be like; to me, all kids draw my home.

I now have a son of my own, Max who is four years old. Stanley Lodge is more of a home to him than anywhere else.

We visit every day, as I want Max to enjoy the freedom and being able to do what I did as a child.

I love to sit in the garden and watch Max play like I used to watch Rob playing. Pushing tractors around, making boxes into farm buildings and using dad's cut grass to replicate a silage pit.

For as long as possible, Max will have the upbringing that I had in Blaisdon and Stanley Lodge. He can enjoy being a child and playing children's adventure games. I hope when he grows up he will look back at Blaisdon and realise how lucky he was to have grown up in such a perfect home & village, like I have done."

Niki & Brian
wedding, 2012.

From the left,
Ben Brown, Brian &
Niki Janneh, Robert,
Pauline & David
Brown, with Max
Janneh in front.
(H. Hawker)

1 STANLEY COTTAGES

1 Stanley Cottages,
with the recent extension nearest the camera.

Following the ownership of the Green family (Volume 2), Mr and Mrs Hyett acquired No. 1 Stanley Cottages in the 1970s and remained there until the current owner moved in in December 1994. Originally Mr John Robert Dyke and Miss Nathalie Hélène Mignotte purchased the house although Nathalie is now the sole owner of the property.

Nathalie Mignotte continues:

"We hadn't properly moved into Stanley Cottages and I was standing in the front room cleaning the house, when I saw this gentleman coming up the front path with two Labradors. As he reached the opened window, he stopped and said, 'Good afternoon, my name is Dick Hawker and my wife will not forgive me if I don't find out who our new neighbours are.' The ice was broken.

John and I moved from Cheltenham to Blaisdon and commuted to work to, what was then, Eagle Star Insurance in Bishop's Cleeve. In 1996, I returned to studying, qualifying as a horticulturist. This was followed by a lecturing post at Hartpury College, eventually becoming the Academic Manager for the horticulture department. I

left the post in 2002 to move abroad. On our return, in 2004, I went back to part-time lecturing and then moved on to a full-time job in a garden centre. John Dyke left Blaisdon in 2006.

Another very important current resident at No. 1 Stanley Cottage is Blacky, my four-legged cat who has been living here for the past 17½ years.

One day, in early 1995, whilst gardening in the front garden, I discovered a French coin dating from the First World War which, being French I found quite a coincidence.

Most of the memories I have of my life, so far, in the cottage mainly relate to the kindness and friendship I have

with my neighbours. In 2002, when we moved abroad for a couple of years, we wanted to keep the house. This was only made possible because of Jean and Peter Adams who looked after the house and the cats while we were away.

In 2005, we built an extension to the house, which allowed for more living space and has allowed me to have my family over to visit and stay with me.

The cottage is where I have lived the longest although I still have a long way to catch up with some other residents of the village! The main thing I would like to say is that I have lived in and travelled to quite a few places, however, when I am being asked whether I go home often, meaning France, I reply that I go home every day, as I look on Blaisdon as my real home."

Top:
Neighbours & friends,
Nathalie Mignotte, right, & Jean Adams.
Above: Nos 1 & 2 Stanley Cottages.

2 STANLEY COTTAGES

Peter and Jean Adams, together with Shelley, their daughter, live in 2, Stanley Cottages:

"We moved to Stanley Cottage in April 1982 from Steam Mills in the Forest of Dean with our children Sebastian, aged 9, and Shelley, aged 6.

Stanley Cottage had been used by the Salesians from Blaisdon Hall as two flats. The upstairs was accessed from the front door. The alcove in the front bedroom had been made into a small kitchen with cooker and sink. The downstairs entry was by the back door, which had been enclosed by a roof to contain the wash-house, coal-shed and toilet. The old washroom had a sink and cooker in it. In the kitchen, the old pantry had been made into a shower room and the front room was used as a bedroom.

The garden was completely overgrown, although we did find some plants surviving along with the plum and apple trees.

Our neighbours were Alan and Lynda Hyett with his two sons, Derek and Darren. The boys were a little older than Sebastian. They were always ready to help with anything we were doing and the boys had good snowball fights in the winters.

No. 2 Stanley Cottages.
(2012)

We knew Shirley and Gary Yemm from Blaisdon Lane Nursery up the lane, as they had lived in Steam Mills while their bungalow was being built and the children had gone to school together.

In Blaisdon, Sebastian and Shelley went to nearby Hopes Hill School with Andrew, Rachel and Denise Yemm. They then went on to Dene Magna, Mitcheldean. Seb then went to Royal Forest of Dean College and Greenwich University where he studied Landscape Architecture. He is now in the family firm, Sports Grange Forestry, with his father.

Shelley studied catering at the RFOD College and works in the Red Hart.

Peter was a motor mechanic in a garage in Mitcheldean when we moved here but set up the business with his brother, who has retired when Seb joined the company. They undertake forestry work as well as land maintenance in schools etc around the Forest area.

I worked at Blaisdon Hall when it was a school for 6 years until it closed, enjoying the family atmosphere created by the Fathers, carers and teachers for the boys.

We have always enjoyed joining in with the many village events such as the fetes, plum festival, cheese and wines with auctions, carol singing and the relatively new christmas markets.

In 2000 we purchased some land across the back of the garden from Mr and Mrs Hawker of Stud Farm. This enabled us after much excavating of soil to create a vehicle access to the rear of the garden and to construct a garage.

The remainder of the land has been planted as a wild flower meadow and orchard, adding to our enjoyment of living at Stanley Cottage.

When we moved here, we had milk delivered every day and the baker came twice a week. We get neither of these now. Also, since Stud Farm moved out of dairy farming, we don't hear the cows being got in for milking in the early hours."

Pete Adams undertaking the mammoth excavations required to create vehicle access behind the cottage.

1. Seb & Shelley with kittens.

2. Pete & Jean Adams.

3. Seb & Shelley warm their feet in the Rayburn.

4. Seb & Shelley asleep on the garden hammock.

STANLEY HOUSE

Jill and Andrew Rodgett moved into Stanley House in July 1985:

"We soon found out that a lot of remedial work needed doing whilst endeavouring to discover the underlying original structure of the house. Now, twenty five years later, the house is undergoing major restoration work with fresh oak replacing the rotten north facing gable end and readying the building for the next three hundred years. Stanley House also enjoys full insulation for the first time, having been recently reroofed.

Stanley Cottage in 2012.

For our daughters, Lara and Francesca, Blaisdon has meant parties in the village hall and in the garden at home. On one occasion we had some sixty people staying over in tents scattered around the lawns and, of course, fireworks. Jill had to ask for the music to be turned down at 1am, 2am and 4am. After that we gave up!! The kitchen looked like a scene from the Somme. Travel to schools meant either a bus ride to Gloucester or a lift from parents. Passing driving tests was a priority!

Most years, we have been running the Bottle Stall at the village fete. We have enjoyed participating in the harvest supper and annual auction raising funds for the church and village hall.

Life as a local general practitioner involved Jill being an out of hours messenger service for the twenty years. This ceased in 2005 when responsibility for out of hours patient care was taken over by the Gloucestershire Primary Care Trust. Many patients have become well known over time!"

Andrew's memories continue:

"Once, when I was on call for medical emergencies, I was called to the red Hart at 11.30pm, only to find a 'lock-in' behind the closed curtains. A patient had collapsed in the bar, most likely due to alcohol intake. I was offered a pint whilst I was there but had to decline as I was on duty throughout the night.

At the Red Hart, Johnny Dunbar's ploughmen's lunches

1. Exposing the inglenook are David Brown, Andrew Rodgett, Jill Rodgett & Pauline Brown.(1985)

2. & 3. The new oak beams in place in the north end of Stanley House.(2012)

4. Exploring the well at the front of Stanley House. (1985)

5. Internal roof timbers.(2012)

6. Bert Daniell mowing the lawn.(1988)

7. The gardens some years later.

were legendary, consisting of half a loaf of bread, a large wedge of cheese and pickled or raw onion. My elderly patients would be lined up on a bench in the bar, drinking cider from china mugs and playing the spoons.

An early and exciting piece of renovation we did in the house was to reveal a large inglenook fireplace that had been covered over for many years. With the help of neighbours, Pauline and David Brown, we removed twelve tons of rubble to reveal it in its splendid glory.

I used to enjoy walking across Stanley Field to go pheasant shooting in Ley Park with our flat coat retrievers, Oscar and Bruno.

There is a well in the garden and we were bursting with curiosity to find out if there was anything of interest in the bottom of it. David Brown and I worked out he could lower me down on a rope attached to the tractor. Whilst we were planning this, one of the Salesian Brothers came along and asked if we had checked for gas? At this point, we decided to get the experts in and the Forest of Dean Caving Club subsequently descended into the depths. Sadly, no treasure was discovered.

Behind Stanley House there used to be a large field of blackcurrant bushes. Sadly, with the collapse of the fruit market some years ago, the E.U. offered grants to remove orchards and they were all grubbed out.

Having kept an eye on the neighbouring fields for cows

Andrew & Jill Rodgett.

calving, we were nominated by Dick Hawker and David Brown as honorary herdsman and woman."

Lara Rodgett adds her own memories:

"Growing up in Blaisdon, all my childhood memories seem to be associated with being outside in the fresh air and playing with my sister, Francesca and friends, Eleanor and Ian Waters, Robert and Ben Brown. In winter, we would toboggan in the fields behind the house with Rob and Ben. Autumn would find us with Ian and Eleanor, collecting as many conkers as we could carry from the trees around Blaisdon Hall. Hot summer's days would mean getting out the builders membrane sheets of plastic and making water slides with a bit of Fairy Liquid added to the stream of water to give extra slide. A special treat was to go to the Tan House and use the swimming pool, again best on warm, sunny days. However warm the day was though, Blaisdon church always seemed to be cold, especially when having to quietly sit through a sermon!

Animals were always part of our life. We would take our dogs, Oscar and Bruno down to the stream with Eleanor and Ian and all of us would come home soaked to the skin. The Waters had 2 pigs that we would visit and feed them apples. Sometimes, we would go down to see the cows being milked at Stud Farm and 'helping' to feed the calves. Playing on the big bales of hay was fun too."

2

3

4

5

1

6

7

8

The Rodgett family:

1. Andrew.   2. Andrew, Francesca & Jill.
3. Andrew, Jill & Lara.   4. Andrew's Medical Practice party.
5. Jill & Francesca.   6. Lara & Jill undertake building work.
                        7. Lara.
        8. Jill & Francesca with Jill's parents, Enid & Phil Clarke.

BRICKHOUSE FARM

Tom and Maggie Board (Volume 2) lived in Brickhouse Farm for many years. It is now split into two houses. Looking from the road, the left side has been the home of Mike and Kirsty Priest since 2002. Paul Williams lives in the other half of the building.

Above & left: Brickhouse Farm.

BRAMBLE ORCHARD

Planning Permission for the new house now known as Bramble Orchard but then called Blaisdon Lane Nurseries was submitted in October 1973 by Gary Yemm then of Steam Mills, Cinderford. Once the house was built, he and Shirley Yemm, his wife, moved into the house and ran a business growing fruit and vegetables in the extensive greenhouses they erected on the land behind the house. Paul and Penny Harris bought the property from Shirley Yemm, who was then divorced from Gary, and her son Andrew and twin daughters Rachael and Denise.

Above:
Bramble Orchard in 2012.
Below:
Blaisdon Lane Nurseries in 2001.

Paul and Penny Harris continue:

"We moved into Blaisdon Lane Nurseries in December 2001 and because there was also a Blaisdon Nurseries in the village, we renamed it Bramble Orchard. We purchased a lovely modern bungalow, together with about half an acre of glasshouses and buildings for the production of tomatoes, runner beans with Majorie's Seedling plum trees in the orchard beyond. These had obviously been a hive of busy productivity in their heyday. Sadly the glasshouses were now in a state of disrepair. We set about clearing the brambles from the orchard and pulling down the greenhouses that were more or less being held up by the brambles. We disposed of over six hundred rotten bean

sticks! Roger Keyse made use of a redundant boiler, pipes, glass and other items. We were told that residents from the village could see our bonfire on returning from Christmas shopping in Gloucester and remarked that they thought Blaisdon was on fire! We repaired the leaking garage roof and put a new dining room on the back and generally brought the bungalow up to date.

Prior to moving here we lived for 29 years in neighbouring Northwood Green where we had brought up our two boys, Stephen and Gordon, who attended Westbury-on-Severn School and then Dene Magna in the 1970s and 80s with several other children from Blaisdon. Penny has spent all her life within the farming community in nearby Ley Lane, Minsterworth and Northwood Green, playing in Ley Park. She remembers some of the older characters from the previous Blaisdon book and attended Abenhall Secondary School in the 1960s with a few of the younger ones.

Having given up dairy farming in 1999, we wanted to keep our roots in the locality where we have friends and family but enjoy an easier way of life. So we brought with us a small flock of sheep for the extra acres we purchased from Olive Davies from Huntley Hill, adjoining our orchard. There is a lovely view from the top of the hill and Paul, with friend Heather Harrington of Prospect House, installed a 'contemplation' seat there for all to enjoy the views of Gloucestershire and beyond after a walk in Blaisdon Wood.

We have enjoyed our 10 years at Bramble Orchard, meeting new friends and neighbours and although Paul is still working, we hope to spend our retirement here."

Top:
The glasshouse from the nursery, now demolished.
Centre:
Rear view of Bramble Orchard during the building of the extension.
Bottom:
Front view during same building works.

IONA

Shirley Brickel and her family moved from Huntley to Iona in 1978 and stayed there till 1984, when she moved to Cherry Rise, also in Blaisdon. The house was sold to the Boyles family, Richard, Zoë and Jeremy. ***Zoë Boyles*** continues:

"We first saw Iona on a cold January day when the then owner, Mrs Shirley Brickel, showed us around and straight away we recognised what a wonderful place this would be to live and bring up our son, Jeremy. We moved from

Above; Iona following modernisation.
Below: Iona in 2002.

our old home in Westbury-on-Severn to Iona on 22nd May 2002 and although it is ten years ago, Richard and I remember the moving day and the run up to it vividly because it was such a roller coaster experience. We had exchanged contracts at the end of April and the moving date was set for 10th May.

Five or six days before the day of the move and surrounded by boxes, our solicitor informed us that the sale had collapsed because the person at the beginning of the chain was unable to proceed. All parties in the chain were now in the uncomfortable position of suing each other because we had gone as far as exchanging contracts. After a 2 week delay all was sorted out and the move for all parties was able to proceed on the 22nd May. Sufficient to say the day of the move was an anxious one, hoping all would go well and so at the end of that day we were completely exhausted.

Our son, Jeremy, was 8 years old at the time of the move and I drove him to St Anthony's School from Westbury in the morning and collected him in the afternoon and brought him back to his new home at Blaisdon. Having had quite a small garden at Westbury, Jeremy found the half acre garden at Iona paradise and it wasn't long before he and his friends had made dens in more than one tree or bush around the garden.

1

The house, although in need of some updating, had a lovely warm feel about it and lots of lovely features like the original pitch pine floors and internal doors and fireplaces. From the moment we first saw Iona and its fabulous location, we recognised the potential it had to make a lovely family home.

Over the last ten years we have completely modernised the inside and outside of the property. One of our favourite aspects of Iona is the garden and the views across the fields to Gloucester. I especially enjoy growing vegetables in my greenhouse and raised beds, and we all have great fun barbecuing with family and friends and playing badminton, cricket or just messing around with a rugby ball.

When we moved to Iona, Richard was the Police Sergeant at Newent and then moved on to be the Inspector for Hester's Way in the Cheltenham area for nearly five years. For the last eighteen months he has been the Forest of Dean Local Policing Area Inspector. I was and still am working as a part-time tutor for what was the Royal Forest

1. Rear of Iona before modernisation.
2. Richard & Jeremy Boyles bricklaying.
3. Richard Boyles on the scaffolding.

of Dean College, now Known as Gloscat, and I recently also started working part-time for Marks and Spencer.

Jeremy moved from St Anthony's Convent School to Sir Thomas Rich's Grammar School and is now an eighteen year old young man who has just finished his A2 exams.

Blaisdon is a fabulous place to live and there are always things going on in the village, which we try to get involved in as much as we can, like the recent Diamond Jubilee celebrations, Summer Fete and our lovely little church. We look forward to many more happy years here."

2

1

3

4

The Boyles family:
1. Zoë, Richard & Ian.
2. Zoë.
3. Jeremy.
4. Richard with a chicken and her first egg!

GREEN COURT

Don Morgan of Oak Field tells the history of the occupants of Green Court, previously known as Ferndale:

"The land that Green Court is built on was originally part of the Blaisdon Hall Estate. Frank Bullock of Nottwood Hill purchased 11.679 acres from Thomas Place of Blaisdon Hall on 21st November 1934.

On 2nd September 1937 Alec Moon of School House, Huntley purchased a plot forty four yards square from Frank Bullock. It is believed that Alec Moon added the house and named it Ferndale. On 29th April 1947 Frederick Brooks, an assistant storekeeper, and his wife Ana purchased Ferndale from Alec Moon. (Volume 2)

They sell on 31st July 1951 to Gerald William Gill a civil servant (Experimental Officer), Norman Leslie Gill (Railway Clerk), and Derrick Jeffery Gill (Electrical Engineer), all previously of Jessamine Cottage, Hinder's Lane, Huntley.

The Gills sell Ferndale to Mrs Alice Dangerfield (Widow) on 30th April 1953. She sells to Mrs Millicent Parrington of 109 Margam Road, Port Talbot, Glam. On 15th

Green Court. (2012)

October 1956.

On 13th May 1965 Ferndale was sold to Gerald James Brobyn, sales manager, of 9a Saint Annals Road, Cinderford.

Mr Nigel Gibbins and Susan Charter bought the house on 13th June 1968 and moved in on their marriage. It was they who changed the name from Ferndale to Green Court. This was an amalgamation of where they lived before, Nigel coming from a farm called Greenway and Susan from Estcourt Road, Gloucester. Nigel was very well known in the area, being an agricultural contractor. His pride and joy was his massive Ford County tractor which he kept in pristine condition. He was able to keep a lot of his equipment at Brickhouse farmhouse and was a great help to us at Oak Field, using his heavy equipment on many occasions.

Nigel's two children, Nicholas and Humphrey were born while they were at Green Court, both being educated at Kings School, Gloucester. Sadly Humphrey was to die at a young age shortly after leaving the area. When Nigel left Green Court in 1986 he had to store all his furniture and worldly possessions while he occupied temporary rented accommodation. In a dreadful twist of fate these were all destroyed when Britannia Warehouse where they were stored on Gloucester Docks was devastated by fire.

On 18th April 1986 the new purchasers were Mr and Mrs C.F. O'Carroll. Chris owned a sports shop in Worcester Street and also organised many road runs in the locality. Bernie, his wife, was a Sister at Gloucester Royal Hospital. They brought up three daughters while at Green Court, the latest being born while living there. It was while here that they enlarged the house into what it is today, by extending out at the back, building a garage and enlarging the upper floor.

Finally on 22nd November 2002 Green Court became the possession of Keith and Sarah Wintle."

Keith and Sarah Wintle take up the story:

"Keith Wintle was born and lived in Bristol until the age of 38. Grandfather was from Newent. Sarah Wintle (nee Giddy) was born in Lichfield and raised in Stroud. We met at a marketing company in Cheltenham and bought Green Court in Blaisdon in 2002. Keith works as an Art Director and Sarah as an Office Manager. We were married

in 2003 in Cheltenham and Connie and Natasha, identical twin girls, were born in 2005 at Gloucester Hospital. We still work in Cheltenham at the same agency, commuting every day. After extensive work to the house to bring it up to scratch, converting the garage into further living space, it is now becoming a very comfortable family home.

Having always lived in the city, when we first moved to Blaisdon we were both struck by how peaceful and tranquil the setting was and each night after returning from working in Cheltenham we began to feel ourselves unwind as we neared the turning to Blaisdon Lane. Another thing that certainly struck us after having lived in a very built up and heavily populated part of Redland in Bristol, was that within only a few months of living in Blaisdon I knew more people to speak to regularly than I ever did living in Redland, where everybody was too busy with their own lives to bother with getting acquainted.

Soon after moving to Green Court, a few of us commenced an annual neighbour's giant sunflower competition, which saw some spectacular specimens over the years and a fair amount of secret formula fertiliser making.

We have watched with pleasure as our girls over their early years have blossomed and enthusiastically embraced the countryside environment in which they have grown. They have developed a profoundly deeper understanding of nature and how things grow than some of their contemporary city dwelling Cheltenham classmates. From birth they have grown up alongside Murphy our 12 stone, black Great Dane. He has been like a big brother to them, ever watchful and present as babies and toddlers and to this day, in his more wobbly twilight years, still follows

Above:
Tashi, Connie & Murphy.
Right:
Keith & Sarah Wintle,
on their wedding day.

them around, at a safe distance, to make sure they come to no harm. He also shares their affections with Guinea Pigs, Snowy and Roger and a tank of tropical fish.

Perplexed by the absence of an open well on the property, when every other house in this rank seems to possess one, we were recently surprised to find that our patio table has been continuously positioned over a fifty foot drop which the attached photo details. The early snowfall clearly shows the position of the existing wellhead, as the air below making the concrete warmer under this spot. After many attempts I've now given up trying to persuade my wife that we should open it up for prosperity. You never know when the next drought is around the corner!

In the ten years we have resided here in the village we have become fondly accustomed and grown to love the ways of the place, from helping to bring in the local hay to the yearly visit to the summer fete and regular forays to the Red Hart Inn; Blaisdon has become an indelible part of our lives. It is the perfect place to bring up a young family surrounded with an abundance of nature, spectacular countryside with countless places nearby to walk that uplift and restore the soul. On a clear summer's evening you'd be hard pushed to find a more idyllic setting."

Above:
Tashi, left & Connie Wintle.
Left:
The well, marked out by snow.

Brickhouse Farm

Blaisdon Lane Nurseries

Iona

Blaisdon Lane

Glasshouses

Oak Field

Glaymar grounds

1987 Aerial View from Hinder's corner looking along Blaisdon Lane. (M. Morgan)

Oak Field

Green Court

Blaisdon Lane

G l a y m a r
outbuildings

1987 Aerial View centred on
Oakfield.
(M. Morgan)

327

OAK FIELD

Oak Field in 2012.

Don Morgan has researched the history of Oak Field and neighbouring houses:

"The land on which Oak Field is built formed part of the Blaisdon Hall Estate. On 22nd February 1934 Thomas Place, the then owner of the Blaisdon Hall Estate, sold to Frank Bullock of Nottwood Hill for the consideration of £230, 11.679 acres of land off Blaisdon Lane, Ordnance numbers 48, 51 and 55. On 30th March 1936 Frank Bullock is shown to be living at 'Stanley Cottage', Blaisdon as a smallholder.

On 1st May 1936 Frank Bullock sells to Frederick Brooks of Silver Street, Mitcheldean, a factory worker, a portion of O.S. 55. It appears the price was a total of £260. The portion of land is ninety nine feet wide and four hundred and forty feet long with a slight bend. These measurements equal one acre exactly.

It is assumed that Frederick Brooks built the original dwelling, as he gained a mortgage through the Gloucester Conservative Benefit Society (Holloway House) using the property as collateral. The dwelling at this time was quite small being thirty feet square and consisting of four rooms with an outside toilet, well water and no electricity. The

well, incidentally, is still in existence and the surface of the water is sixty feet below ground level.

On 19th May 1947 Frederick Brooks now shown as living at Ferndale, Blaisdon, sells Oak Field to Percy and Beatrice Pugh (Volume 2) of 2 Church Cottages, Longhope. Mr Pugh is shown as a factory worker. George Robins Joyce, a retired schoolmaster, of the Tan House, Blaisdon, witnessed the conveyance. Mr Pugh died in 1969 and was shown as working in an Aircraft Maintenance Department.

On 27th September 1973 Herbert and Valerie Tovey purchased Oak Field, moving from Dinney Pig Farm, Minsterworth and while living here doubled the length of the house by constructing a new living room, kitchen and dining room. As well as working as a lorry driver Bert

Don & Ruth Margan
outside Oak Field
prior to their alterations
being carried out.

pig house. Sadly Bert was killed in a road accident and the alterations were not fully completed.

On 8th July 1977 Oak Field changed hands again, being sold to Kenneth Gordon Griffin who moved from Poulza Farm, Jacobstow, Bude, Cornwall. The alterations were completed and the property reroofed.

On 19th October 1984 the property was purchased by Donald and Ruth Morgan who came from Pentire, Cainscross Road, Stroud."

Don continues with an account of the years he and Ruth have spent at Oak Field:

"I was shortly to retire from my job of Divisional Officer in the Gloucestershire Fire and Rescue Service and Ruth brought her well-known, prize winning, herd of British Toggenburg goats. Our two sons Mark and Matthew had, by this time, already left home but our daughter Megan came with us and stayed for three years.

Meanwhile Ruth continued to show her goats at many agricultural shows, and exported breeding stock to many countries of the world. It was while she was holding a large meeting of the Gloucestershire Goat Society that, by chance, Mrs Pugh had stopped outside with her daughter. We invited them in to show them what the place now looked like and Mrs Pugh told us that the large array of narcissi planted behind the house was planted by her to pick and sell. This she did by taking them on the bus to Cinderford market but very often she had sold them before she got to Cinderford.

and Valerie Tovey kept a number of pigs in a purpose built We continued with our agricultural interests by expanding and rearing a small number of beef calves and a pedigree flock of polled Dorset sheep replaced the goats. As more land became available we took on a commercial orchard of dessert apples. These apples were picked, graded, packed and taken overnight to St. Philips market in Bristol to be sold the next day. In this we were helped by Ron Suckling, a much respected local man who worked for many years in the orchards around Blaisdon and Huntley when they were owned by Bert Knight and later Gerald Akerman. The orchard has since been turned over to grassland for the sheep and making hay.

In 1991 a new tarmac drive was laid and in1994-5 half the house was demolished and a two-storey section constructed by Clive Phelps, a local builder from Old Hill, Longhope. A brick built feed store was replaced by a new garage, which completed the major alterations. The property now consists of a four bedroom, two storey house with a large living room, hall, kitchen/dining room, two bathrooms and a large landing which doubles as an office. With the inclusion of a high level of insulation, treated woodwork throughout and electricity and water laid on it is a far cry from the original four roomed bungalow but, hopefully, an improvement which is in keeping with the locality.

In Volume 2 of Blaisdon Memories of a Country Parish, mention was made of the well, which is sixty feet deep from ground level to the surface of the water. In 2012 a new and safe wellhead was constructed and is now a pleasant feature of the property. Also at this time a large array of solar panels was installed to bring Oak Field into the 21st century."

Opposite:
The Morgan family celebrating Ruth's 60th birthday:
1.Nick Whalley (Ruth's brother).
2. Tatiana.
3. Margaret Baron (Cousin).
4. Simon Finch (B.-in-Law).
6.Mark (Son).
7. Matthew (Son).
8. Myriam Whalley.
9. Megan (Daughter).
10. Ruth.
11. Beverley (Daughter-in-law).
12. Don.
13, Mitchel (Grandchild).
14. Heather (Grandchild).
15. Tristan (Grandchild).
16. Paula (Grandchild).
17. Rachael (Grandchild).

GLAYMAR

William and Mary Hatch lived in Glaymar from 1957. After their deaths, the house was sold to the Oldham family.

Sue, Mark, Dan (16) & Becky (10) Oldham viewed the property 'Glaymar' is September 2001, loved the location and purchased the property in December of the same year. **Sue Oldham** continues:

Above & below; The new Glaymar in 2012.

"We moved from a large Victorian house that we had renovated over several years in Pembury Road in Gloucester

While originally the intention was to renovate and extend Glaymar, the property was in such a bad state that we decided to apply for planning permission to knock the bungalow down and rebuild. We gained permission for a five bed detached house with detached triple garage and triple stable block for Becky's yet to be chosen pony.

Work to demolish the bungalow started in February 2002, and building commenced shortly after. During the start of the build we remained living in Gloucester. We moved out to Glaymar to live in our caravan October 26th 2002 on the stormiest, windiest night we could have chosen!! During that winter we encountered mud twelve inches deep, snow and ice and more rain than we would have liked but it was a dream to build our own house. Christmas 2002 was very interesting; cooking a full Christmas lunch with all the trimmings for five (we had company) in a caravan oven, transporting it to the room above the garage, which had been transformed into a lounge/diner, was extremely challenging but rewarding!!

The build was almost completed by March 2003 and we moved in on Easter Sunday that year, firstly completing the children's bedrooms followed by the kitchen and bathrooms.

When we moved to Blaisdon, Dan attended Sir Thomas Rich School and Becky Harewood Junior School both in Gloucester. They both continued their education to finish at their respective schools. Dan went on to become an electrician and Becky attended Dene Magna School for her secondary education completing her 6th form studies at Beaufort Comprehensive in Gloucester.

We are property landlords and Mark has a maintenance company, I work as a School Business Manager at Tuffley Primary School in Gloucester. The commute to work in the mornings is tedious sometimes taking over an hour to get to work!

I supported the Blaisdon Village Hall committee becoming treasurer for approximately three years until other commitments became too great.

We have had lots of adventures, changes, social gatherings and still finding things to do. Dan now lives in Adelaide, Australia and Becky is still at home but thinking of flying the nest not too far into the future. Mark and I are still here and will be for the foreseeable future."

Top:
Sue & Becky Oldham in front of the Old Glamar bungalow.
Above:
Aerial view of the original Glaymar showing the many outbuildings around it.

1

2

3

4

5

6

7

The Oldham family:
1. Starting the demolition of Glaymar.
2. Demolition of the old cottage is underway.
3. Becky receives digging instruction
4. Master driver Sue!
5. Mark & Dan on a well earned break.
6. Dogs and dinner.
7. Mark, plus friends.

HINDERS LODGE

Hinders Lodge, formerly known as Hinders Farm sits just outside the present parish boundary. Although it is technically in Huntley parish, its former and present owners feel that they are more connected to Blaisdon, situated as it is at the top of Blaisdon Lane. For some years, the house was occupied by Richard Heulin and his family, who were noted for their collection of Volkswagen Beetle cars, some with personalised number plates. They moved to France some years ago and the house was sold to Nicholas Lowe and *Joanna Kelly*:

Hinders Lodge in 2012.

"We moved to Hinders in 2008, just before the Financial Crash: we were one of the last mortgages our Mortgage Company concluded, as within days the housing market was in trouble. We lost £150K on the house price the following month of moving in, but things are looking up now.

We knew at the time we may be paying too much for the property but it ticked all the boxes, as we owned several horses, which we point to pointed and raced. We had moved from Westbury-on-Severn with our children, Tarron, Darcy and Toby, having lived there for 25 years. That was when the last property bubble burst; a definite theme seems to be emerging here! There we had been managing with 1 acre and 8 stables in the garden. Hinders

has fourteen acres, a large garden and two lakes surrounded by trees and the most magnificent views.

Hinders was a property we had looked at when we moved twenty five years earlier but it too expensive for us then. So it felt like fate when we looked at it early in 2008. We decided to change the name from 'farm' to 'lodge' as it was no longer a working farm.

The house needed a lot of work and although the mature gardens were pretty, they were slightly overgrown. We are definitely NOT gardeners but we have done a lot of work tidying and doing hard and soft landscaping. Hinders was also covered in Virgina Creeper which looked lovely but was pulling off roof tiles, breaking the guttering and invading the bricks and loft, so it had to go. We also moved the drive from the back of the house to the front where the aspect is outstanding. There is still more to do. The upstairs could benefit from enlarging and it would be nice to put glass around the back of the house to really encompass the exceptional views. Tarron works as Assessing Engineer for a company based in Weston Super Mare and travels this part of the country and Wales in his work.

Darcey attends Newent Senior School, more for their art status as she is an exceptional artist. Although she has not decided what to do for a career it will be interesting where her path takes her. Toby attends Dene Magna as he is more focused on practical applications not academia and this school suits him. He is far more focused and would like to enter electrical engineering as an apprentice. Tarron, now 26, has moved into his own pad. Nick is now semi-retired. Jo works at Three Choirs Vineyard in Newent in sales and is never short of a glass/bottle of wine!

The main place to meet and socialise is the Red Hart pub in Blaisdon, and where everyone learns what is happening in the village. We love living here and could never contemplate moving into town after having all this space and quiet living. The children love having the space to have their friends over and be 'away' from the adults. We mainly stay around the area and take full advantage of our outside space, not really needing to go on holiday as we have everything right here. We must sound quite boring to outsiders but we love our lives here."

1. The Virginia Creeper!
2. Creeper removed.
3. Stable occupant.
4. Nick with a trailer load of boys!

ROUGHLEAZE

Mark and Ann Hopkins have lived in Roughleaze since 1984, though Mark has spent all his life on Nottwood Hill, having been brought up at The Mount. Prior to 1984, the cottage had been owned by Mark's father, George, and been rented out to various tenants. Mark and Ann had lived in Nottswood Cottage before moving to Roughleaze. Whilst living there and bringing up their three children, Amber, Rowena and Lydia, They have extended and improved the cottage.

Plums used to be a major crop for them. In the older days, they would have seasonal plum lickers collecting the crop by hand. The need to improve efficiency to get the crop quickly to the jam making purchasers such as Robinsons, led to automation and tree-shakers were used after spreading nets below the trees. The fallen fruit was then gathered quickly into containers. Now, with imported fruit and concentrates, the market has disappeared apart from those people who still make their own jam.

Mark and Ann also own five other properties on Nottwood Hill. These have been rented for many years and, with one exception, it has not been possible to contact them for this book. The houses are summarised on the following pages.

Above: Rough Leaze. (2012)
Below: Ann Hopkins with plums & cherries. (1976)

1. Lydia & Amber Hopkins. (1990)
2. Mark Hopkins driving tractor with Harvey Atkinson & Rowena Hopkins plus a load of cider apples.
3. Rowena Hopkins. (1995)
4. Mark Hopkins & tree-shaker. (1980s)
5. Plum picking. (1978)
6. Plums on the sheet ready for gathering. (1970s)

Above:
Roughleaze in 1988.

Right:
Roughleaze in 1982.

FREEDOM COTTAGE

Freedom Cottage was formerly known as Rose Tree Cottage but was changed to avoid confusion with nearby Rose Cottage. It and West View are attached cottages.

Above:
Freedom Cottage with West View to the right. (2012)

WEST VIEW

Above: West View & Ann Hopkins in 1976.
Left: West View in 2012.
Far left: The old wash-house (now demolished)
behind West View & Freedom Cottages. (c1970)

THE OUNT

Above and left: The Mount.

OTTSWOOD COTTAGE

Two more houses rented out by Mark and Ann Hopkins. The Mount was the home of Mark's parents, Edgar and Molly and before them, his grandparents, George and Rebecca.

Nottswood Cottage continues the debate over whether there is an 's' in the Hill's name. Mark and Ann say there is an 's' in the cottage's name anyway.

Nottswood Cottage. (2012)

ROSE COTTAGE

A snowy Rose Cottage.

Vicki Handley was one of the tenants in Rose Cottage and has a lovely tale to tell of her time on Nottwood Hill:

"I'm originally from Ashleworth, near Gloucester. My then boyfriend and I rang up with an interest in renting Rose Cottage, though unfortunately another couple had beaten us to it by only half an hour. We ended up living in Longhope and I began working at the Nursing Home there. Everyone was lovely and I have some fond memories of the people I cared for, and the staff.

One staff member in particular, Alex, was the kitchen assistant and born and bred in Longhope. Both our existing relationships ended and gradually Alex and I began chatting and formed a friendship. Everyone around us could see the spark between us. There would be a lot of banter at work, and I couldn't help but smile when I saw him. At the Christmas party Alex told me he liked me and I felt it too, but we weren't ready for a new relationship yet, so he walked me home and we continued our friendship.

On Christmas day, Alex and I shared our first kiss under the mistletoe. It was on Boxing Day that I found out it was he that beat me to Rose Cottage! I was 24 and Alex was 29 when I moved in with him, a month later as we both needed to share bills. Our friendship blossomed into a relationship and we fell in love in Rose Cottage. We lived there together for three years, loving the summers and surviving the winters. The house would be nice and cool in the summer, which we would enjoy after a day of trying to keep the countryside out of the garden; it was like a jungle sometimes! We had barbeques most weekends and family round for dinner and drinks.

We had a fantastic view from Rose Cottage, miles and miles of countryside, and you could also see Gloucester cathedral from our house. The sunrises were so beautiful, coming back from night shifts to see the sun rising and the mist throughout the countryside made me feel so peaceful.

Vicktoria Handley, right, with
Brother, Stephen Handley, centre, Alex Cox, left, and
Lucia Handley at the back.

The winters were hard though; two of the three winters we spent there we had heavy snow. Access was, at the best of times, difficult, so when it snowed we had to park our cars down on the main road. The house was so cold and drying our washing was a nightmare, hanging our clothes off the beams, and the constant battle against condensation and mould was frustrating. But we knew it was all worthwhile to get through to spring and see all the flowers coming up and the birds in the garden, and to spend our days off in the sunshine. It was like the house came to life in the summer."

RAMCREST

A snow covered Ramscrest in January 2010.

Susan Green tells of her life at Ramcrest:

"My name is Susan Green and when I was little I lived at Pittstowe Cottage on Nottwood Hill, before moving down to Ramcrest:

Ramcrest was then owned by Philip Green (Volume 2), who had lived there since the 1950s. We became friends in March 1982 and although I had known him since I was a child, we fell in love. I moved in with him in November 1982 after I arrived back from Israel, where I lived and worked on a kibbutz for five weeks. Although it was lovely living in the Forest of Dean countryside with lovely walks and so on, locally there was no or very little work.

Many years earlier, Philip had also been to Israel, or Palestine as it was then known, for two years. It was a strange coincidence that we both went there to get away from here for a bit and to see the rest of the world, as we both wanted more from life than just staying in one place. So, even though what we did was years apart, we both felt the same, that living in Blaisdon was not enough while we were young but lovely to come back to when our travels were over. It was as though we were destined to be together, just as we both went back to Nottwood

Hill to live. However, my travel bug never went away so I continued to travel but was always glad at the end to get back to Blaisdon and Nottwood Hill to Philip and the animals where we were most happy together.

Philip went to work at RAF Quedgeley in Gloucester where he worked after training to be an engineer. He got there and back by bus, which a lot of people used in the 1970s and 1980s to get to work. However, Philip took early retirement after he met me because he said that he wanted to make the most of his time with me. He concentrated on changing the outside of Ramcrest by planting ornamental trees, building a greenhouse and summerhouse and having lots of animals. He no longer wanted to travel, as he was content to be at home and go for long walks around the wood with me, which is why we got together in spring

1. Philip Green on a frozen reservoir, Blaisdon woods. (1984)
2. Philip clearing paths on Nottwood Hill. (1990)
3. Susan Green at Blaisdon Hall. (1990)
4. Shep in the woods. (1992)
5. Susan & companions in Blaisdon woods. (2001)

1982. It was love at first sight, so we never wanted to waste any time and we were living together by November 1982 and would have got married but I said not yet. So that's why we married in 1984. After marrying Philip, I worked at Blaisdon Hall for a while as a cleaner to get extra money for holidays etc.

We changed things in the garden while living here, planting trees and changing the garden outside as well as opening up the fireplace inside the living room but other than that the house is pretty much the same except for different colour paint on the walls and windows.

We had chickens, cats, rabbits and three dogs. We would take the dogs for long walks around Blaisdon woods and Philip would keep the paths around the wood and Nottwood Hill clear, with help from Oscar Jones, so people could take their dogs or go for walks without having to fight through overgrown brambles and so on. We also went blackberry picking in the wood, as there were loads of them everywhere. Also, the dogs used to love swimming in the old reservoir. We also liked chatting with the neighbours and catching up on all the local gossip and seeing people come and go over the years. Philip was fifty seven in 1982 and now would have been eighty six but sadly passed away in January 2012.

So, I have lived here since I was a child, as did Philip after moving here from Gloucester to another house on Nottwood Hill with his parents."

Susan & Philip Green
ouside Ramcrest. (1997)

HILLSIDE

Simon and Amanda Drake extended the original cottage significantly during their time in Hillside before the property passed to the Venn family, from High Wycombe in May 2006. The family comprises Kyron and Kate with children Emily (9), Jacob (6) and Samuel (3).

Emily Venn, writes about living at Hillside:

"My name is Emily and I live in Blaisdon with my family and pets. I was born in High Wycombe and when I was three we moved here, when my first brother Jacob was born. We love living here. There are woods and beautiful views all around and we have a big garden which means we can have lots of pets.

Above:
Hillside with Emily, Samuel & Jacob Venn. (2012)
Below:
Hillside, some years earlier.

I have a dog, named Bailey; he is my pal. I also have two cats called Hally and Cleo. I did have three chickens named Minnie, Mabel and Penny but sadly Mabel and Penny disappeared so we got a new chicken, so now it is Minnie and Charlie chickens. We have two rabbits called Humf and Star, which we got at Christmas.

Talking about Christmas, every year we go up to a tree in the woods and hang decorations on it and every Christmas night we go outside and enjoy the lights and falling snow, if there is any. This Christmas we went to the Red Hart with some friends for a Christmas dinner.

1

2

3

6

4

5

7

The Venn family:
1. Kate & Kyron with Emily, Jacob & Samuel.
2.-5. Emily, Jacob & Samuel.
6. Kate with Emily, Jacob & Samuel.
7. A tired Samuel resting.

Sometimes there is some wild weather here on Nottwood hill; for example trees blowing over, deep snow which means we can't get the cars down the hill, so we don't have to go to school. We all go to Hope Brook school together in Longhope but Sam is still in playgroup and Pippins.

We have lots of rainy and sunny days up on my hill and usually lots of friends like coming over because we have a kids caravan, a playhouse and animals. My dog-loving best friend Alicia likes to play with Bailey when she comes round. We sometimes go geocaching in the woods. Geocaching is where we use a Global Positioning System and maps to hide and seek containers, called geocaches.

Where I live is a beautiful place."

Left:
The family Christmas tree in the woods.
Above:
Samuel, Kyron, Emily & Jacob Venn.

HERRY TREE COTTAGE

Harold Brain and his wife, May, lived in Cherry Tree Cottage for many years. ***Llivia Hales,*** age 10, their great grand daughter interviewed her family after she went to visit her family home.

Brenda Hales (nee Brain), my grandma, said:

"We never really had a favourite time of year at Cherry Tree Cottage although in the spring time we used to cut the lawn, weed the garden and just generally tidied it up. At summer and autumn we

Above: Cherry Tree Cottage in 2000.
Below: Cerry Tree Cottage in 1993.

used to go for walks around Nottwood Hill. In the winter it was hard to go to Cherry Tree Cottage because the lane was impassable due to snow and ice, on the other hand if we did go we used to have snowball fights and build snowmen."

Daren Hales, my dad said:

"I was born in 1968. My Nan and gramps, your great grandparents, lived in Cherry Tree Cottage for many years. I have fond memories of this lovely homely cottage as I spent many a weekend there with my sister Cindy. Most of the time in the summer was spent fruit picking in the plum orchard and having plenty of fun with the plum boxes; we would stack them up and then hide in the garden from our mum and dad for hours on end entertaining ourselves. I would also play on top of the hill and often I would pick blackberries and hazelnuts with my Nan, I would run away through the Ferns and explore the bushy trees searching for twigs to play with. At teatime we would make our way back to Cherry Tree Cottage for homemade cake and lemonade.

There was a room in the house, which was extra special, and I was not allowed in it. This was the front room and it was for best and only used on special grown up occasions. Everything revolved around mostly two rooms in the house the kitchen and the living room. On a Saturday afternoon my great granny and I would snuggle up and watch the wrestling on the TV together which I enjoyed very much."

Llivia Hales, age 10, continues:

"My Nan moved away from Cherry Tree Cottage after she got married in 1964. For two years she lived at Orchard Bank Farm and then, in 1966, she moved to Whiteshill in Stroud where she and my granddad still live today. My Nan visited Cherry Tree often to keep an eye on her parents. She sometimes mowed the lawn and weeded the garden with her sister, Wendy, and her brother, John. When my dad was small he and his sister Cindy, my auntie, used to stay at Cherry Tree Cottage many weekends.

In 1977, they remember how excited they were when they were told that they were invited with their Nan, grampy, mum and dad to the Queen's Silver Jubilee in London. My great, great uncle Harry Moseley worked for the Queen in the Royal Mews. They saw all the horses, carriages and

The State Coach:
Top, from the left:
Peter Hales, Daren Hales, Cindy Hales, May Brain, Harold Brain, Lil Moseley whose husband was a footman & rode in the Silver Jubilee procession.
Bottom:
Brenda & Cindy Hales.

the beefeaters and they also got to keep a royal horseshoe. This year's Diamond Jubilee bought back many memories for my family.

On Saturday 10th June 2012, my dad, Daren, my mum, Rachael, my brother, Oscar, and I went on a walk to May Hill on the way back my dad took us to Nottwood hill and there we went to Cherry Tree Cottage. Whilst we were there Liz Perry, the owner of the house, invited us in. I was amazed at the sight of the wonderful place where my great grandparents used to live. The owl stood proudly at the top of the garden overlooking the hills just like the terrace on top of the house. My favourite part was the bread oven, which has a village in it and a snowman. Outside are pots that my dad made when he was younger. Tall trees, long green grass and beautiful sheds full with magical statues, it was a place anyone would dream of living.

Down a lot of steps surrounded by trees each side you would come to a place where Winnie the Pooh lives, it is truly a wonderful place and hopefully one day the cottage will return to our family. This was the first time I have ever been to Cherry Tree Cottage and I would really love to live there one day. Even though there were a lot of things in the garden it was all colour co-ordinated and beautiful. The big and enchanting cottage also known as Cherry Tree Cottage on Nottwood hill will stay in my mind forever and never leave. It felt sad to be there, as I never knew my great grandparents but at the same time happy because the house is so well looked after."

3 generations on the steps outside Cherry Tree Cottage:
Top: Llivia & Daren Hales.
Far right: A young Daren with his dad, Peter
Right: Peter on the steps of Cherry Tree Cottage

Cherry Tree Cottage

The long grass grows through all seasons along with beautiful trees and flowers.
A shy little robin hops onto the windowsill waiting for food.
An old cat strolls past and hisses, trying to scare him.
The red breasted bird flies away spreading his wings.
Dolls sleep in the bedroom of a lovely kind lady as she sleeps too.
The morning sun shines through the window as she awakes.
Another nice day at Cherry Tree
The house that means a lot to me

Llivia Hales (2012)

Elizabeth Perry (nee Etherington) spent her childhood at the Forge, Blaisdon (Volume 2) but was drawn back to the area later in life:

"Having left Blaisdon in 1963, I returned with my Husband Geoffrey Perry in 1996, when we purchased Cherry Tree Cottage on Nottwood Hill. After four years of extensive renovations we actually took up residence in the Cottage in 1996. Sadly Geoff died in July 2004 but I am still enjoying the joy and beauty of all that surrounds me here on Nottwood."

Working under her maiden name, Elizabeth was instrumental in the production of the book, ***'Blaisdon Memories of a Counry Parish 1935-64'***. She and Margaret Hogg were able to contact many folk from Blaisdon and Nottwood Hill whom they had known during those years. With their encouragement, these people wrote down their memories and produced a unique archive of pictures from those distant times.

Elizabeth Perry with copies of Blaisdon Memories & a calender produced from pictures within the book.
(2011)

Above;
Geoffrey & Elizabeth Perry,
outside Cherry Tree Cottage. (1996)
Right:
Elizabeth's grandchildren, from the top left:
Amy, Rachel, Jessica,
Kate, Tom, James,
Hanneh, Cassie.

Below: Cherry Tree Cottage. (2000)

ILLVIEW

Christine Barnard tells the continuing story of her family at Hillview:

"My parents, Claude and Margaret Barnard (Volume 2), had moved into Hillview after their wedding in 1958. The original house was built in 1808 with wattle and daub walls and had no running water. They set about renovating and extending the house on a very restricted budget. Over the years, the house has been double glazed and central heating and a conservatory have been added but the original walls remain and the original house remains as uneven as when it was built.

Claude and Margaret with the help of children, Christine and Michael, were self sufficient in vegetables and Margaret loved to grow her annual flowers. Some produce was also sold at Gloucester market. Fruit picking was a regular family job with plums being picked and sold to Ron Walton (Volume 2), though now the remaining plum trees just provide the fruit for jam and plum vodka, a favourite family tipple at Christmas. In the summer we would spend days picking apples and blackcurrants with mum and Nan Rose. The Hill was our playground, making dens and mud pies. Unfortunately a lot of the Hill where they used to play is rather overgrown.

Hillview. (2012)

Michael and I helped with the animals of George and Rose Beard (Volume 2), and grandparents, at The Priestleys. They had hens, pigs and sheep. Christine would help plucking chickens for market. Today, the orchard is rented out for sheep grazing.

Michael and I went to nearby Zion School. It had two classrooms with outside toilets. Christine then went on to the Royal Forest of Dean Grammar School and Michael to Abenhall School.

We went to Gloucester only on special occasions and it was a treat to go to Cinderford. Once a fortnight the family would go to Claude's parents in Mitcheldean for tea. Nan Elsie would have lemonade delivered by the Corona man and as a treat we would share a glass.

Holidays were a friend's caravan at Uphill, Weston and later with a borrowed car to caravans in Devon and Wales.

I have lived all my life on the Hill and remember fondly the parties that we have been to over the years. Claude and Margaret liked to throw parties to celebrate birthdays, anniversaries etc. The last party was their golden wedding anniversary at the Latchen Room in Longhope.

Michael has left home but I remain at Hillview with my father, Claude. Margaret sadly passed away in June 2012 after bravely fighting a number of illnesses over many years."

1

2

3

4

5

6

1. Golden Wedding of Claude & Margaret Barnard.
2. Claude & Margaret Barnard
George & Elsie Beard, Elsie & Frank Holford
Christine & Michael Barnard.
3. Claude & Margaret in their garden.
4. Claude with Christine & Michael Barnard.
5. Party time at Mitcheldean Community centre.
6. Christine Barnard in the orchard. (1988)

PRIESTLEYS COTTAGE

In 1975 **Clive Rodway** and his wife Miriam Rodway bought Priestleys Cottage. At that time it was a small bungalow with only four rooms and an outside toilet. In the back two rooms there was a railway carriage, which had been the original accommodation on the site. Due to this being in poor condition it was removed and the entire property was renovated. The house now comprises four bedrooms, a study, a playroom, lounge and kitchen, also three bath rooms (two en-suite) and a separate toilet. Since the original renovation a large double garage with a granny annexe has been added.

In 1983 Clive and Miriam had a little boy named Michael Andrew Rodway. When he grew up he moved to live and work in Cheltenham. After twenty years of marriage Clive and Miriam divorced, however they still remained friends and kept in touch. Miriam settled down later at 'Mirestock' in Lydbrook with her new partner. Clive remained at Priestleys Cottage, but in 2004 went to Cuba for a holiday to learn Salsa.

As luck would have it in Cuba he had his own Salsa teacher, Anabel, who just happened to be young and pretty. Eighteen months later Clive invited Anabel to come to the U.K. for a holiday. After several more visits they got

Above: Priestleys Cottage
Below: Priestley Cottage before modernisation.

married in October 2007. Shortly after in 2008 they were both delighted to have twins, a boy and girl named Samuel and Nia. At the time of writing this book the twins are now 4 and a half years old and are just about to start school. Clive will be sixty years old in August and Anabel 38 years old in September, but as Clive says, age is only a number! Especially when your wife is twenty two years younger!!"

From the left:
Michael, Anabel & Clive Rodway
with twins, Samuel & Nia.

PITTSTOWE COTTAGE

Susan Green writes about her parents:

Beryl and John Little moved into Pittstowe Cottage about 1963 from Orchard Bank Bungalow, Little London. It was a 2-bedroom house, to which they later added a 3rd bedroom, as by then they had 2 children, Susan and brother Nigel. They also put a conservatory up, as with a growing family they needed the extra room.

Like her mother before her, Beryl worked at Blaisdon Hall as a cleaner when it was a Catholic school run by priests and John worked at Gloucester Royal Hospital and then Permali as a boiler man as by that time he had to go to Gloucester to find work. Both children went to Zion

Left: Pittstowe Cottage. (2012)

Below: Nigel & Beryl Little.

primary school then Abenhall secondary school. Susan lived there till 1982 and Nigel lived there till 1998. Beryl and John moved out in 2003.

Father did the gardening and I had rabbits and guinea pigs, which lived in the garden. We also we had a cat and dog. Most people around here had a garden with vegetables, as there was no local shop, so it was easier then getting on a bus to Gloucester. Now everyone has a car, so hardly anyone has a productive garden but as the recession bites people are doing small plots or pots to grow things again now, so its gone full circle.

My brother Nigel used to go to the Red Hart pub at Blaisdon on a weekend, which he got to by walking over the wood by the church and on down to the pub. Nigel also had to go to Gloucester to work. He still works there at the Walls factory. I went to Israel then later got married after moving into nearby Ramcrest.

Present occupants of Pittstowe Cottage are **Neil Smith and Jenina Millar:**

"We bought Pittstowe Cottage in December 2007. Our first son, Jack John Millar, was born in January 2008 and we moved in when he was six weeks old. I am originally from Cambridge and Janina is from Surrey. We are both serving Police Officers with Gloucestershire Constabulary. I transferred from the Metropolitan Police in 2007. Janina works from Tewkesbury and I work in Gloucester.

Our second son, Max Henry Millar, was born in May 2009. They both go to Sunbeams Day Nursery in Mitcheldean. Jack starts at Hope Brook Primary School in September 2012.

Our cottage was built in the 19th Century and was in need of significant work when we moved in. It still needs a lot of work doing to it, something we will get round to in time, children permitting! This year we bought a black Labrador puppy called Scooby. Since having him we have discovered wonderful walks around Blaisdon Hill. It takes us about forty minutes to walk over the hill to the Red Hart in Blaisdon, though it takes us longer to walk back.

We have found all the community on Nottwood Hill to be extremely friendly especially our next door neighbour Liz."

From the top:
Pittstowe Cottage c 1968.
Pittstowe Cottage c 2000.

WALNUT TREE COTTAGE

Walnut Tree Cottage.

Andrew and Judith Vickers, relative newcomers to Nottwood Hill give their first impressions of their new home:

"We moved into Walnut Tree Cottage over February and March 2012. The previous owners had lived here we believed for twelve years and have moved to Longhope.

The house has a beautiful setting with literally stunning views to the Severn, the Cotswolds and Gloucester, whether it is dawn and the sun first appears, through to evening when the lights of distant villages and towns are twinkling. The garden is better described as grounds, covered in roses and colour, numerous trees and seating areas. The house, originally from 1675 has now a modern sympathetic extension and conservatory, is very gezellig.

Gezellig is a Dutch expression suggesting a place is cosy and warm and references that Judith is Dutch, being born in Rotterdam in 1946. She lived as a child in Argentina and then in The Hague whilst a teenager. I am from Surrey and we met at work where we were social workers both specialising in mental health.

Judith retired a couple of years ago and our move to Nottwood Hill follows my retirement from work. We had been living in Dorset where I managed the community mental health services in Weymouth. We have four children and six grandchildren between us.

We had no real knowledge of this area but seeking something new, now look forward to many years of enjoying our new home and local area. Life on the Hill is obviously different from years past where, from the descriptions in the earlier version of the book, life appeared hard but generally people seemed accepting and got on with its challenges. I recognise many of the descriptions of children playing from my own 1950s childhood in Surrey. Today we expect much more, immediate rescue when things do not work, ease and comfort. There are still echoes of the past, unmade roads, now traversed mainly by 4x4s, the sweet smell of burning wood from the chimneys, now protruding from solar panelled roofs.

Top right:
the fantastic view from
Walnut Tree Cottage, looking
over the River Severn towards
the Cotswolds.

Top left: Judith Vickers.

Right: Andrew Vickers.

In a few weeks here we have experienced power cuts when the electric line came down, snow and hail, rainbows in the valley, daffodils, primroses and forget-me-nots in the warm sunshine. We particularly look forward to staying young on Nottwood Hill, remembering and learning of the past, enjoying the day and keeping up with the ever increasing pace of life.... and at some point writing again in the next edition of this book."

EW TREE COTTAGE

Julie Buckley describes her family's time in yew Tree Cottage:

"We moved to Yew Tree on the 17th February 1978 from the West Midlands. Paul and I had been very fortunate that even though we lived in the city, our parents, Travers and Joan, had taken us away for many holidays, camping, caravanette then caravanning and experiencing the wonders of the countryside. Therefore although we were a little apprehensive about the move we were looking forward to living in the country.

When I had finished school our parents had decided to move to the countryside. After viewing several houses we eventually moved to Yew Tree Cottage. It had recently been rebuilt by John Dowding from one and a half original walls and extended to a three-bedroom property. It had been refurbished but with no original features. So since moving here thirty four years ago, Yew Tree has taken on many changes and extensions to its original demeanour, with us adding traditional character to reflect the buildings original age.

Moving from the West Midlands was a bit of a culture shock first off for my brother and I. Our parents didn't appear to be affected, only by the fact that Dad still had to

Yew Tree Cottage. (1999)

commute to Birmingham for work. We had to make new friends and I found this all very daunting after leaving my friends and boyfriend behind. I also had to find a job, which was hard at first being a school leaver. I shouldn't have worried really, as we both soon made friends with locals our age and we would go out in a large group to many local places and enjoy local gatherings for Carnivals and Fetes. This sort of thing didn't happen where we use to live, so the Plum Festival and Mitcheldean floats were fascinating events to us at that time. The first Christmas we had at Yew Tree was brilliant, and when the carol singers arrived at our door we were amazed. There was so many of them and having the traditional lanterns made it a wonderful thing to remember

Our neighbours at Walnut Tree Cottage, Cuthbert and Gwen Dowding were very helpful and supportive and

Above: Yew Tree Cottage in 1980s, top, & 1990s, below.
Left: 2 views of the garden from the 1990s.

such radiant characters. We soon became accustomed to Mrs Dowding's wonderful chocolate cake and homemade wine. Gwen would always have a glass of sherry within minutes for my Mum whenever she popped down to see her, even at 9.00am in the morning! Cuthbert was always keeping the garden and surrounding area in tiptop condition, despite his age and so would Gwen. They had lots of stories to tell and made us feel like we had been around for years and not new to the village life. Once we got to know the other residents on the hill there appeared to be such camaraderie among them. This was very apparent when anyone needed help or assistance, or under the weather. Everyone would be so willing to make sure you were ok and had anything that you needed.

The Buckley family from the left:
Kurt Danson (Julie's son). Joan, Julie, Travers & Paul.

view from Yew Tree Cottage, and I would sit outside at night and sketch the moon and the cloud formation, captivating and mesmerizing at the same time. I would also lie on a camp bed at night and watch the sky, looking for shooting and falling stars. Before I found a job I would walk up to Blaisdon woods and climb the Yew Tree by the gate to the blackcurrant field and read my book. I found this to be very tranquil at a troubled time for me and would check out the reservoir for newts and other water life.

It was lovely to become friends with most of the folk on the hill who are mentioned in your previous publication. We would also see lots of people on regular occasions, including Karen, Rita and Brian Pearce, as well as Sandra, Richard, Joyce and Oscar Jones with their homemade Elderberry and Plum wine. Oscar was another great character always used the old paths around the hill with his dog in tow, keeping them clear. Sue, Nigel and Beryl Little and Phil Green who always liked to have a chat and tell you of times gone by on the hill. My favourite character was Albert Pithouse. I could hardly understand him when we first moved but I loved to sit and listen to his stories on the hill or down at the Red Hart in Blaisdon. He would always cheer you up and make you laugh.

This came to light too when we experienced our first heavy snow fall. We all mucked in and cleared lanes on Nottwood Hill, carrying the grit up in buckets and chipping away at ice so that we could hopefully get vehicles up and down. This was pretty hair raising trying to get up or down without damaging our vehicles. I loved going for walks in the woods on the hill with snowfall. Sometimes I couldn't sleep, so I would get up during the night and take our dog Tana for a walk. No torch needed, as it was light enough with the moon reflecting on the snow. We have a fantastic

Paul Buckley was on the Blaisdon Parish Council for 20 years, which again introduced us to more local folk. We also had the opportunity to visit Blaisdon Hall, what a splendid building it is.

With the very bad winter of 1981-82, we had a very heavy snowfall with over six foot drifts on the corner and the lane being inaccessible. Dad was stuck on the Monmouth bypass with frozen diesel. We had no electricity or water for over three days. We melted snow and boiled this on the wood burner for drinking and washing. Dad stored and kept our food fresh in a snowman. We have had power cuts in the past, but this was a real challenge.

Paul and I worked in Gloucester and they could not believe how much snow had fallen and that we needed to try and get in. We walked down the hill with black bin liners taped to our legs and body and into Huntley, but the buses were unable to drive either, so we were stranded. We took photos to show that we were not exaggerating with Mum standing near the snow. Our vehicles could not be seen under the snow. My great Uncle Ernie was living with us then. He was an adorable man. He would stand outside with his walking stick and take it all in. When we would come home from work, he would make us a cup of tea god bless him, even though he was in his eighties.

Sandra Jones and Paul worked together around twenty years ago, and are still doing so to this day. Dad retired from HGV long distance to follow his love of gardening, fishing, carpentry and dancing. Mum stopped working in 1993 and joined Dad in the same pursuits, but formed a large pond in the garden rather than fishing! This has proved to be hard work, but very rewarding to sit and enjoy the fish and their antics. Mum enjoys walking too, and adores all animals. I have worked mainly in the office environment Receptionist/Secretary etc. Paul has done painting and decorating since leaving school. Mum was a carer for elderly folk, and then worked for Contact a Family.

With the busy lifestyle that most folk lead now, means there is less time to get to know neighbours on the hill.

None of us regret our move to Blaisdon. Being close to the Forest's and wildlife is so exhilarating. Mum and Dad are very knowledgeable and taught us what was safe and not safe about flora and fauna. Moving to where we are has enabled us to witness some fascinating wildlife including snakes, slow worms, glow worms, lizards, buzzards, kestrels, herons, pheasants, squirrels, badgers, woodpeckers, dragon and damsel flies, boar, muntjac, brown deer and white deer. Including the more common creatures you find in woodland. I still find that I will be looking something up in a book to find out more about it. We see so many different varieties of birds too. When we had not long moved to Yew Tree, we woke up one morning to find a load of sheep munching their way through what we had in the garden. Also on two separate occasions have had a horse in the garden, which wasn't ours but an escapee!

We are immensely grateful to our parents for giving us this opportunity to experience what some people may take for granted. A fantastic view to study for hours with binoculars, the fragrance of crops being cut, rapeseed blossom and many other smells that fill you with fond memories to treasure of our teenage years on the hill. It is still a very special place to be whatever age you are."

PROSPECT HOUSE

Above: Prospect House in the snow.
Right: An aerial view of Prospect House. (2011)

Heather Harrington lives in Prospect House:

"We, Hank and Heather Harrington, purchased Prospect House in 1991 from the Parish family who had owned it from 1986. Prior to that the Burns family owned it from around 1970.

We were living in Dubai at the time and as it was becoming increasingly difficult to accommodate a family of 6 and the associated baggage during our holidays, we decided that we needed our own house instead of invading various relatives' homes. In April 1991 we stopped overnight at the Hatherly Manor hotel and while we were there we took down the addresses of some local estate agents and contacted them when we returned to Dubai.

The details for Prospect House were faxed to us and we decided that we would like to know more about it despite it being a terrible photo. We asked relatives to visit and look at the property for us. The feedback was positive and so we decided to go ahead with it and on our return to the UK for the summer we took all the children to see the property and get their approval! It was a resounding success and we set about sorting out the purchase.

We had six weeks to arrange the mortgage, complete and exchange before returning to Dubai. Everything was in place when the surveyor for the building society decided that the roof would only last for a couple of years (it's still there after twenty!), there was damp in one of the rooms and most peculiar of all that the cellar was below ground! This meant starting the paperwork and survey again for a different mortgage company and consequently had to leave the solicitor to complete the purchase for us.

Over the next fifteen years we came back every summer as well as some Easter and Christmas holidays and the house was also used for many relatives to stay in for their holidays and for my eldest stepdaughter to live in while she was doing her teaching qualification. All the children have good memories of their holidays here. It was during

367

these visits that we got to know many of the hill residents, among them, Oscar Jones who had been born in this house. He would often stop by for a chat mainly about life on the hill when he was younger.

Other than a new sun room and a few new windows and doors the property is more or less as we bought it. Some of it has been re-plastered which caused some interesting moments when it was discovered that the joists of one of the upstairs rooms were resting on the plaster instead of the wall. We also found some wattle and daub that looked to be original as it was made out of whole hazel sticks. As with all old properties there are always surprises.

The garden at the front of the property has been changed with new steps leading up to the front door and a new patio. There is also a small pond. Unfortunately the old pear tree by the gates had to come down as the roots were knocking down the garden wall, which I then rebuilt.

My daughter and I returned to the UK permanently in July 2004 and since then have made some good friends on the Hill and in Blaisdon Lane. These friends are always there to help with any of the problems that arise living in an old property, along a track that is always in need of DIY maintenance and of course to share a cup of tea with at any time! We are lucky to live in a beautiful place with such a fantastic view."

LFRED HOUSE

After being occupied for many years by the Jones family (Volume 2), **Sam & Amanda Spencer** moved to Alfred House, in 2009:

"At the time of first setting eyes on Alfred House, who would have thought within 3 months we would become the new owners. This was back in August 2009, Sam and I were living in Longlevens, Gloucester. Sam discovered Alfred House and the For Sale by auction sign when he attended an electricity line fault on Nottwood Hill, through his job as a lineman. A visit from my Dad, a retired builder followed and the rest is history. We became the new owners on the 28th October 2009 after a tense auction experience! Prior to moving to the Hill we had no family, friends or connections with Blaisdon and were in fact not looking to move at all.

We soon learned about the history of Alfred House in particular the previous owner Oscar Jones (Volume 2), who had been a pillar of the community and remains in the hearts and minds of the village today. Whilst we were not able to meet Oscar, his memory remains. Alfred House may still be referred to on occasion as 'Oscar Jones' old place', over the short time in comparison we have lived in the small community of Nottwood Hill and Blaisdon. We have received a very warm welcome and Alfred House

Above: Alfred House. (2012)
Below: Alfred House before recent alterations.

is definitely our home, along with our black Labrador, Jasper.

Life for us has changed dramatically, moving from surburbia to living rurally up a track on a hill. It is a very different challenge, getting to and from work when the weather is bad. However it has a greater feeling of a sense of community. The Red Hart pub where we catch up with the many friends we have made locally, the views across the Slad to Bredon Hill , watching the weather come across the valley and Blaisdon Woods all make living in Alfred house such a privilege.

After a gruelling eighteen months of living in a caravan watching the transformation of the old cottage, extending it into a larger three bed-roomed cottage, was a nerve racking, challenging but the most amazing journey. Support on the hill during this time was tremendous. Ironically when the contractors started work on the house we had the worst winter for thirty years, but they struggled on regardless.

Many weekends were spent with Sam & I putting stone down on the track to make sure the contractors could reach the house safely. Mike, Wayne and Tim, experienced builders we can quote said it was the coldest temperature they had ever worked in, especially when they ran round the scaffolding naked when it was snowing as a dare. I don't think the neighbours spotted them!

No treasures were found during the build sadly however when the old cottage was being dismantled, a note was found that has been placed in one of the walls by Sandra Jones (Oscar and Joyce's daughter) when she had done some DIY many years prior.

Our history with Alfred House is very short and therefore anecdotes are few however it has made an impression with us that will last forever."

OUNT HOUSE

Martin Webb tells of his time on Nottwood Hill, starting in 1981:

"In 1981 the much loved Albert Pitthouse (Volume 2) died and Albert's sister and executor Ivy Marshall put the Mount up for sale. I was born in Bath and Gill was from Coventry and we moved to Gloucester when job in Architecture. Gloucester was a good centre for my hobby of Hang Gliding. On a Friday in October details on the Mount House arrived from E. W. White where David Marshall, Ivy's son worked. We were due to exchange contracts on the following Wednesday on a lovely cottage at Tibberton, which would have been perfect. Just from looking at the details I immediately told Gill we are going to have to forget Tibberton we are going to buy The Mount House and so we did.

Above: Mount House, rear elevation, both extensions completed. (1994)
Below: Mount House. (1984)

Albert had two friends living nearby. One was Doug Gurney who had his caravan near the gate at the bottom of the drive. When we bought the house we insisted Doug moved away so we had full vacant possession. In retrospect I felt guilty and thought I should have adopted Albert's more laid back approach. Ivy sold us Albert's little caravan, which we moved into, as the house needed gutting. However it was a very cold and snowy winter so we soon moved into the house to have a fire.

The house had been well built in the late 1700's. On the ground floor was the main Living Room/Kitchen, with a beautifully built twin bread oven and a small Parlour Room. Between the rooms, stairs led up to two bedrooms.

Beneath the Parlour was a cellar entered by wide stone steps from the Kitchen/ Living Room. In 1807 a two story extension was added with a date stone which reads 'JAW 1807'. Unfortunately in building this extension they partly destroyed the bread ovens, but it did add a new large Kitchen and extra Bedroom above. The house had been neglected and the only service connected to the mains was a weedy water main, which needed replacing. No electricity or drainage, even the old outside WC earth closet didn't look as if it had been used for years.

a lovely set of friends and neighbours we were about to acquire. I still enjoy recounting the various battles with John Burns over his casual fire setting, which set fire to our boundary hedge and field. A big part of our enjoyment came from standing in the shadow of the Pitthouses and of course, Albert. The family would regularly turn up on a summer's day to relive their past or come and pick plums in the lovely productive orchard that Albert planted in 1947. Ivy who lived at Rose Cottage became a very special and much loved friend. When she eventually left for

Left:
Mount House. (1981)

Right:
Chicken Coup in the snow.
(March 1985)

Those were challenges I was eager to face because it was just what we were looking for and in a fantastic position within an idyllic settlement. Everyone has his piece of land for a few animals, vegetables and orchard. They are far enough away not to tread on their neighbours toes but near enough to help in time of trouble and to keep up to date with the gossip. Although just at present I don't live on Nottwood it is always in my thoughts. I have two dogs buried there and my father's ashes are scattered on the Hill. It will always be my ideal kind of place to live.

We knew it was good but what we didn't know was what

Gloucester we took in Albert's rather wildcat and Tessie his lovely old Collie both of which Ivy had looked after since Albert died. When Tessie died we got another Collie called Nellie and she was a lovely cunning character.

I spent evenings in the house working by the light of paraffin, Tilley lamp at my drawing board deciding how to extend and renovate the house. We decided to take out the staircase to open up the Living Room a bit by building an extension on the north side to contain the new staircase, a small dining area and bathroom on the first floor. The walls were to be cavity block then faced with local stone. The first tasks were to renew the water supply, bring in electricity and build a septic tank so that we could refurbish the outside loo, so much easier than continually digging holes in the garden!

Within the year the land next door, which Albert's brother, Ted, owned then came up for sale upon which sat Gamekeepers Cottage so we purchased it jointly with our new friends Mark and Ann Hopkins of Roughleaze. Mark was always ready to help and advise and we often called on his services with his tractor. They both worked hard on the farm and improving and maintaining their cottages but there was always a cup of tea and friendly chat whenever we called.

There was one little problem however with our purchase. Albert had his other friend Foster Yemm living in a small garden shed in the corner of the field by the wood down below Gamekeepers Cottage with his terrier called Vomit. Now we didn't know Foster but we knew that he was handy with a shotgun to help feed himself from the local wildlife. So just before we purchased the land it was with great apprehension that we all four knocked on his door and asked him to vacate!! Thinking how long it would take him to reach for and load the shotgun behind the door we scuttled off sharpish but I couldn't believe it the next day when the shed had vanished leaving no sign that he had been there at all. I later met Foster several times down at the Red Hart and he rightly used to take the micky out of me. Again I knew that Albert had it right and I wished that I had left Foster in his shed. The Red Hart now is a great and thriving pub with excellent food but I am grateful to have experienced its less busy old times when Johnny Dunbar had it and enjoying a glass of cider in the

company of Albert's mates such as Foster and Tommy.

Gill and I did the entire main building work, helped now and then by both sets of parents and only using contractors for the final finishing trades. She laboured hard in her long school holidays mixing mortar for pointing and my stone laying and concrete for foundations and floors. Of course the access did pose a few problems. We dug out for the foundations and I decided that mixing and laying 20 tons of concrete would be a bit much even for us so we took the short cut of ordering Readymix. As luck would have it we had a fine day ahead but unfortunately there was a light drizzle first thing. At 8am I ran down the hill after hearing labouring engines only to see the rear of the two mixers disappearing back to Gloucester! Never mind Hales soon delivered the materials and we set to. It took us a day and a half but it's all good experience. Another time I asked for a delivery of special sand from Gloucester making it exceedingly clear that it had to be delivered in at least two small wagons. I was at work that day but I understand that it took Richard Reeds recovery vehicle quite some time to extract their ten-ton wagon, which had fallen down the bank just below Prospect House.

A major task was finding suitable matching stone. There are no quarries open for the hard grey-green sandstone with quartz that is local to Nottwood Hill and Huntley. I was fortunate to find a fine source at Deep Filling on Huntley Hill, which I purchased from The Huntley Estate. There was a lot of work to do, clearing trees and turf to extract the stone and then transport it with tractor and trailer.

We finished the work in 1984 and were then able to relax and enjoy occasional house parties at the Mount House

1. Gill Webb, her mum & Martin Webb, bring stone from Huntley Hill.
2. Gill webb & Ivy Marshall with Albert Pitthouse's collie, Tessie.
3. Gill with wet cat, Wally.(1982)
4. Martin's dad, Martin & Gill Webb.
5. Sarah Jane Webb in Mount Meadow.
6. Stonework to North extension nearing completion.
7. Roof tiling in progress.

with the whole Hill invited. They were great times and with Ivy Marshall as star attraction, especially when doing her broom dance not to mention the time she was only prevented by her son, David, from completing her striptease! The last party I had there I rang Ivy to see if she was well enough to come but she sounded miserable and I thought she sounded near to death. Then she suddenly perked up a bit and said, 'Why are you ringing me? Your not having another party are you?' At that her voice changed and on the night she was her usual old vivacious self again.

In 1987 I went self-employed working from The Mount House and we had Sarah Jane born at the same time as Amber Hopkins. In 1989 we divorced and Gill left for Gloucester but I managed to hang on to the place I loved. Gill and Sarah took our young cat Wally with them but I still had Albert's old cat Puddy and my lovely Border Collie Nellie for company. Puddy the spitting wildcat we had inherited had become a more placid creature, now completely blind but otherwise fit. I used to let her out for an hour at a time and keep an eye on her but she just walked in circles so couldn't get too far from the house anyway.

On a bright April spring day in 1991 went for a very memorable days hang gliding near Merthyr Tydfil circling in and around the clouds. I returned at dusk on top of the world only to realize that I had let Puddy out in the morning but in my rush to get away had forgotten to get her in again. Well she couldn't be far away. I searched the fields and hedgerows until midnight and was worried that she could be defenceless prey for a fox but I hoped to find her in the morning. I was up early and searched till the afternoon but she was nowhere to be found and I was losing hope fast. I was working from home that day and the next but I just had to face the fact that my carelessness had done for her. It was dry and there was no water anywhere for her to drink even if she could somehow have survived. On the third day even though I knew she must be dead, every now and then I would still go out to look just in case. Then suddenly there she was just one hundred yards into the field plodding round in circles!

The house was too big for me on my own so I built another extension for myself so that I could let the main house out as Holiday accommodation to help pay the mortgage. This was a single story extension to the east, which replaced a range of poorly built single storey outhouses that had been added over the years. First had been an open sided stone hayloft, then a block/ brick/ stone pigsty and finally Albert's famous "Jeep" house which was mainly corrugated iron, off which the roof used to blow now and again and have to be put back on. Whilst we were renovating the house I rigged up an electric shower in the hayloft and remember after showering running naked through the snow and into the house to get warm and dry by the fire!

The new annexe contained a decent sized Living Room and Bedroom together with small Hall, Kitchen and Bathroom, built with the help of great friends, Phillip Green and Oscar Jones. Although I still had a fairly good stock of stone I needed additional quality stone and especially quoin stones. Fortunately I had now discovered a new source. I had been looking at old RAF aerial photos of the Hill one day and noticed on a 1960 photograph a house standing in the orchard between Preistleys and Nottwood Cottage, which I had been unaware of. Miriam Rodway allowed me to purchase the stone and I set to digging out many tons of fine. I left for posterity the base of the chimney, which I assume is still there. I was fascinated to see that it looked as if the rounded chimneybreast had been built first and then the rest of the gable built onto it. If so then this would fit with the old stories of squatter building and getting smoke out of the chimney before nightfall. Unfortunately I haven't found anyone who knows the name of the house but David Marshall told me that his grandmother, Nellie Marshall, lived there before moving to Nottwood Cottage.

By May 1994 and I had been living in the main house and letting the single story annexe out for holiday lets. I had just been for a lovely walk in the Black Mountains on an exceptionally warm and beautiful spring day with my lovely Nellie who had been my constant companion for the past ten years when I had been through so much. She had been running down the mountain chasing sticks, not quite as fast as she used to, but not bad for a ten year old Collie. The next day she had gone off her food and didn't look too well but I put it down to over exercise in the heat. However the next morning I became concerned enough to take her to my Vet, Mr Jones at the Globe. He gave her all the shots but said she didn't look too good. By the evening she kept collapsing and I returned to Mr Jones and we decided to put her down. I had people staying in the Annexe and I always wonder what they thought, if they even noticed, what was happening just outside their window at the top of the drive. I was digging a hole by the light of the old Tilley Lamp, swigging frequently from a bottle of red wine and crying my eyes out for my lovely Nellie who a day before had been so vibrantly alive.

In 1991, I very reluctantly sold the Mount House to Howard and Anne Lowe so that I could fund the purchase of a business in Gloucester. I then turned my attention to Gamekeepers Cottage"

Martin Webb's much loved collie, Nellie
on Pen y Fan.
(1992)

GAMEKEEPER'S COTTAGE

Gamekeepers Cottage. (2008)

Martin Webb bought Gamekeepers Cottage whilst living at Mount House. When he sold Mount House, he started renovating Gamekeepers Cottage, subsequently living there till he moved to the Isle of Man.

"Gamekeepers Cottage had been mothballed by the Blaisdon Estate since the First World War but had been kept weatherproof by Albert, so was reasonably intact. It had exactly the same twin bread ovens as the Mount House and thought to have been built at the same time but had a different layout. The main house was slightly smaller but otherwise identical to the Mount House, including the cellar although this one had a separate external entrance. However at the rear was an extension with the roof carried down to a lower level housing a dairy and stable on the ground floor and above this a third Bedroom and externally entered Hayloft. By this time the Cottage was fast deteriorating and before it fell down completely I nagged Ann and Mark into selling me their share.

After a tussle with the Planners but with the fantastic support of all my neighbours I had obtained permission to reuse Gamekeepers Cottage and by 2008 the renovation was complete. I renovated it almost exactly as it had originally been with the exception of squeezing the staircase into the rear annexe, converting the dairy into a Kitchen, the Stable into a Cloakroom/Hall and Hayloft into a Bathroom. None of this work would have been possible without the very hard graft, wisdom and guidance of my great friend Geoffrey Williams. Geoffrey and Cynthia of course lived at Nottwood Cottage until a few years ago.

The character of the hill is largely due to orchards and sheep. When we first arrived the Blaisdon Plums were still being picked commercially especially by Mark, Ann, Molly and Edgar Hopkins. In our first year or two we too picked industrial tons of plums and sold them until we

fell foul of some stupid EU rule and lost heart. Sadly the market dwindled anyway and much now goes to waste, however fortunately the sheep are still keeping things tidy. Of course Albert Pitthouse had his sheep and then we had a series of Sheep Badgers over the years, some were better than others but the recent ones have been excellent. These shepherds although not resident in the village are a vital glue to the community because they are working and maintaining the land, always vigilant and ready for a natter.

Since I first came to the Hill it has lost many great characters like Edgar and Molly Hopkins, Phillip Green, Oscar and Joyce Jones. Then most recently Bill Edwards and Margaret Barnard. All friends who helped to make Nottwood so special but it has the attraction to draw in a certain kind of similar people who can appreciate what the community has to give such as Sam and Amanda Spencer who have done such a lovely job in extending and updating Alfred House."

Top:
Gamekeepers Cottage. (1993)
Above:
Roof repairs. (1994)
Right:
New windows & doors in place with
builder, Geoff Williams.

WOMEN'S INSTITUTE

Blaisdon WI continued as a small but friendly group of neighbours and friends throughout the second half of the 20th century. The group decided in 2009 that it was no longer viable to keep going due to falling numbers. The branch was therefore closed with the remaining members joining a neighbouring WI at Longhope.

In its time however, Blaisdon WI was very successful. In 1975 the members produced the first history of Blaisdon. Their illustrated portfolio won first prize in a competition run by Gloucestershire WI. This is now in the Gloucester Records Library. They would also enter many other competitions from the more usual flower displays, to the unusual, such as the foil bird made by Lynne Hogg and Rosemary Wagstaff. They also fielded a rounders side for a WI competition and, more importantly, had a reputation for producing the best parties in the area!

Above: Foil Bird.
Below: Final Meeting.

From the left, back row:
Jean Adams, Pat Higgins, Sue Booth, Pauline Brown, Hilary Hawker, Shirley Yemm.
Front row:
Sue Gent, Jean Waters, Louise Hawker.

Rounder's Team, from the left:
Megan & Debbie Kear, Sue Gent, Shirley Yemm, Jean Adams, Sue Booth, Lynne Hogg, Jill Rodgett, Pauline Brown.

LEDISLOE CUP

The Bledisloe Cup competition was run from 1937 to 2008 and was Gloucestershire's best-kept village competition with 3 categories depending on the size of the village. Blaisdon competed in the small village category and was successful on 4 occasions, 1971, 1989, 1993, 2002 and 2006. In addition, the village was runner up in 1992 and 2004.

The competition assessed the following:
- Appearance and maintenance of public places and buildings.
- Appearance and maintenance of residential areas and private premises.
- Community effort and initiatives to improve the appearance of the village.
- Map and report.

The effort and dedication required by the villagers cannot be understated. In order to get through the different stages of the competition, the village was visited on various occasions and had to be pristine on each of them. However, the assessment went further than the outward appearance of the village, taking into account its community spirit and charitable work. A sample village report, compiled by Sue Booth in 1980 also gives an insight into the village at that time:

Above:
The Bledisloe Cup Competiton sign that was erected in the winning village for 1 year, with Dick Hawker & Rosemary Wagstaff.

Right:
PC Chairman, Gerald Kear, receives the Bleisloe Cup. Vic Woodman looks on.

The main public areas the Church, the War Memorial and Village Hall (formerly the Village School) are well looked after. The churchyard is kept in good order by members of the Parochial Church Council and other volunteers from the village.

The social calender of the village seems to have been a little quieter this year, probably because last year additional fund raising events were held to pay for the new floor at the village hall. This work has now been completed together with the exterior paintwork, W.I. Members, husbands and other helpers will shortly be embarking on a mammoth spring clean to finally bring the hall Into tip top condition.

The work by volunteers to paint the war memorial railings is now complete and looks considerably better for a coat of paint.

Villagers are also keen to keep in good repair the Church as well as the Village Hall, the main fund raising being the Village Fair, the stalls are placed through the village, usually between The Lodge and Sunnyside when the villagers provide a variety of side-shows, bargains, strawberry teas and many other traditional forms of entertainment associated with summer fairs. Other charities have not been neglected and The Red Hart Inn held a successful Harvest Home when harvest produce was sold by auction and the proceeds going to kidney research. A Christingle Service at St. Michael's and All Angels Church was held in December, the proceeds of this and that raised by carol singers went to the Church of England Children's Society.

The Village Hall provides accommodation for evening classes, Parish Council meetings, W.I. Meetings, Parochial Church Council Meeting's, and is also used for private parties, wedding receptions and similar everts, including the Harvest Supper.

One particularly successful annual event is the Spring Pantomime, this year's production is Sinbad the Sailor. ,The proceeds usually go to needy children. Local people work in conjunction with the school staff on the production and when ever possible local girls also take part.

Blaisdon Hall's extensive grounds provide excellent camping for Scout- and Cub Groups from many parts of the country, this and regular visits by old. boys of the school have resulted in many lasting friendships with villagers.

The grounds of Blaisdon Hall, are kept in good order by their own gardener, but the properties owned by them, such as St. Michael's Close, are usually cared for by the residents. These are often short term, and therefore, there is not always the continuous care given to the gardens as there might be.

The telephone kiosk is kept clean by courtesy of our local postman.

The War Memorial and the flower bed to the front of the village hall come under the province of our active WI, two members of which spend many an afternoon carefully tending the flowers and plants. Other W.I. activities include regular visits to the Old People's Home at Westbury Court, Westbury-on-Severn and providing transport to and from the doctor's surgery. Members also attend group events and some are able to join in county and national events.In recent weeks, Blaisdon was host for the first round of the County Quiz. They also do fund raising for charity by selling Christmas and birthday cards throughout the year. The big event this year is a Cheese, Wine and Pate Evening to be held at Flaxley Abbey in June, the proceeds of which will go to kidney research and to WI funds.

Like other small communities we have our problems, particularly relating to the cutting of grass verges, road repairs and similar matters. These are usually not carried out through lack of funds at county level, in spite of continued requests by the Parish Council for the work to be done.

Many properties owners are working on their properties carrying out home improvements, the cement mixer and piles of building materials have become a familiar sight and it is very rare to walk through Blaisdon without seeing them at least once.

In conclusion I can only say that the majority of the villagers are extremely keen to keep their own gardens and the village in good condition.

1. George Keyse accepts the Bledisloe cup. (1971)
2. George Keyse working on his garden border prior to Bledisloe Cup judging. (1971)
3. Gerald Kear, right, & Rosemary Wagstaff accept the Bledisloe Cup from Major Tim Hayward, left and His Honour Judge Hutton, centre.
4. Bledisloe Cup.
5. Erecting the Bledisloe Cup winner's sign.
6. Paper cutting reporting Blaisdon's victory in 1971, (Source unknown)
7. Villagers watch on as the cup is awarded.
Opposite: Extracts from Report for 1980 competition.

PLUM FESTIVALS

In the 1980s, Blaisdon held three Plum Festivals, starting in 1982, then 1984 and finally in 1988. These were 3-day events over the August bank holiday weekend. This was no small thing to achieve in a village of about 100 people, including children. At this time, there were few similar events to give hints and inspiration to the organisers, so most of the ideas came from within the village. However, the entire community pulled together with Sheila and Ceri Evans leading the way, helped by an enthusiastic committee, including Sue Booth, Nigel Hogg, Vic Woodman and John Dunbar (apologies to any who haven't been named) but they were really village affairs with everybody involved.

The Salesian community at Blaisdon Hall also leant their wholehearted support to the events, allowing the use of the Hall and opening their grounds for walks etc. Each of us spent time manning the various stalls, preparing and serving teas and food and, most importantly, plums had to be picked daily. Thankfully, these were in good supply for all three festivals.

In those days, plums were still picked commercially. Most of them were bought by Robertson's who used them to make jam. For the last plum festival in 1988, they donated

King & Queen Plum.
Made by Vic Woodman.

a large Golly. At the time this was the symbol they used on their jams and generations of children had collected the brooches they made. The Golly was an instant hit with a young Eleanor Waters who would give it a big hug every time she saw it. The Golly was taken around the village during the weekend and tickets sold in order to raffle it. Eleanor's mum and dad lost count of the number of people who said that if they won it they would give it to her. They also bought tickets each day. Amazingly, it was one of Eleanor's own tickets that came out of the hat and she took proud possession of a Golly bigger than she was.

In 1982 the village produced a Blaisdon plum recipe book, with every conceivable way to eat plums and in

1984, also produced its own newspaper, The Blaisdon Chronicle, with articles about the village, its people and its history. There was a plum making competition won by Vic Woodman's King and Queen Plum. The festival weekend of 1984 even saw its own village wedding when Debbie Kear from Woodgreen married Olly Rowe with a procession through the village too.

Each festival raised money for the church and village hall. The first festival was organised in part because of the need for extra funds for the church to finance some urgently needed repairs, a perennial problem for old church buildings. Over £1,600 was raised for the village church by the 1982 festival. In addition, in 1984, almost £1,000 was donated to the Pain Clinic Fund at Gloucester Royal Hospital. Now an established unit, it was then in its infancy, being developed by the Anaesthetic and Intensive Care Department of the hospital.

The weekends followed a similar pattern with exhibitions of art and historical documents in Blaisdon Hall with a cheese and wine viewing on the Friday evening. On the Saturday and Sunday, the village would be 'open' all day with plum stalls, craft fairs, flower festival in the church, farm walks around Stud Farm and refreshments served and made by the Blaisdon ladies. Saturday evening would see a concert in Blaisdon Church and the weekend would finish with a choral evensong, again at the church.

The evening concerts were given by the Cadenza Singers. In 1988, the Sunday church service was treated to The Church of God Prophecy Choir from Gloucester bringing their enthusiastic gospel singing to Blaisdon Church to the great enjoyment of the congregation.

Although in the following years, events on this scale have not been repeated, the village continues to celebrate the plum harvest with smaller fetes around the time the plums ripen. The memory of the original plum festivals and what they achieved will last for a lifetime and, perhaps, one day, will be repeated by another generation of Blaisdon folk.

Programme cover to 1982 Plum Festival.

PORK CHOPS WITH BLAISDON PLUMS

6 pork chops ½" thick   salt and pepper

3 medium sized onions grated rind and juice of 1 large orange

1 level tablespoonful plain flour 1 lb plums

12oz cooked beetroot

For the Garnish -   1 large orange   a sprinkling of caster sugar

a few drops cooking oil

Cut skin off the chops. Fry the backs of the chops to a golden brown by standing them upright in a frying pan. Once the fat is brown, lightly brown the meat on both sides, then remove from pan. Peel and slice the onions thinly, and fry gently, stir in the flour. Meanwhile peel and grate the beetroot on a coarse grater and stir it into the onions. Add salt and pepper then the grated rind and juice of the orange. Nestle the plums into the beetroot and arrange the browned chops round the dish. Cover with kitchen foil and cook for 50 minutes 400F Gas Mark 6. Take off foil, slice the orange and arrange in centre of dish, brush lightly with oil, sprinkle with sugar and lightly brown them under a hot grill. Serve with plain boiled noodles.

HOT BLAISDON PLUM TRIFLE

1 swiss roll   1 lb cooked, stoned Blaisdon plums

pkt vanilla blancmange (made as directed) or a pint custard

2 eggs (separated)   3oz caster sugar

Slice swiss roll and arrange in the base of an ovenproof dish and pour over the plums. Make up the blancmange as directed, beat in the 2 egg yolks and pour over the plums. Whisk the 2 egg whites until stiff, whisk in 2oz of sugar and then fold in the remaining 1 oz. Pile on top of the blancmange and bake at 400 F, 200 C, Gas mark 6 for 10 minutes until the meringue is golden brown. Serves 4-6.

BLAISDON SPECIAL PLUM WINE

1 gallon Blaisdon Plums plus 1 gallon water

4lb sugar & 1/2 pint brandy per gallon liquid

Remove stalks and cover with boiling water. Stir 3-4 times daily for four days. Drain off liquid. Add sugar and brandy and when sugar is dissolved leave under fermentation lock until fermentation ceases. Seal container for 12 months. Then rack off and bottle.

BLAISDON PLUM GIN

2 lb Blaisdon plums

1 bottle gin

2 lb sugar

Prick the fruit with a needle and place in demijohn, together with sugar and gin. Seal and leave in a warm place for three months. Strain liquid and bottle. Eat the fruit.

THE "BLAISDON" COCKTAIL

Per person

½   glass of Blaisdon Plum Gin   small piece of lemon peel

½ glass gin   crushed ice

10 drops of orange bitters

Half fill a tumbler with broken ice, pour over it the ingredients and shake well. Place lemon peel on top and enjoy the warm taste of Blaisdon hospitality.

An alternative to using the Blaisdon Plum Gin is to use the fresh juice of the Blaisdon Plum.

Recipes taken from the Blaisdon Plum Recipe Book.
(1982)

Bank Holiday Weekend
August 25th, 26th, 27th

Open 11.00 am to 5.30 pm

Admission, including Car Parking,
£1.00 Adults, 50p Children (over 5 years),
Children under 5 free.

FESTIVAL PROGRAMME

BLAISDON CHURCH

Flower Festival
Saturday, Sunday and Monday

Choral Evensong
Sunday at 6.30 pm

Concert by The Cadenza Singers
(Founder Frank Wombwell)
Monday at 8.00 pm (Tickets £1.00)

BLAISDON HALL AND GROUNDS

Cheese and Wine Evening
includes preview of Exhibition of Paintings by Local Artist,
Exhibition of old local Photographs and Exhibition of Craftwork.
Friday 24th August at 8.00 (Tickets £1.50)

Exhibition of Paintings, Photographs and Craftwork
Sunday 1.00 pm to 5.30 pm and
Monday 11.00 am to 5.30 pm

Country Walk
Saturday, Sunday and Monday

BLAISDON VILLAGE HALL

Craft & Antique Market
Saturday, Sunday and Monday

BLAISDON HOUSE

Morning Coffee   Ploughman's Lunches
Afternoon Teas
Available throughout the Festival Weekend
from 11.00 am until 5.30 pm

RED HART INN

Plum Market
Saturday, Sunday and Monday

Children's Entertainment
Each Afternoon

OTHER ATTRACTIONS

"Made in Blaisdon" Day
Saturday

Ice Cream Parlour
Daily 12.30 to 5.30 pm

Blaisdon Chronicle
Available each day

Farm Visit
Each afternoon 3.30 to 5.30 pm

1. Programme for 1982 Plum Festival.
2. Blaisdon Chronicle. (1984)
3. Entrance ticket. (1984)
4. Cheese & wine ticket. (1984)

1

Blaisdon Chronicle

2

Commemorative Issue   Plum Festival 30p   August 1984

Plum Festival CHARITIES

The three recipients of money raised at this year's PLUM FESTIVAL will be Blaisdon CHURCH, Blaisdon VILLAGE HALL and the PAIN CLINIC FUND based at Gloucester Royal Hospital.

The Pain Relief Clinic was set up to help patients whose suffering cannot be helped by treating the condition causing the pain. Patients may be dying from an incurable cancer or be suffering from nerve damage, following shingles, or incapacitating back pain which will plague them for years.

Traditional treatment by drugs, even well tried and tested ones, can be upsetting to some individuals who cannot cope at home because the drugs make them too sleepy, too sick or they loose their effect too soon.

The advent of the microchip and marvels of modern technology

have encouraged the development of new tools. In spite of their apparent simplicity, such devices as the portable syringe pump which provides continuous pain relief, can allow a patient to stay mentally alert and physically active for as long as possible, before dying in comfort and dignity at home.

The priority for spending on items that can help only very few people is understandably low, but for someone in constant pain, every extra day is distressing, and those who are dying cannot wait.

The Pain Clinic Charity was formed for relatives and friends of patients who wished to help the National Health Service improve the facilities available in this county. To minimise running expenses, it is administered under the auspices of the Intensive Care Unit Charity (Registered No. 275009) as Pain Clinic Fund No.3.

Nineteenth Century Blaisdon

As it was in the beginning
......of the 20th century
by Ruth Magee

PROGRAMME INSIDE

3

BLAISDON PLUM FESTIVAL

25th, 26th and 27th AUGUST

OPEN 11.00 am to 5.30 pm

*(Blaisdon Hall opens
1.00 pm to 5.30 pm Sunday and
11.00 am to 5.30 pm Monday)*

ADMISSION TICKET
to
ALL DISPLAYS

**£1.00 ADULT
50p CHILDREN (UNDER 5 FREE)**

FREE CAR PARKING

Blue Ticket – Saturday
Pink Ticket – Sunday
Buff Ticket – Monday

4

Blaisdon Plum Festival 1984

Cheese & Wine

at Blaisdon Hall

ON FRIDAY 24th AUGUST

at 8pm   Ticket £1.50

Bank Holiday Weekend August 28th. 29th. 30th.

Open 11.00a.m. to 6.00p.m.

(Blaisdon Hall opens 12.00 noon Sunday 29th.)

This is the first Blaisdon Plum Festival and we hope it will be attractive to all who appreciate "Village Life" It is a cooperative event to which all Villagers contribute and we will be more than satisfied if we provide an interesting and relaxed Day out in the Country.

The Village

Blaisdon a small rural parish of 900 acres lying 7 miles west of Gloucester. Not mentioned by name in the Domesday Book but described as a Hamlet of Longhope. Known in 1166 as Blenchendone. A Parish Church is recorded in the 13th. cent. when 3 Oaks were granted by the Crown for repairs and later rebuilt in the 19th. Century. The Manor was granted in 1537 to Sir William Kingston and later held by the Wade family till 1793. Fire destroyed part of the village in 1699 40 houses & 180 people recorded in 1710 A Tannery is recorded as being sold in 1787.

The Blaisdon Red Plum

The Blaisdon Red plum was discovered in the 19th. century by Mr. John Dowding of the Tanhouse Farm, Blaisdon, Gloucestershire. Origins obscure, it grows on its own rootstock. Extensively planted in Blaisdon and surrounding parishes during the first thirty or forty years of this century. About three hundred acres grown in the district in and around Blaisdon c.1948, but now much reduced. Commercial picking starts third week in August, ripe end August/early September.
Uses dessert, culinary, jam making, canning, pulping, also used for making wine. Fruit oval and medium sized, claret red in colour, looks almost blue when fully ripe.

Festival Programme

A FLORAL DISPLAY IN THE CHURCH

EXHIBITION & SALE OF PAINTINGS IN BLAISDON HALL

EXHIBITION OF LOCAL HISTORICAL DOCUMENTS IN BLAISDON HALL

CRAFTS FAIR IN THE VILLAGE HALL

**ADMISSION TO ALL OF THE ABOVE INCLUDING CAR PARKING
ADULTS £1.00 CHILDREN (3-14 YEARS) 50p**

BLAISDON PLUM FESTIVAL

Special Events

FRIDAY 27th. AUGUST 8.00p.m.

A Review of Painting & Document Exhibition at Blaisdon Hall

Cheese and Wine Tickets £1.50

SATURDAY 28th. AUGUST 8.00p.m.   Tickets £1.00

A Concert in the Church

By The Cadenza Singers - Gloucester
(Founder Frank Wombwell)

SUNDAY, 29th. AUGUST 6.30p.m.

Choral Evensong

Preacher: Rt. Rev. BISHOP BROWNFIELD PORTER
Choir: THE COTSWOLD SINGERS

PLUM MARKET : RED HART ORCHARD

OPEN DAILY 11.00a.m. to 6.00p.m.

BLAISDON RED PLUM RECEIPE BOOK
ON SALE AT ALL DISPLAYS & EXHIBITIONS Price 50p

1. Programme for 1982 Plum Festival.
2. Locally grown plums.
3. Programme for concert given by Cadenza Singers with soloists Megan Kear, Derek Davies & Jean Waters.
(27th August 1984).

Choir:	Early One Morning	English trad.
	O No John	arr. Eric Thiman
	Sweet Nightingale	arr. Roberton
	L'il Liza Jane	arr. Gordon Lawson
	Watching the Wheat	arr. Henry Geehl

GUEST ARTIST: MEGAN KEAR

Choir:	Loch Lomond	Scottish trad.
	All in the April Evening	Hugh Roberton
	Celtic Lullaby	arr. Fanshawe
	Joshua Fit de Battle of Jericho	arr. Roberton

Solo: Derek Davies

Choir:	Tumbalalaika	Yiddish Folk Song
	My Love Dwelt in a Northern Land	Edward Elgar
	I Know Where I'm Going	arr. Russell-Smith

Choir:	Little David, Play on Your Harp	arr. Sargent
	Were You There?	arr. Roberton
	Steal Away	arr. Roberton

| Quartet: | Michael, Row the Boat Ashore | arr. Gardner |

Choir:	Golden Slumbers	arr. Roberton
	Little Bo-Peep	arr. Gardner
	Little Polly Flinders	J. Michael Diack
	The Goslings	Frederick Bridge
	Go Lovely Rose	Eric Thiman

GUEST ARTIST: JEAN WATERS

| Choir: | As Torrents in Summer | Edward Elgar |
| | King Arthur | arr. Roberton |

CONDUCTOR: BOB SCOTT   ACCOMPANIST: ANN SCOTT

1

2

3

4

5

6

7

8

1. Cedric Etherington explains an historical document.
2. Document display in Blaisdon Hall.
3. Craft fair in village hall.
4. Punch & Judy.
5. Concert in Blaisdon Church.
6. Painting display in Blaisdon Hall.
7. The plum stall, manned by Mike Wagstaff.
8. Two views of childrens games in Red Hart orchard.

Flower
arrangements
from Plum
Festivals.

Blaisdon folk at the Plum Festivals:

1. Ed & Frank Booth, Andrew Hogg.
2. Vic Woodman & Doug Inger on entrance duty.
3. Pauline Brown, Louise & Hilary Hawker.
4. Andrew Hogg gives Amanda Trigg, Miss Forest of Dean, a basket of plums after she opened the Plum Festival.
5. Newspaper sellers, Andrew Hogg, centre with Frank & Ed Booth. (1984)
6. Jean Waters takes a break from washing to sample the produce.
7. Steve Waters enjoying a glass of wine.
8. Lynne Hogg does likewise.
9. Ben Brown with a sample of Blaisdon plums.

Villagers at the Plum Festivals:
1. Dave Lilley & Niki Kear (1984)
2. Olly & Debbie Rowe. (1984)
3. Peter, Frank & Ed Booth with Andrew Hogg and Fido.
4. Andrew Hogg, Frank & Ed Booth.
5. Andrew Hogg.
6. Cedric Etherington.
7. Louise Hawker with Robertson's Golly.
8. Pony rides.
9. Dick Hawker keeping the village clean.
10. Tea break at Stud Farm with Louise Hawker, Jean Waters, Dick & Mike Hawker.

FETES

For many years, Blaisdon village fete has been a summertime feature of the villagers' year. Its aim has always been to provide a few hours of gentle enjoyment with traditional fete day stalls and events. Far from becoming more sophisticated, the fete and the villagers have retained the traditional elements that make a good old-fashioned village fete

It is interesting to look at what was on offer 50 years ago. According to the village hall records the stalls proposed were as follows:

Extract from Blaisdon Village Hall minutes.

1968 fete in August. Stalls were to be:

New Stall	Bottle Stall
Hoopla	Cakes
Jumble	Raffle
Guess cake wgt	Produce
Hidden mystery	Fishing
Skittles	Teas
Balloons	Plants
Donkey rides	Children's sports
Childrens' fancy dress	Novelty stall

3 Scarecrows at the Blaisdon fete:
Abigail Cross, Emily Atkinson & Elizabeth Cutler. (2005)
(N. Atkinson)

Nowadays, a lot of the items on this list are still to be found at a Blaisdon fete. This does not mean that the village has been slow to innovate. In recent years, there has been a Dr Who theme as well as a Worzel Gummidge inspired scarecrow theme and the never-to-be-forgotten, 'men in dresses' day. Children's games have returned with the centrepiece being the 'plum and spoon' race. This is just as difficult as using an egg and, unless the plums are very ripe, avoids messy clothes.

Entertainment is sometimes brought in, such as the local brass and silver bands and local troupes of Morris Men.

The Plum Festivals in the 1980s highlighted that the Blaisdon Plum was a good focus for promoting the fete and in recent years the fete has been held in late August, just as the plums are ready to pick. There is still a good demand from people for the Blaisdon plum, whether to make the best plum jam or just to eat with custard, cream or both!

For many years, the fete benefited from the plant stall of Vic and Enid Woodman. Their fuchsia plants were so in demand, queues would form before the fete opened. Indeed their stall would often raise more than the rest of the fete put together.

The fundraising aim of the fete has been and remains to raise funds for the village church and hall, proceeds being divided between the two.

The location of the fete has moved around the village over the years. It was held in the grounds of Blaisdon Hall some time in the past and similarly, it was held in the garden of New House at Stud Farm. For some years it was positioned along the road from the village hall to The Forge with the stalls in gardens along the way. In recent years, it has been held in and around the village hall, as well as the grounds of the Red Hart Inn.

Perhaps the unique nature of this event is in its appearance and disappearance. Barely 2 hours before it is due to open, there will be the first stirring around the village. Tables will appear and goods, produce etc will be laid out. The kitchen in the village hall will become a hive of activity, as ploughman's lunches will be laid out alongside slices of homemade cakes and scones. Tea and coffee will be brewed

and soft drinks produced for the children. By opening time, the village is a maze of activity with stalls here and there around the village hall and grounds of the Red Hart.

A few hours later as the event has drawn to a close, the packing up begins. Just as efficiently as earlier, everything disappears back into homes and the village hall. Almost miraculously, the village returns to its pristine state. The villagers return home for a tea or a well-earned drink at the Red Hart, where they will discuss the fete and what to do next year.

Map around Blaisdon Village Fair (1969)

1. View of Fete in New House garden
2. Village fete, early 1970s.
3. Fred Mason, honorary Blaisdonite who was fete treasurer for many years. (Brother in law of Brian Jones, Halt Cottage)
4. Frank Baylis in costume.
5. Band playing in garden of Parkwood. (1983)
6. Three photos of Morris Men in school yard c2010.

VILLAGE SETTING FOR FAIR

Bellringers rang a peal from Blaisdon Church to open the Blaisdon village fair.

Instead of confining the stalls to a hall or a field, the various amusements were spread throughout the length of the village. In addition several gardens were open to the public for viewing.

The Gloucester Boy Scouts Band paraded through the village and provided entertainment, as did the parade of the Cotswold Vale Farmers' Hunt hounds; fortunately the weather could not have been betterer for the tractor and trailer rides up and down the village, which were extremely popular.

An art exhibition in the studio of the "Forge," and an arranged by Hilary Etherington, attracted a great deal of interest. Drawings and paintings were contributed by: Joy Griffiths, of Drybrook; Roger Etherington, of Blaisdon; the Rev. David Bick. of Flaxley; Mr J. Green, of Blakeney (paintings by the mouth); Mrs Jennie Green, of Gloucester; Hilary Jayne of Blaisdon; Mrs Ivy Davis of Blaisdon; Sonja Howard-Williams; pottery from John Drinkwater of Gloucester; with a fine display of woodwork and ceramics from the Blaisdon Salesian Boys' School.

A dance was held in the village hall in the evening.

Review of Blaisdon Fete taken from unknown newspaper source indicating some of the other attractions that have been offered over the years c1970.

Top:
Emily Scarecrow Atkinson.
(N. Atkinson)

Below:
Evans family from Blaisdon Court in Dr Who.

Fun at Blaisdon Fete.

1.4.6. Nigel Hogg, Roger & Clare Keyse on the plum & produce stall.

2. Zoe Boyles & Lynne Hogg on Ploughman's lunches.

3. Jan Royall serves afternoon tea toNathalie Mignotte & Katie Baker.

6. Cake Stall with Nicola & Stephen Atkinson.

7. Peter Adams & Stuart Gent on burgers.

8. Foot care was a new attraction for 2012 with Tracey Batham & Louise Lisseman.

9. The Bottle Stall with Jill & Andrew Rodgett.

10. Face painting.

11. Plum Race from the left:
Andy & Liam Selwyn, Emily & Stephen Atkinson, watched by Brian & Alison Evans. (2002)
(N. Atkinson)

12. The human fruit machine, gambling with a twist.

12a. A tour of the grounds of Blaisdon Hall, another popular addition to the fete attractions. (2012)

11

12

12a

1

2

3

4

5

6

7

8

9

10

1. Dr Stuart Gent Who & assistants
with a real TARDIS!
2. Ladies hat competition in front of Blaisdon House.
3. Happy fete organisers, from the left:
Angela Baker, Nathalie Mignotte, Stuart Gent, Jean & Shelley Adams, Emily
& Katie Baker & John Higgins.
4. 'Ladies in Dresses' with Nigel Hogg, centre.

SILVER JUBILEE

GOLDEN JUBILEE

Church kneeler made by Rosemary Wagstaff to commemorate the Golden Jubilee of Queen Elizabeth II.

Blaisdon Village celebrate the Golden Jubilee.
Taken in the garden of Blaisdon House.
(2002)

◗IAMOND JUBILEE

Blaisdon clebrate the Diamond Jubilee of
Queen Elizabeth II.
Taken in front of the village Hall.
(2012)

Blaisdon Beacon answers those on the Cotswold escarpment in the distance.
(4th June 2012)

INDEX